Responsible children make responsible adults.

FAMILY RULES

shows you how to handle unruliness—without losing your temper!

From preschool problems to adolescent annoyances, it's all here, and it's all clear. End the slapping and yelling. Adopt a controlled approach to helping your children deal with drugs and sex. *Family Rules* helps you do it!

"Kenneth Kaye's advice...fills the gaping void in today's literature for parents. Those who feel besieged by their children's natural, often intolerable, testing of limits will now see clearly what to do and when to do it." —T. Berry Brazelton, M.D.

"One of the strengths of this book is the inclusion of many true-to-life examples of parent-child confrontations, with suggestions for how to settle differences to everyone's satisfaction."
— *Practical Parenting*

Kenneth Kaye, a developmental psychologist, is associate professor of clinical psychiatry at Northwestern University Medical School. He is also a faculty member of the Family Institute of Chicago.

FAMILY RULES

RAISING RESPONSIBLE CHILDREN

KENNETH KAYE, PH.D.

ST. MARTIN'S PAPERBACKS

Acknowledgments for permission to quote from copyrighted material:

Bettelheim, Bruno. *Dialogues With Mothers.* Macmillan Publishing Co., Inc. Copyright © 1962 by The Free Press of Glencoe. Reprinted by permission of the publisher.

De Saint-Exupéry, Antoine. Excerpt from *The Little Prince.* Copyright © 1943, 1971 by Harcourt Brace Jovanovich, Inc. Reprinted by permission of the publisher.

SADD (Students Against Driving Drunk) Marlboro, Massachusetts. *Contract for Life.*™ 1983. Reprinted by permission.

Committee on Drug Abuse. *Parties: A Practical Guide for Parents and Teenagers.* Reprinted by permission of Township High School District 113, Highland Park, Ill.

Published by arrangement with Walker & Co.

FAMILY RULES

Library of Congress Catalog Card Number: 83-40434

ISBN: 0-312-92369-4

Printed in the United States of America

Walker & Co. edition published 1984
St. Martin's Paperbacks edition/February 1991

10 9 8 7 6 5 4 3 2 1

For my parents, Saul and Juanita Kaye

Acknowledgments

As a psychologist, I have worked with several hundred families, some in research studies on child development and others in family therapy. Although they cannot be thanked by name, they are the principal people from whom I have learned about human interaction, change, and growth. A few have also helped me learn how to write for parents, as they read parts of this book and gave valuable feedback.

The system of child-rearing recommended here is drawn from the insights of many professionals. Along with those mentioned in the text and those whose books are suggested, special acknowledgments must go to Rosalind Charney, Rachael Cunningham, Bill Pinsof, and Sherry Tucker, who transformed me from an ivory-tower researcher into a real-world therapist and who continue to share their skills with me and shape my thinking.

Susan and Peter Friedes's encouraging response helped keep me laboring when the manuscript was at an early stage. Finally, I am grateful for the enthusiastic support of Walker and Company, especially for Richard K. Winslow's and Julie Glass's thoughtful, painstaking efforts on behalf of the reader.

Contents

Part III. Special Topics 293

What the king fundamentally insisted upon was that his authority should be respected. He tolerated no disobedience. He was an absolute monarch. But, because he was a very good man, he made his orders reasonable.

"If I ordered a general," he would say, by way of example, "if I ordered a general to change himself into a sea bird, and if the general did not obey me, that would not be the fault of the general. It would be my fault."

"May I sit down?" came now a timid inquiry from the little prince.

"I order you to do so," the king answered him.

—Antoine de Saint-Exupéry, *The Little Prince,* 1943

CHAPTER ONE

Introduction

Children are not a constant joy. They are often a great deal of aggravation and worry. To help them grow into happy, self-respecting adults, we try to be patient, understanding, generous parents. Yet these virtues are not enough. They can produce irresponsible, unhappy children—unless we also show firmness, consistency, and clarity. Children need the security of clearly enforced rules before they can begin to handle freedom.

Clarity begins at home

Al and Betty have two boys, ages eight and eleven, and Betty's fifteen-year-old daughter from a previous marriage. At times, any one of the three children can make Al and Betty feel frustrated and angry; more often, though, the feeling these parents are left with is worry.

"If only we could be sure that they knew how to take care of themselves," Al says. "This is not the world we grew up in. Everything today seems so much more catastrophic, so much less certain."

Betty observes her daughter Cathy's friends: "They aren't realistic. Sometimes they don't seem to believe that they have full lives ahead of them to look forward to."

Because they are sensitive to the confusion and pressure their children experience away from home, Al and Betty have tried to create a relaxed, low-pressure atmosphere at home. They are not interested in punishing the children. Unfortunately, they often wind up nagging them instead. Look what happens, for example, when the family comes down for breakfast one morning:

"Whose night was it for dishes?" Al nods toward the full sink and the unwashed pots and pans on the counter. He will try not to get upset, though he knows that his patience has limits.

"Mine, I guess" is eleven-year-old Doug's reply. "I'll do them after school."

"He'll have some excuse by then," mutters Betty. "It's always the same: I get home at five, the dishes from the day before are still piled up, whoever was supposed to do them is outside somewhere, and I have to wash them before I can make dinner."

MISTAKE: Al says, "You're supposed to do them after dinner, Doug. Not the next day. Immediately after dinner, you understand?"

"I couldn't, Dad. I had to finish my book report."

This familiar excuse does not satisfy Al. "If you had so much homework, how were you able to watch TV last night?"

Doug has an answer to that, too. Finally, Al lays down the law: "Listen to me. Those dishes better be done before your mother gets home today, *or else!* Do you understand?"

BETTER: Al and Betty could announce that from now on, anyone whose night it is to do the dishes may not use the telephone or television until the kitchen has passed inspection. Anyone who disobeys this rule will lose TV and phone privileges for twenty-four hours. The "or else" becomes clear, specific, and enforceable.

MISTAKE: As the boys get ready for school, Betty hears Doug calling Brad stupid.

"Doug," she complains, "I've told you a hundred times not to call your brother names. When are you going to stop being such a brat? And I don't like you wearing that faded shirt."

BETTER: Betty should have a standard penalty for name-calling—for example, a ten-cent fine. (*Never* call your children names yourself; their self-esteem depends on your respect.) As for the faded shirt, Betty should have a rule about what the child can wear to school and enforce it, not merely complain. If she doesn't have a rule, that means the choice is the child's; again, she shouldn't complain about it.

MISTAKE: Al stomps upstairs. "Get up, Cathy. It's seven-thirty. You're going to be late for school."

"I don't feel well."

"You don't feel well because you didn't get to sleep early enough. You should have thought of that last night, while you were driving around with those scuzzy friends of yours. How much beer did you drink?"

"Leave me alone, will you?" Cathy yells.

Al's patience, stretched thin by the daily argument about the dishes, and even thinner because he overheard Betty's impatience with Doug, finally bursts: "You're grounded tonight. I'm sick of you not coming home when you're supposed to." Cathy makes no reply.

Betty can foresee the whole scenario that will unfold this evening. Cathy will argue about the time she was supposed to be home last night, what time she actually came in, why she did not call ("I didn't want to wake you up!"), and why it is unfair to ground her. In the end, because Betty and Al have a party to go to—and will be afraid of Cathy sneaking out after they leave—they will let her off with another warning. Al and Betty will probably not fight about this until later at night, when Cathy is once again out past her curfew ("It's not a school night!") and when Al, anticipating Betty's criticism of him, will accuse her of not being firm enough. (She'll wince when he says, "She's *your* daughter.") Then they will discuss Doug and Brad, and the dishes that Doug will not have washed, and the bicycles, which were left out all night in the rain, and the concerned notes from Brad's teacher, and the boys' constant bickering that drives Betty crazy. ("They don't do it around me," Al will say, "or I just whack 'em both." "When are you ever around?" will be her response, and the battle will escalate.)

This book is designed to teach all parents to stop nagging, stop complaining, stop yelling, stop growing frustrated with their kids and then with each other, and even to stop whacking. The secret is clear communication and sensitivity to children's feelings, combined with firm, consistently enforced rules.

Al and Betty obviously care about their children, but they are simply not clear enough about their expectations. They rely on the meaningless "or else." They don't state specific consequences of misbehavior and follow through with them.

On the other hand, they miss opportunities to be constructive, to be sensitive, to instill confidence. Doug's book report, which his father could have read and praised, is drowned in Al's annoyance about the dishes. In Betty's frustration about Doug's name-calling, she winds up calling him a name. As both parents grow frustrated, tense, and angry, they have little energy or warmth left over for any of the three children.

The label "overly permissive" applies to parents who set few limits on their children's behavior. The children of permissive parents generally make more and more demands on them, and the parents capitulate—until they reach their breaking point. At that point the parents scream and yell, attack the children emotionally and sometimes physically, apologize and revert to permissiveness. Unfortunately, despite all they are "getting away with," these children often do not get the sense of security and acceptance that every child needs. They grow up to be, at best, unpleasant, and, at worst, seriously disturbed.

At the opposite extreme is the "authoritarian" parent, who has strict rules for the sake of having strict rules and who exacts obedience for the sake of having obedient children, even when there is no reason for concern about the potential disobedience. This parent tends to use punishments that are more severe than necessary to get the children to conform. Authoritarian parents rule by fear rather than by love. Some children of authoritarian parents become passive, withdrawn, ineffectual adults; others are hostile and aggressive; many become authoritarian parents themselves.

≡Being firm

Quite separate from these two extremes—not a half-and-half mixture but a type distinct from either the permissive or the authoritarian parent—is the "authoritative" type. Authoritative parents are firm and clear about issues that are important for the child's safety, development, and respect for the rights of others. But they are not interested in unnecessarily strict controls. Based on studies by Professor Diana Baumrind, a University of California psychologist, we know that authorita*tive* parents raise more responsible, independent, and competent children than either permissive or authorit*arian* parents. (In this book, I shall call authoritative parents *clear* parents, because the word *authoritative* looks too much like *authoritarian*.)

I think the biggest difference among these types of parents is in how certain they are that they are right. *Authoritarian* parents are quite certain (or at least *act* certain) that they are always right. Their word should be law. *Overly permissive* parents feel helpless: Resigned to not knowing what is best for their children, they cave in to the pressure of the moment. *Clear* parents don't feel helpless, but they don't feel infallible either. They can be convinced by their children about many issues, through reasonable discussions. On certain issues, however, the parents are prepared to set limits. They will change the rules as their children's needs change. They are more interested in being rational than in always being right.

Many permissive parents are inspired by all the best intentions. They are bending over backward to avoid being authoritarian. They are trying to show respect for the child's independent judgment. They want to generate an atmosphere of equality and democratic decision-making. Those are worthwhile goals, but only for certain kinds of family decisions (what restaurant to go to, for example, or what book to read at bedtime). When more important concerns are involved (health, safety, education, responsibility to others), a family cannot work as a democracy. It has to be organized as a hierarchy, with the more competent members—the parents—at the top. At the same time, the structure has to be flexible enough to acknowledge the child's growth and increasing competence. It has to permit open, supportive communication between parent and child. It has to emphasize the fundamental task of parents: not to control children's lives but to enhance the development of young people who will soon control their own lives.

A built-in paradox. Chances are, this is not the first book you have read on being a good parent. If it is not, then you have already encountered many of the ideas in Part II, about building self-confidence and competence. Part I, about restrictions and discipline, may be new to you. But the two parts of the job go together. Parents who nag, complain, and fail to make clear, enforceable rules inevitably undermine their children's self-esteem.

This book is about both aspects of parenthood: the restrictive part and the constructive part. It is especially about how to weave together both roles, without sacrificing either part of the job for the sake of the other.

At the root of parents' concern is a built-in paradox, for in all children, three psychological needs conflict with one another.

1. They need *attention* from their parents. They need to be stimulated and they need to be responded to. They need affection, praise, and adult models with whom they can identify. They need to know that their parents care about them, and they need someone wiser than themselves to monitor their growth and changing needs. But all this attention conflicts with the next need:

2. They need *autonomy*: This requires more and more independence as they grow older. Children must gradually acquire a feeling of being responsible for themselves, along with the feeling that their parents want them to be so. The process of achieving autonomy begins in infancy. It cannot be suddenly thrust upon the child at age eighteen or later. Unfortunately, the need for autonomy conflicts directly with the next equally essential need:

3. Children need *limits*. They need the security of knowing that someone more competent than themselves is in charge. They lack the knowledge or experience to make certain decisions. They also need to know that someone cares. Parents who don't set limits, who act as though their children's behavior does not matter, imply that the children themselves don't matter to them. Another reason children need limits—perhaps the most important reason—is that they need a structure in which to "be good," that is, to be able to behave in such a way that they can feel good about themselves.

The conflict among these three needs can only be resolved if we realize that restricting children goes hand in hand with building strengths within them.

≡Being constructive

The first part of this book is about the job of being restrictive; the second part is about being constructive. Since both parts are absolutely essential to being a parent, I wish it were possible for you to read both parts of the book at once. Building up children's skills and self-confidence, the subject of Part II, is really the rationale for the system of rules and discipline described in Part I. This section briefly summarizes that rationale.

Building in self-esteem. Most of the parents I know would list among their deepest hopes for their children:

Motivation: That their children strive to achieve the best they are capable of, in school, in outside activities, and later in their chosen walks of life.

Decency: That they grow up to be "good people," earning respect for their humanity and trustworthiness, not just their achievements.

Self-preservation: That they manage to traverse the obstacle course of adolescence and young adulthood without succumbing to drugs, delinquency, unsavory friendships, depression, and other self-destructive detours.

Self-esteem: That they feel good about themselves.

The way to help children toward *all four* of these goals is to concentrate on the last one. This is because the first three can only be built into your children indirectly. The motivation for achievement—in school, work, sports, the arts, or community affairs—has to be built into a person. Positive human values, and the resources with which to care for others, also have to be built in. So does the instinct for self-preservation.

The first three goals come fairly naturally to a child or young person who is high in self-esteem. A person with good self-esteem feels: "I am competent—if I work hard, I can succeed" (motivation); "I am a good person" (decency); "My loved ones value me and see me as someone special, so I should take care of myself" (self-preservation).

With low self-esteem—with doubts about one's competence,

worth, or importance to loved ones—it is difficult to be motivated, decent, and self-preserving. Many people low in self-esteem do poorly in school and in later work. Others become high achievers but have personality problems that annoy and alienate the people who work or live with them. Still others with low self-esteem are well liked and appreciated, yet they turn against themselves through alcoholism, drug abuse, eating disorders, or other psychological problems.

Since you are certain to have an enormous effect upon your child's self-esteem, it is your best ally in helping to enhance the child's achievements, personal qualities, and ability for self-preservation.

Imagine that your child is in his or her* early teens and is offered a ride home from a party by an acquaintance who has had too much to drink. Will he get in the car? Or imagine that someone offers him a little pill and assures him that it will provide a terrific high with no side effects. Will he try it? If he believes that his life is worthwhile and that he has a bright future, and if he knows how important he is to you, he is likely to say, "No, thanks."

It is the young people with little self-esteem who are willing to risk their lives and the lives of others for a moment's pleasure, or to bring an unwanted life into the world, or to throw away their educational prospects. Parents who devote too much energy to worrying about those dire possibilities—for example, trying to crack down on drugs while doing nothing to help their children feel good about themselves—generally do more harm than good.

This book is based on the premise that our children's success and happiness will depend, ultimately, upon what we *build into them*—in the form of motivation, intelligence, and moral character—rather than what we *lay on them* in the form of specific demands. Yet we do have to demand that they behave in certain ways, and not in other ways, when they are young; and the clarity of those rules plays an essential part in helping them grow up to be self-controlled, self-motivated, self-respecting.

How can you build children's self-esteem? It depends upon their age and the kinds of activities they engage in, but two prin-

---

* Almost everything in this book applies equally to girls as to boys. It is awkward to keep saying "he or she," however, so I will sometimes make use of the generic "he" where the child's gender does not matter.

ciples stand out as most important. One is to use praise, as sincerely, as specifically, and as often as possible. Negative criticism undermines self-esteem. The ideas in Part II should help you convey your values and motivate your children while *increasing* their self-esteem.

The other principle is to listen. Sometimes it takes a special effort to listen compassionately, understandingly, and nonjudgmentally, especially to a family member. (We all know people who are excellent listeners at work or with friends but who fail dismally with their own parents, spouses, or children.) However, there is something even more important than understanding your children. On certain points, it is essential to make *them* understand *you*.

≡The job of restriction

The problem with the restrictive part of our job is that we love our children. We want life to be easy for them. We want to protect them from the ruthless world outside the home. We do not want a ruthless world inside the home. We want to be kind, generous, understanding parents. We want our children to love us. At the same time, we need to ensure our children's compliance with basic rules, and that means establishing a certain degree of authority.

This dilemma faces parents all across America: rich and poor; married, single, divorced, and remarried; black, white, and of every ethnic group. We place a high value on individual freedom. We have a distaste for authoritarian regimes of any kind. Yet, as parents, we do sometimes have to discipline our children.

Unfortunately, many of us feel so ambivalent about the whole idea of discipline that we do it in an unsystematic, even arbitrary, way—and we often find that it only makes our children's behavior worse. This is because we garble the messages that we are trying to send them.

Part of our ambivalence is that while we want our children to obey certain rules, we don't want them to do it because they are coerced. We want them to follow our rules *of their own free will!* We are not satisfied with reluctant compliance: We want *willing* compliance—children who come home on time because *they* think it is important. As the psychoanalyst Bruno Bettelheim expressed the dilemma to *our* parents:

> Life was much easier for my parents: they knew what a child was supposed to do, and he had jolly well better do it. But things are different with us. We want our children to live according to their own lights, to develop their personalities in freedom. This we do because we believe in freedom and know that coercion is bad. At the same time, we want their development to lead to goals we have set for them. Fearful of spoiling their spontaneity and happiness, we refrain from imposing our wishes on them; yet we want to end up with the same results as though we had.*

The dream child would respect our rules, would want to abide by them just because he sees how reasonable they are. We are afraid to force our children to do things they do not really want to do, and we are afraid to prevent them from doing things they do want to do.

A system of rules. In Part I of this book, I am going to show you how to make and enforce a set of rules consistent with your own values. I assume that each set of parents will have their own ideas about what limits they need to place on their children's freedom. This system will work for any family. It deals with *how* to be firm and consistent, *how* to translate your specific concerns into rules. The question of *what* rules to make will be left up to you.

You may be liberal or conservative, modern or old-fashioned, permissive or strict. My task is to teach you to translate your own values into clear and consistent rules: enforceable rules that provide freedom to live together and grow.

I have no opinion as to whether your daughter should be home by 5:00, 9:00, midnight, or whenever she pleases. Your rule must depend on her age, your neighborhood, your lifestyle, and the degree to which you can trust her judgment. I have no opinion as to whether your son should be required to do his homework before he turns on the TV, whether he should be allowed to invite friends over without asking you first or to smoke dope on school

* Bruno Bettelheim, *Dialogues with Mothers*, New York: Free Press, 1962, p. 11.

nights. Instead, I shall try to help *you decide* what rules to set up for your family.

If you already have a few firm rules, if your children know what the rules are, if you follow through with consistent consequences when the rules are occasionally tested, and if you don't nag or complain about other things, then you are not having trouble with your kids. You may skip to Part II. On the other hand, perhaps the principles make sense to you intellectually but you simply have not been able to put them into practice. Do you find yourself being inconsistent about rules, unable to enforce them, unable to monitor whether the kids are obeying them or not? Or perhaps you are getting into power struggles about things that are not really important. Part I is for you.

This system has helped many different kinds of families. Some were families whom I counseled when their kids were only mildly obnoxious; others were in deep trouble. I cannot claim much originality for the system. Every day, thousands of family counselors help parents to draw up lists of rules for their children. If your family is having a crisis, then you need professional help (see chapters 20 and 21). But I decided to write this book when I realized that for every family in need of professional counseling, there are dozens of other parents who can put a system of rules to work *before* a crisis occurs, with far less emotional and financial cost.

I put the restrictive part first because I think other books on child-rearing don't say enough about it. However, you need to be *both* restrictive and constructive. The principal purpose of this book is to show you how to integrate the constructive part with the restrictive part of your job.

≡In a nutshell

This book is not radical or avant-garde. It is not based on new discoveries. It is based on fundamental, well-established principles of psychology, child development, and family relations. Its three most important principles can be stated quite simply:

1. Children, like adults, will make responsible decisions, protect themselves from harm, and work to achieve their potential only if they have a strong sense of self-esteem.

2. Children, like adults, respond poorly to criticism of

their personalities. They respond much better to suggestions on how they can change specific behavior to get specific results.

    3. Children, like adults, choose to act in ways that lead to pleasant consequences and not to unpleasant consequences.

I don't know any psychologists who would disagree with those principles. For that reason, I will not be citing many other authors to support the statements in this book. At the end of Part I and each subsequent chapter, however, you will find a list of suggested books for further reading. (In making these suggestions, I have limited myself to full-length books, currently in print, which contain additional material on topics I may have treated too briefly. Each book is listed only once, though most could have been listed in connection with several chapters. Unless otherwise indicated, the recommended books are addressed primarily to parents, rather than to psychologists or educators.)

Is this book different from the dozens of other self-help books for parents? It is different in two major ways. In one way, it is more specific. It avoids generalities, which make sense while one is reading a book but are not so easy to translate into practical measures. As much as possible, I shall present *methods* for making and enforcing rules, for making children feel good about themselves, for listening to them and getting them to listen to you.

In another way, this book is *less* specific than any other book I know, because the methods offered have nothing to do with the content of your rules, punishments, or values. The system helps *you* decide on *your* rules, helps you enforce them, helps you talk with your children about those rules and about your preferences and concerns. You can use this system whether you are conservative, liberal, religious, agnostic, or "none of the above."

Later in the book, to be sure, many of my own attitudes will be obvious. It would not be possible to hide them, nor would you want me to hide them. They are derived partly from professional experience and partly from my own successes and mistakes as a parent. But what my wife and I think is right for our kids may not be right for yours. What you need is a system for making and enforcing your own family rules, based on your own values.

PART I.

A System of Clear, Firm Family Rules

Part I deals with the restrictive aspect of parenting. Not all children require written rules with specific consequences, but if one of your children does, then you need to write a set of rules for each child in the family. Although two parents can have different opinions about most things without creating any problems for their children, they have to come to a definite agreement about rules, because rules are the things parents *insist upon*.

You should start with as few rules as possible, with consequences that are relatively small. Then you can add rules as needed, and you can escalate the consequences until they are sufficiently persuasive. After an overview of the system in chapter 2, chapters 3 through 10 deal with making rules, enforcing them, and changing them over time.

Throughout this part of the book, I deal with the dilemma of how parents can be authoritative without being authoritarian: how to be firm about certain things and open about others, how to rule by love and respect rather than by antagonism and fear.

CHAPTER TWO

Restrict
to Make Free

This chapter presents the main ideas of Part I. The most important idea is that children need restrictions in order to be able to handle freedom.

A developing child's proper goal is to acquire the liberty that adults enjoy. Adults in a free society have a great deal of freedom, as long as we obey the law and respect the rights of others. Infants begin with no respect for the law or for other people's rights—and with no freedom. They learn how to be free, within the law and in cooperation with other people. Their parents' long-term goal, therefore, is not to control the child. It is to *relinquish control* to him, gradually, sensibly, and sensitively.

Defining children's and parent's goals that way—in terms of freedom—leads us to three principles:

1. At every age, make the limits on your children's freedom clear to them. Too much freedom is scary. They are afraid of hurting themselves or others. A few well-defined restrictions are reassuring. Children often are uncomfortable when they do not know what the rules are. It makes them unsure where they stand with other people. Do others, particularly their parents, care what they do? Will others, particularly their parents, think them good or bad? It is just as important for parents to be restrictive *enough* as not to be overly restrictive.

2. Allow more freedom only when your children demonstrate that they can handle the freedom they already have. Greater autonomy is the child's *reward* for respecting the rules.

3. When you have to punish a child in order to make it clear that your rules are to be taken seriously, the best kinds of punishment to use are those involving extra restrictions. Children's disobedience usually indicates that they are not mature enough to handle the freedom they have and that they need a little more restriction to feel secure.

Ways of restricting freedom are different at different ages: A seven-year-old might be sent to his room, a twelve-year-old grounded, a seventeen-year-old denied the use of the car. Having an allowance, being allowed to have a friend sleep over, watching television, and talking on the telephone are all forms of freedom that children cherish.

Some frequently used methods of punishment that are *not* restrictions of freedom include spankings, humiliation, and deprivation of basic needs, especially food. I don't advocate any of those methods. Such methods cheat parents out of the opportunity to get across that important message about freedom. Furthermore, they aren't effective. And they often create worse problems than the ones the parents are trying to solve.

With these principles in mind, you can become a perfectly clear parent with a minimum of effort and aggravation, freeing yourself to concentrate on the more constructive aspect of the job, which is to build competence and self-confidence.

≡How to be a clear parent: Eight steps

It may sound like an ambitious task, proposing to teach you how to change your whole manner of dealing with problem behavior in your children. We can break the system down into eight steps:

1. Read this entire book, and discuss it with your spouse or partner. (If you're a single parent, discuss it with a friend.) If you're not having any problems with your children right now, then you don't need written rules; con-

centrate on the ideas in Part II, and save what you learn from Part I until it is needed.

2. If you are concerned about certain behavior problems, make a list of rules for each child, based on those current problems. Start with as few rules as possible; you can add more later as needed. (It is only the "standing" rules that need to be written down. Those are the ones I shall emphasize in this book, because once you learn how to make enforceable written rules, the one-time spoken rules, such as "We're not going to the beach until the family room has been cleaned up," will come naturally to you.)

3. For each rule, think of an appropriate consequence to impose if the rule is violated. ("If Sandra doesn't wash her dishes before going off to call her friends, she loses phone privileges for twenty-four hours.") A *consequence* is a specific punishment that the child knows about in advance. Start with the *smallest* consequence that you think might be sufficient to enforce the rule.

4. Formally present the list of rules to your children. Some rules will apply differently to each child, depending on their ages and individual needs.

5. Don't panic if the children test your rules. You can expect them to. Show them that you are serious by following through with the consequences you promised.

6. Amend the rules as necessary.

7. Escalate the consequences as necessary. Start with the *smallest increase* that you think might get the message across.

8. When your children catch you nagging them or complaining about actions that you have not dealt with in your written rules, admit your error. Apologize, and either leave them alone or establish a new rule that will apply in the future.

Each of those steps will be discussed and illustrated in the following chapters. The first thing to make clear is the distinction between *rules* and *preferences*.

≡Rules versus preferences

Rules are the things you insist upon. Each rule states what a child must do (or must not do) and what sort of consequence will follow if he ignores that rule. *Every rule involves consequences.*

Preferences, on the other hand, are essentially suggestions; although you may try hard to convince a child to follow those preferences, they are ultimately matters of the child's own discretion.

Now you can see how the restrictive part of this system and the constructive part (Part II) are each indispensable to the other. In making your rules clear, you provide firmness and security. At the same time, you make it equally clear which of your statements are merely preferences, not rules. That builds the children's sense of having choices and having to take responsibility for their own decisions.

By drawing up a set of written rules, stated clearly and enforced consistently, you get a double benefit: Your children follow the rules, and in the areas where you are not making rules, they learn to handle freedom.

These two areas of your children's lives will be treated quite differently from each other in this book. Part II deals mainly with the area outside your rules, where you have preferences but allow your children to make their own decisions. That is the area in which you give them most of their moral education, social skills, positive feelings about themselves and others. Rules and discipline, our concern in Part I, have little to do directly with right and wrong or with whether the child is good or bad in any moral sense. Their purpose is merely to provide a structure. They are for safety, convenience, family harmony, peace of mind. They guarantee the child some experience at meeting the parents' expectations, while becoming less necessary as the child grows up.

You may think that you already have rules, but I'll bet you don't. You don't have rules unless every rule and its consequence are written down and clearly understood, and unless you always follow through.

> MISTAKE: Joe and Patty claim to have three rules for their eleven- and thirteen-year-old boys. The boys "must" do their homework before they are allowed to watch TV in the evening. (Actually, all that happens when the children

decide to put off their homework and turn on the TV is that sometimes they get away with it and sometimes they get yelled at.) They "must" practice the piano half an hour every day. (If they miss a day, they had better have a good excuse; if they miss a lot of days, they get yelled at.) They "must" cut the grass every week. (Their father keeps nagging at them until they do it; when he gets tired of nagging, they get yelled at.) This is not a system of rules; it is a system of nagging and yelling.

BETTER: Joe and Patty decide that they can be more explicit about a homework *rule*: The boys are not allowed in front of the TV until they have shown their homework to one of the parents. If either of the boys tries to watch TV before showing his homework, he must go to bed.

They can also eliminate the nagging and yelling about the lawn. If the grass is not mowed by noon on Saturday, neither boy gets his allowance that week. Dad announces that it is not his responsibility to remind them to do their chore.

The parents decide that they cannot insist on the piano lessons, since both boys have shown a lack of enthusiasm for practicing. They make a rule about practicing, with the only consequence being that the lessons will stop if the boys do not practice. Of course, the parents would *prefer* to have the lessons continue, but not at the price of nagging and yelling. They tell the boys their reasons for valuing music lessons so highly, and they say that they will stop paying for lessons if the amount of practicing the teacher recommends is not done each week. They will still sometimes remind the boys to practice, but they will not take the responsibility upon themselves to ensure that the boys meet their requirement. They leave up to each boy the decision about whether to continue the lessons, on those terms.

If these children were yours, you might make different decisions. That is why I am not interested in telling you what rules to make or what consequences you should impose. Instead, you can apply this system to your own values and concerns, and to the specific problems that come up with your own children.

The differences between rules and preferences. Rules are the things you *insist upon*, whereas preferences are the rest of the things you have *opinions about*. There are several important differences.

- Mom and Dad don't have to have the same preferences; they do have to agree on rules. One parent may think pierced ears are terrible while the other thinks they are okay. The child can be aware of both parents' views and make her own decision. If either parent wanted to make a *rule* about it, however ("All girls in this family must [or must not] have their ears pierced before age fifteen"), he or she would first have to get the other parent to agree.

- Preferences do not have to be consistent; rules do. Children can live fairly comfortably with the fact that we adults are often inconsistent or changeable in our preferences. I might state flatly that video games are an awful waste of a child's time yet turn right around and have a great time playing Cosmoblast with my son. He will infer something like "Adults are often inconsistent in what they claim to approve or disapprove of," which is true. But I must not be that way with rules. With rules, I have to be consistent.

- A rule has to be perfectly clear, whereas a preference can be conveniently vague. To a child who is going outside to play, you might say, "Don't go too far." That is only a preference, because it leaves the meaning of "too far" to the child's own judgment. If you want to make it a rule, you have to say, "Don't leave the yard" or "Don't cross the street" or "Don't leave town." Similarly, saying, "Don't go too far," to your teenage daughter, referring to her boyfriend, would only be a preference. A rule—if you could enforce it—would have to state explicitly whether turning out the lights is "too far," whether taking off clothes is "too far," and so forth.

- The most important difference is that when rules are ignored, the child is going to be punished; when preferences are ignored, you may get upset, you may give a lecture or burst into tears, but there is really no consequence for the child unless you decide to make a new rule for the future.

How strongly do you feel about pierced ears? Strongly enough to punish your child for going against your wishes? If not, then it isn't going to be a rule. And it doesn't have to be a problem either, unless you continue to make an issue of it.

Many of the difficulties parents get into with so-called "problem children" can be traced to the parents' failure to make that last distinction clear. The children are yelled at or nagged at about all kinds of things, but they do not get the idea that their parents care much more about some of those things than others. They do not see the difference between "opinions about" and "insist upon." With a set of rules, you make that special set of concerns crystal-clear, thus freeing the whole family from the destructive burden of nagging, arguing, and resentment.

Every rule should be written down. You do not have to think of every rule you might need, in advance. (In fact, the fewer rules, the better!) You can add them to the list as they become necessary. But no child should be punished for actions that are not explicitly prohibited. This means that the first time your fifteen-year-old helps herself to a beer from the refrigerator, or the first time your two-year-old draws on the wall, if that kind of behavior is not mentioned in the list of rules, you should tell the child not to do it again, but you should not punish her. Show the child that you are writing, "No alcoholic beverages," with a consequence, or "No drawing, painting, or marking on anything except drawing paper," with a consequence. (Don't worry about two-year-olds not being able to read; they will remember what you tell them it says.) And the *next* time it happens, you punish the child as promised.

≡Liberty versus Probation

The system proposed in the following chapters is based on the principle that children should lose freedom when they act irresponsibly, gain freedom when they demonstrate responsibility. This involves two fundamentally different modes of life, which I call *Liberty* and *Probation.* Each mode has its own set of rules and consequences, and there are also rules about how a child can move from one mode to the other.

Liberty. Within the Liberty mode, parents assume their children are following the rules and telling the truth, unless evidence arises to the contrary.

In a free society, none of us is entirely free; the law restricts us, and there are laws that restrict some of us more than others. There are laws applying only to psychologists, other restrictions applying to physicians, broadcasters, beauticians, union members, government employees, and many other groups. Minors are subject to the greatest restrictions. They are denied the rights to vote, to drive, to buy liquor, to choose not to go to school, and to refuse medical treatment.

Despite all the restrictions of the law, liberty is still a great privilege. If we abuse it, we lose it. The idea behind Liberty for children is the same: They can enjoy a great latitude, trust, and freedom of choice within the boundaries created by certain rules. Their parents must make those rules clear and consistent, and keep amending them as the children mature.

As the diagram indicates, if the first consequences you apply don't change the child's behavior, you can escalate the consequences. Still within the Liberty mode, you experiment to find out how much restriction the child seems to need.

If the child continues to repeat the undesirable behavior despite escalating punishment, something must be wrong—with the child, with the rules, with you, or with all three.

Problem assessment. Suppose those minor punishments (the routine consequences listed in your rules) are not working. The decision about what to do next requires a family meeting in which everyone tries to discover any reason why the child *cannot* do what you expect of him. It is not a question of why he *chooses* not to obey but of whether there is any physical or psychological impediment. Here are some possible circumstances in which you would *not* impose Probation:

LIBERTY

1. Ask for cooperation without formal rules.
2. If problem persists, make formal rules.
3. If problem persists, escalate consequences.
4. If problem persists, assess whether professional help is needed or whether the child needs to lose certain privileges (Probation) until more responsibility has been demonstrated.

PROBATION

1. If successful, return to Liberty.
2. If unsuccessful, seek professional advice.

PROFESSIONAL HELP

Pediatrician
School psychologist
  or social worker
Family therapist

1. The child is physically ill. In that case, he should be treated as in "Sick Bay" (a temporary mode requiring a special set of rules) until well enough to return to the Liberty mode.

2. The child is emotionally disturbed, learning-disabled, or has some chronic organic impairment. You need to get therapy or remedial help for the child.

3. You have not really resolved to control the behavior; you are giving confusing or inconsistent messages. The child's payoff for continuing the obnoxious behavior may be greater than the cost of abandoning it. In this case, the whole family needs counseling. Chapter 21 deals with how you can tell when problems with children have gone beyond what you should be able to resolve on your own and when you need professional assistance.

The remaining possibility is that the child does not believe you are really going to take charge. He or she is afraid that in the face of chaos and antagonism, you may back down. There may also be a fear that your resolve on this one issue will be negated by weakness on other issues. Children do not want weak parents; they want strong parents. A strong parent is one who stands firm on important matters yet is strong enough to refrain from taking an authoritarian stance on matters that should really be up to the child.

The way to reassure the child that you are as strong as he wants you to be is to let him know that you do not think Liberty is working and that you are putting him on Probation.

Probation. Any occasional punishments, or even a series of escalating punishments, fall within the mode of Liberty. I use the term *Probation* to refer to the times when freedom has been lost for a period; the child can no longer simply obey the regular rules, and he must earn his way back to Liberty by *proving* himself under more restrictive conditions.

Probation is a totally different mode of family life because the burden of proof is now on the child. He will have to regain your trust before he can return to Liberty. Chapter 9 is devoted to Probation.

Problem reassessment. If the extra restrictions of Probation are not sufficient incentive to the child, and if you are not willing to accept a standoff, then you need to consider the same four possibilities listed under *Problem assessment* above. There is a third mode, *Crisis*, which combines the third and fourth of those choices: professional help and (if so advised) an even tougher stance.

In chapter 20, "Crisis," we shall talk about the ToughLove movement and other parent support groups for families whose teenagers are out of control. The purpose of these groups is to make an adolescent dissatisfied with the condition into which he has gotten himself and to make sure he knows how he got in as well as how to get out. At this point, the parents absolutely refuse to make any accommodation to the child—refuse to be victimized by abusive behavior—until there have been radical changes. The Crisis mode, besides involving more onerous conditions for the child, requires an intensive commitment of time and energy by the parents to solve a severe problem. We hope you are not going to need chapter 20. This book is a crisis *prevention* system.

Are you really going to have to "get tough"? No. For the majority of children whose parents resolve to be clear about rules and consequences, the years from birth to age eighteen will consist of a total of about seventeen years and eleven and a half months of Liberty, plus maybe a week or two, total, of Probation. Only a few families will have to resort to Probation more extensively. Of those, a very small number will actually reach what I consider a Crisis. Your children will live in the Liberty mode most of the time. The value of the other modes is to provide something you can fall back upon if needed. So long as both you and your children realize that the other modes exist, as viable but less desirable alternatives to Liberty, you won't need the Probation mode much or the Crisis mode at all.

You are also likely to find that you need *fewer* rules after reading this book than you had before and that you seldom have to punish your children. A few clearly stated rules, consistently enforced with mild consequences, are far more effective than a long list of *do's* and *don'ts* maintained only by nagging, or by ignoring misbehavior for a while, then cracking down with an excessive punishment.

CHAPTER THREE

Who Makes the Rules?

Parental clarity involves three types of "management" decisions: writing rules in the first place, deciding on punishments when the rules are violated, and amending rules if they are not working as intended. In all three cases, *the parents together* have to make these decisions. Even if you disagree about other things, you must be a united front with respect to the rules.

There are some circumstances in which one parent may delegate authority to the other—for example, when a challenge to the rules has to be dealt with immediately by whichever parent is home at the time. Even then, however, it is really a decision of the management team (one parent agrees to support the other's ruling, whatever it might be), and the children must not be allowed to undermine the team's authority by appealing to the one who was not around at the time the ruling was made.

A child's *parents*, for this purpose, are not necessarily the mother and father as defined by law (the biological or adoptive parents). They may be mother and stepfather, father and stepmother, one parent and a live-in partner, foster parents, even grandparents or grown brothers or sisters if the original parents are dead or absent. What matters is that they are the adults whom the child recognizes as having parental responsibilities. Even if only one of them is related to the child, that parent's spouse or partner living in the same home usually has to act as a coparent with respect to rules.

In the simple, intact family, mother and father have to make the rules together as a team. This cannot be said too often. For example, it is almost impossible for a mother to enforce a set of rules if the children's father lives in the home but has no part in creating the rules or does not back up his wife when she tries to enforce them. It is equally impossible for a father to succeed with such a system without the active participation of his wife.

Your family may not fit the standard model (mother, father, and their mutual children). If not, you will want to read chapters 17, 18, and 19, which deal with the special challenges you face. But at this point in the book, you need to decide to whom the word *parents* refers in your family.

> EXAMPLE: Sandy, a single mother, is living with her children in her parents' home. The grandparents have made some rules about their house ("No jumping on the furniture" is one), but Mother alone is the decision-maker about bedtimes, homework, fighting among the kids, and other rules affecting their welfare. Sandy's boyfriend, her parents, and her ex-husband are only consultants.

> EXAMPLE: Bill and Sue are divorced. Sue and her new husband make the rules for their home, while Bill alone makes the rules that apply when the children are visiting him.

In a divorced family with remarriages or equivalent long-term relationships, each set of partners has to make rules autonomously for their own household.

> EXAMPLE: Ron and Linda have a "his, hers, and ours" situation. His three children from a former marriage and her two children live with them, as well as the children they had together. Both parents function as a team with respect to all the children. Their *relationships* are naturally different with the individual children, but the way they make and enforce *rules* is not different.

If you are among the millions of divorced parents with new partners in our society, the commitment to move in together and cooperate in the management of a home has to mean a joint commitment to parenting, even if you aren't legally married. The issues are not legal ones. Married or not, you might be tempted to say, "She's your daughter, so you be the parent; I just want to be her friend." That usually creates more problems than it solves.

I don't mean to say that a stepparent should try to have the kind of relationship with a stepchild that a full parent can have (see chapter 18). The role of stepparent is a different role, never taking over the natural parent's role.* But so far as enforcing rules is concerned, it is *family management teamwork* that matters, not biological ties or depth of feeling.

In other words, a team consisting of a natural parent and a stepparent should handle rules and punishments exactly as any other parents should. It is not as easy, of course. But the best ways for stepparents to communicate clear rules are the same as for natural parents. In fact, in Part II, when we take up the task of building self-esteem and competence, I shall again be saying the same thing to stepparents, foster parents, grandparents (and so forth) as to biological parents.

Regardless of how they are related to the children, some parental couples are going to have trouble agreeing on rules or punishments. That is when many couples give up the idea of teamwork. The father lets his wife deal with the children, or the mother resorts to "wait until your father gets home." *This is guaranteed to make the children act up.* If the parents can sit down together and debate the pros and cons—no matter how long it takes—so that they finally come up with an explicit written rule which both agree to enforce, and if they proceed to stick to it without undermining one another later, their children will almost always shape up.

What should you do if you can't get your partner to cooperate in this effort? Perhaps your spouse travels a great deal or feels hopelessly incapable of managing children. Don't give up. Make up a set of rules on your own as if you were a single parent, but then show them to the other parent and get at least a tacit agreement. Then you can present them to the children as coming from both of you.

The time your rule-making team needs professional help is when you cannot agree on rules or when you yourselves break the rules because you keep getting embroiled in extraneous conflicts. We shall have more to say about that in chapter 21.

---

* An exception is when a stepparent legally adopts the children; then they drop the "step-."

≡Some nonexceptions

There are certain "special" situations that can increase stress upon parents, children, or both—and which usually increase the necessity for a clear set of rules. However, these variations will not be treated as exceptional in this book, because what I have to say applies just as well to them as to all other families.

Working mothers. Historically, most mothers have also had to produce food or to earn income for their families. The mother whose only job was to manage a home on her husband's income was the exception. In recent centuries, her "privileged" position became a kind of upper-class fashion (against which women of achievement had to fight), and in our parents' generation it became a middle-class pattern. Now it is going the way of all fashions. As Dr. Spock recognized when he revised his 1945 *Common Sense Book of Baby and Child Care* in 1975, methods of child-rearing that require mothers to stay home all day are no longer adequate for the majority of families.

Accordingly, I do not assume that mother and father are the only people who will be taking care of the children when they are not in school. However, no matter who else is involved in caring for your children, the rules we are concerned about in this book are the rules you, the parents, make. You may decide to ignore some of the things the baby-sitter or day-care worker handles differently than you would. You may also decide to incorporate some of his or her suggestions in your rules. And there may be other rules that are so important to you that the sitter must cooperate in enforcing them: "If you don't do it our way, we'll have to find someone else."

In loco parentis. On the other hand, what if you have the charge of someone else's children in their home, or in yours, or in a day-care center or nursery school? Or what if you are a foster parent? The methods in this book are perfectly applicable to you. Only be sure to clarify with the children's parents (or with the agency that has custody of them) where your responsibilities begin and end. The difference between "at-home" rules and "elsewhere" rules, to be explained in the next chapter, will be particularly important for you.

Special children. No matter what is special about your children—whether they are adopted, physically or mentally handicapped, exceptionally intelligent, or emotionally disturbed—they still need rules. You are still the parents who must make the rules. Everything in this book applies to your family as much as to any other.

Some parents who feel sorry for such children, or awed by them, may unconsciously try to compensate by being overly permissive. Not only can this make the children feel even more different from other children than they are, but it also makes them feel insecure, because they are denied the structure any developing child needs.

Undoubtedly you have already learned a great deal about your particular child's special needs. Insofar as rules and discipline are concerned, *every* child has special needs. This system allows you to tailor the rules to a child's age, capability, and personality. It is flexible enough to be used with special children, too; the methods are the same.

CHAPTER FOUR

Making the Rules

Let's begin with the question of *when* you need rules.

Not everything you want your children to do has to be laid down in the form of a rule. You can ask children to do things simply because they are sensible things to do ("After your bath, please hang up your towel to dry") or because they will make your life simpler ("I'd appreciate it if you'd write all my phone messages on the pad in the den"). If that doesn't work, *then* you need to translate those preferences into rules.

> EXAMPLE: Dad is a contractor who works out of his home. His telephone messages are important. He has mentioned this to his children several times, but still his clients and suppliers complain in disbelief, "Didn't you get my message? Your kid said he was writing it down."
>
> This is the time for a rule. Not for detective work to figure out which child is guilty. Not for complaining, yelling, or threatening. Dad merely tells the children calmly (after discussing the problem with Mom), "Failure to get my messages has become a big problem for me. Every message must be written on this pad. If you're not in this room when you take the call, ask the person to hold while you come in here so that you can get all the information down on the pad. The rule is, if anyone tells me they called earlier and I didn't

get the message, Mom and I are not taking any messages from any of your friends for forty-eight hours."

Dad chooses the duration of punishment, forty-eight hours, after giving it some thought. It is long enough, he guesses, so that a few calls will probably come in for the children. (Even if they are home, he can tell the friend politely, "I'm sorry, I can't call Bob to the phone tonight; we're having a problem about the phone. Call back tomorrow.") On the other hand, it is short enough not to build up a grudge. If it proves to be too short—if the kids are still careless—Dad can make it seventy-two hours next time.

In this case, Dad has decided that all the children should suffer the penalty if any one of them fails to take a message. Since the penalty is so mild, the amount of unfair "suffering" won't really do any harm. There are two advantages: Dad does not have to play detective, and it will be in the children's interest to cooperate with each other in seeing that no one forgets.

In short, when a problem develops that makes you feel like nagging, yelling, or imposing some vengeful punishment, don't. Instead, sit down with your partner and translate your most important concerns into rules.

Like Dad's rule about phone messages, every rule should be in the form "If . . . then. . . ." It states what you plan to do next time. The child can feel secure about not being punished without advance notice. And you can feel secure, too, having a rational, effective plan ready to deal with any repetition of the problem.

≡Logical consequences

Dr. Rudolph Dreikurs, a child psychiatrist who wrote many books for parents a generation ago, made an important point about consequences. He discussed the difference between logical and arbitrary consequences. *Logical* consequences are restrictions that have an obvious meaningful relation to the problem a parent hopes to solve. It is logical to withhold allowance from a child who has not done his chores, because you can easily point out the connection between sharing family resources and sharing family tasks.

Arbitrary consequences lack that logical connection. They should be parents' second choice because they have less educational value than logical consequences. If you withhold allowance from a child who calls his sister names, you are teaching him about acceptable and unacceptable behavior in the family, but not about any direct connection between money and name-calling in the real world. A logical consequence for name-calling might be to send the child to his room; name-calling is antisocial.

Dreikurs further pointed out that the best logical consequences are *natural* consequences, which not only have a logical connection to the problem behavior but actually follow automatically upon it if the parent lets them. For example, a child leaves his bicycle unlocked in front of the house, violating a family rule. A natural consequence would be "If your bicycle is stolen, it will not be replaced."

Try to use natural consequences whenever possible. They are the best way for children to learn the contingencies of life itself, without feeling resentment against their parents.

Sometimes, however, there are no natural consequences. Suppose the child doesn't make his bed. If bed-making matters to you, then you will have to try to think of a logical consequence (for example, not being allowed to bring friends into the house, because the house is "not presentable"). Even when logical consequences are not immediately apparent, creative parents can almost always think of some sort of logical rationale. For example, taking twenty-five cents off your daughter's allowance for not making her bed would be an arbitrary consequence: but if you subtract it from her allowance and add it to her brother's for making her bed *and* his own, it becomes a logical consequence.

Sometimes natural consequences are not feasible because they are too severe. If your son misspends his bus money for the week and his school is five miles away, you may not feel he should have to walk there and back. A logical consequence might be to advance him the bus money and take it out of his allowance over the next few weeks.

Another example is a six-year-old who crosses the street without watching for cars. No parent is willing to wait for the natural consequence of that. Instead, we impose a logical consequence whenever a child of that age runs across the street without looking, whether there is a car coming or not: We suspend his or her earlier-won freedom to cross the street. Until further notice, the child has to ask permission and have an adult watching.

The same behavior in a two-year-old has no logical consequence, because the child has not yet earned the freedom to cross the street. So we have to resort to an arbitrary consequence, a spanking. The Dreikurs method is to try natural consequences first, if they are feasible. If not, then try to think of logical consequences that you can impose. Use arbitrary consequences as a last resort.

> EXAMPLE: Ten-year-old Barbara is slow at getting ready for school every morning. The carpool usually has to wait for Barbara, and sometimes all the children are late for school.
>
> *Natural consequence*: Leave without Barbara, if it is feasible to do so without creating other problems. Otherwise:
>
> *Logical consequence*: Make Barbara go to bed earlier so she won't be so groggy in the morning.
>
> *Arbitrary consequence*: Fine Barbara ten cents per minute after the time when she should be in the car. This is the least desirable method because there is no logical connection between the fine and the problem behavior.

≡Written rules for each child

Why do standing rules have to be written down? Because unwritten rules are never explicit enough. Even if you announce a rule explicitly at the dinner table when you have everyone's attention, the next time you remind someone of the rule, you won't word it exactly the same way. Did you say "in bed" by 9:00, or "in the bedroom" by 9:00? Did you mean "in bed, lights out" or "in bed reading"?

Many families post the standing rules on the refrigerator door. Others keep them out of sight of visitors, since they are no one's concern but the family's. Either way, I think it is a good idea to do a neat, impressive job; at least have the family member with the nicest penmanship do it, and redo the sheet whenever amendments become numerous. You may want to use extra-large sheets of paper or posterboard. If someone in the family knows calligraphy, this is a chance to practice it.

It might also be a good idea to keep a copy of the rules in a safe place, in case anyone destroys the public copy.* In practice, that happens rarely; even when the children may not like some of the rules, they come to appreciate having them written down for the sake of clarity and consistency.

Of course, you will also make some rules that apply on a single occasion; for example, "If there is any more fighting in the back seat, we are going to turn around and go home" or "If the stereo is turned up again, your friends will have to leave." These are not the sort of rules that one would write down, but everything else I say in this book applies just as much to single-occasion rules as to the more permanent, written rules. Once you establish credibility as a clear and consistent rule enforcer, with a written set of standing family rules, your children will respect the spontaneous, temporary rules as well.

If you write down rules for one child, you should write some for every child in the home, even if the other children are presenting no problems. Otherwise the rules will only increase the "problem child's" feeling of alienation. If he does ask, "How come George never has to . . . ," the answer can be, "You follow the rules we make for you, and let George worry about the rules we make for him."

The rules are different for different children because of disparities in age, maturity, proven capabilities, and special needs. You will continually reassess the rules for all your children as they mature.

Following are some sample rules for a family with four children: Karen (age seventeen), Bob (thirteen), Laurie (ten), and Billy (eight). The list for this family is organized in eight categories, which you may find helpful as you think about areas of concern in your own family. However, there is nothing sacred about these categories; there could just as well be two, or five, or only one category. Don't feel that you have to have rules about any of these particular issues; every family is different.

Some of this family's rules will strike you as too liberal, others as too strict, still others as just plain silly. That is to be expected: Your rules will depend on your values, your lifestyle, your

* You don't need a rule against that. As long as you have a copy of your rules, the children are going to be held responsible for them even if they "lose" the public copy. You needn't replace it unless they ask you to.

community, your family type (intact family, single parent, step-family, etc.), your income level, and, most of all, upon the maturity of each child.

You should start with fewer rules than these. I imagine the following list as having evolved for this family over a period of several months.* Don't make any rules unless you need them. In those areas where you have not found yourself nagging or complaining to your children, you don't need rules.

Rules about taking care of yourself	Consequences
Bedtimes (in bed, lights out)	
school nights—Billy 8:30, Laurie 9:00, Bob 10:30, Karen no rule	Bedtime 15 min. earlier next night
other nights—Billy, Laurie: 9:30; Bob, Karen: no rule	
Baths or Showers	
Billy, Laurie—Saturday nights and all school nights	If late bath makes you late for bed, see above
Toothbrushing (Billy)	
Remember without being told	If caught forgetting, Mom or Dad will brush

There are two good reasons for bedtime rules. One is that young children are not always wise enough to go to bed early enough to get the rest they need. They do not think ahead to what time they have to get up in the morning. The other legitimate reason for sending children to bed is that parents need some time for themselves at the end of the day.

However, it may not be important that your child always go to bed at a particular hour. You may feel it is more important that the child should go to bed whenever you say it is time. In that case, your rule should say, "No arguing, tantrums, or dawdling when told to go to bed." Specific times for each child, as in the example, are merely a convenience so that parents do not have to defend their judgment night after night.

In most families, the discipline issue only arises if the child delays when *told* that it is bedtime. The consequence for that can

---

* In fact, I went out of my way to think up many different kinds of rules for this illustration. I have never known a real family to need this many rules.

be flexible. Write "to be determined" in the consequence column, so you can make it follow logically from the specific circumstances.

> EXAMPLE: "I can't—I haven't finished my homework."
>
> "Then you will take the consequences at school for not having done your homework. You shouldn't have waited until 9:30 to start it."
>
> Or: "Then you may finish it, but for the rest of this week you will have no TV in the evenings."
>
> Or: "Then you may finish it, and we're writing down a new rule: 'From now on, no video games until all homework is done.' "

This kind of flexibility allows parents to tailor the consequences to the circumstances in which the rule was not observed. The main advantage of leaving punishments "to be determined" is that you keep your options open. The disadvantage is that you have to make and defend a decision every time, with infinitely varying extenuating circumstances.

With bathing and brushing teeth, the purpose is different from that of the other rules. Karen and Bob have already had the natural consequences (body odor, rotten teeth) so deeply ingrained that they are self-motivated, and need no rule. Billy and Laurie must bathe on certain nights, early enough so they can get to bed on time. The *natural* consequence of late or slow bathing is that one will not satisfy the bedtime rule, which in turn will have its logical consequence. (If, instead, a child began refusing to take baths at all, one would need an additional consequence for that.)

These parents have found an effective consequence for the child who habitually forgets to brush his teeth. He would rather do it himself than have someone else do it to him. After one or two times when a parent follows through as promised, Billy will take this responsibility upon himself. In the next edition of the rules, toothbrushing will no longer need to be mentioned.

Rules about when to be home	**Consequences**
After school, time expected home:	
Billy, Laurie—3:30	If late without asking
Bob—4:30	permission, must come

| Karen—6:00 | home directly from |
| | school, next three days |

Evening curfew:
    School nights—Bob 9:00, Karen
        10:30
    Other nights—   Curfew set earlier by
        Bob midnight, Karen 1:00 A.M.   the number of minutes
        (unless arranged in advance)   late, for one week

Rules involving times—whether they be mealtimes, bedtimes, curfew times, or times by which one is to have done something—can be handled in a much more straightforward way than most parents realize. The secret is to *make the child take the consequences even for circumstances beyond his control.* I will explain why this is fair and reasonable in the next chapter.

The consequence when Bob or Karen is late—setting back the curfew—is the quintessential punishment in this system. The logic is clear: "We seem to have given you more freedom than you could handle responsibly, so we'll take back a little." The reward for respecting the rules is to gain gradually more freedom. That process is temporarily reversed when the amount of freedom seems to be too great.

There is also something else that makes this punishment effective. It allows you to start small. When Karen is ten minutes late, her parents do not need to ground her for a whole evening just to make their point—and make her resentful. Instead, they set her curfew back ten minutes, for a week. As I shall explain later, it is the consistency of consequences, not their intensity, that gets the message across. If, after Karen tests the rule a few more times, they conclude that this has not had the desired effect, then they can change the penalty to "two minutes earlier per minute late" or change the duration of the penalty to two weeks, three weeks, and so forth. *When you start with the smallest consequence that you think might work, you have room to escalate it as needed.*

Why did the parents write down an explicit consequence for missing curfew? Why not be flexible, as I suggested they could have done with the bedtime consequences? Although it is convenient to be able to use your discretion in some situations, there are two important advantages to spelling out the consequence in advance if you can. First, the decision does not have to be made in the heat of anger when the child is testing you. When you have been waiting up anxiously for a child whom you imagined lying dead on the highway, and who now strolls in unscratched, there is a chance that you might overreact and overpunish, which would be counterproductive.

The other advantage is that when children know exactly what will happen if they fail to comply with your limits, they can give their friends a convincing explanation for wanting to comply. When a curfew violation has a fixed penalty attached, the teenager has no difficulty explaining to her friends why she wants to be home by a particular time. Instead of telling them, "I'm supposed to be home by 10:30," she can say, "If I'm not home by 10:30 I won't be able to go to the basketball game Friday night." The consequences of violating curfew have to provide the rationale not only to the child but to the peer group as well. (Adolescents often tell their friends that their parents have made a stricter rule than is really the case. They use the parents as "bad guys," to get out of social situations they do not feel ready for.)

In general, it may be best to spell out consequences clearly, in advance, for major rules having to do with the boundary between parental authority and peer temptations (curfews, drinking, drugs, etc.) and to be more spontaneous and flexible about punishments for minor disobedience of rules such as those concerning bedtime and chores.

Rules about freedom of movement	Consequences
Billy & Laurie—parent who is home must know where you are; if neither of us is home, call Mom at work	Grounding—duration to be determined
Bob—we must know your destination, time to expect you home; railroad tracks are OFF LIMITS	" "
Karen—we must know where you are in evenings; location of parties, etc.	" "

These are what I call *elsewhere* rules, rather than *at-home* rules. They can only be enforced if and when it comes to the parents' attention that they were violated. In theory, any of the children could lie about where they are going or where they were. However, if lying has not been a problem in your family, you should assume that your children are going to continue to tell the truth. *Trust each child to the full extent that he has shown himself trustworthy in the past.* (I will have more to say about trust in Part II.)

On the other hand, these children know, without needing to have it spelled out, that if something were to happen when they were not where they were supposed to be—if Billy had a flat tire on his bicycle, for example, on the other side of a road he was not supposed to cross—the consequences would be serious. One incident might be handled by grounding, but by the second or third incident the child would have lost the parents' trust, and his mode of life would be changed from Liberty to Probation.

Chores	Consequences
Breakfast, lunch, snacks—everyone does own dishes	If dishes left in sink or kitchen a mess, you take one of Dad's nights

Dinner dishes:
    Mon., Tues.: Bob & Billy
    Wed., Thurs.: Karen & Laurie
    Fri., Sat., Sun.: Dad	

Bob & Karen—grass cut & raked by noon Saturday, except when Dad says not needed; shovel snow within twelve hours	$5 of allowance revoked that week
Laurie & Billy help Mom fold & deliver clean laundry to rooms every Sat.	Lose 50¢ of allowance
Put your own dirty clothes in the hamper	
Bedsheets—help each other change as needed	

The schedule of chores is best worked out at a family meeting. The parents announce what has to be done but give the children maximum participation in deciding who should do what, and when. That puts the burden of proof on the children to show that the plan they work out is a good one; if it does not work, then Mom and Dad will come up with a plan that the kids like less.

There are dozens of different ways to handle the dishwashing problem. In some families, everyone helps after each meal. In some families, the job rotates by the day or the week. I know families in which Mom does all the dishes (as well as the cooking), others in which it is Dad's job with a different helper each night. And there are many families who rarely eat together; they all take care of their own meals and dishes.

Whatever system you and your children work out, you need a clear procedure to follow when someone "forgets." This family has decided that if the omission is discovered in time, the person who forgot can be summoned back from whatever he or she is doing, even if that means interrupting a TV program or a phone call. If the person has already escaped, then someone else will wash the dishes, but the offender will have to take over one of Dad's weekend dinners.

At the family meeting, you can veto any proposal that would be unfair to someone or that would not get the jobs done in good time. However, it is worth trying it the kids' way whenever their plan has a reasonable chance of succeeding. You can let them know in advance what Plan B will be if they don't make Plan A work.

In this family, the consequence for not putting dirty clothes and sheets in the laundry hamper is a *natural* consequence: They will not be washed. If that is not a sufficient incentive in your house, then you will need an additional consequence, such as a fine.

Allowance (Irrevocable + revocable = total/wk.)

	Irrevocable		revocable		total
Billy	.25	+	.75	=	$1
Laurie	.50	+	1.50	=	$2
Bob	5.00†	+	5.00	=	$10
Karen	11.00†	+	5.00	=	$16

†Only when school is in session

Giving allowances is not really a rule—it is something the parents promise to do each week. It is convenient to write the allowance on your list of rules because, like the rules, it will be different for each child and because a specific portion of the allowance can be listed as revocable if chores are not done.

I think it is a good idea to treat part of the allowance as "irrevocable," to be given to the child even if the other portion has to be withheld as punishment. Older children may need bus fare or lunch money every schoolday.* Everything beyond that is extra spending money.

Once you give the children their allowance, you are giving them the freedom to spend it as they choose. Otherwise, it is not really their money. So there should not be any rules about how the allowance is spent. Don't require the kids to get approval for every purchase; if you think they *routinely* misspend their allowance, you can reduce it. For the same reason, it makes little sense to require children to save part of their allowance. If you want to teach them about saving, open savings accounts for them and give each child money for regular deposits; but that is not an allowance.

Notice that Karen gets no more spending money than Bob. In fact, many teenagers get no allowance beyond what they need for school. Their parents feel—and I strongly agree—that adolescents should earn their spending money. (When they have a job that brings in more than a few dollars per week, there is nothing wrong with requiring them to save most of their earnings or, depending upon your family's situation, contributing toward the household expenses.) In this hypothetical case, however, the parents find it convenient to give Bob and Karen an incentive to get the yardwork done promptly.

Some parents go too far with the idea of allowance in exchange for chores. Getting the chores done is probably not your main purpose in giving an allowance. Your primary goal may be to give your children the experience of being responsible for some money of their own and learning that money is a finite resource requiring choices: "If I play any more arcade games, I won't be able to buy that record." The purpose of chores is to make children carry a fair share of the work involved in maintaining a home, whether they need the spending money or not.

Therefore, if Bob and Karen start to shirk their lawn-mowing duties and forgo their allowance, the parents will have to change

---

* Treat it as a *per diem*: no school, no lunch and bus money for that day.

the rule. One thing they can do is insist upon the chores and use some logical consequence other than money (for example, they might stop doing certain favors for Bob and Karen). On the other hand, if they think the children are being helpful enough around the house and are taking their other work seriously, they can simply hire a neighbor's kids to do the lawn. That would probably be cheaper than what they were paying Bob and Karen in allowance.

Priorities for use of time	Consequences
Everybody—finish homework before TV, phone, etc.	No TV or phone on following night
Bob & Karen—participate in at least one formal extracurricular activity involving at least two practices, rehearsals, or meetings per week—or an after-school job	
Everybody—if problems with grades, priorities will be reestablished after each report card	

Rules such as "homework before TV" are easy to enforce, if a parent is home in the evening. Obviously, it requires some thought as to how to design the rule so that you can enforce it in your family. But you don't need to worry in advance about all the possible evasions that might occur behind your back. The fundamental principle of the Liberty mode is trusting children until or unless they violate your trust. Make the rule only as iron-clad as it needs to be for that particular child.

It is worth asking *why* one thing should be done before another. In this family, homework was habitually put off until there was not enough time to do it carefully. Your child might be more responsible about homework, even if he does watch a favorite TV show right after dinner. Your real purpose is to support the *long-term* priority: Education is more important than entertainment. That does not necessarily have to be reflected in the order in which things are done, so long as they *are* done.

An entirely different reason for priorities, besides getting things done, is that they express the parents' values. Children need to know where their parents differ from the predominant values of their society. Some friends of mine never open Christmas presents until after church; once a year, they get a reputation for being hard-nosed, but they communicate a symbolic message to their children about their values. Similarly, some families prohibit TV except on the weekends. The children may complain, but they also enrich their lives by finding other things to do. *You can make any rule about priorities that you can justify in terms of your own values, as long as you are prepared to follow through.*

The rule about extracurricular activities might have been written to combat an "I don't care" attitude on Karen's part. Mom and Dad are saying, "You have to care about something. You can choose—or we'll choose for you." The consequence is implied. If Karen or Bob were to decide to test the parents on this, an explicit consequence would be needed—perhaps curtailing informal recreational activities in which the parents see no value.

Not all parents would go that far, but some go even further, demanding participation in such specific activities as football or choir. That might be unreasonable. Your judgment about the child's aptitudes for, and future benefits from, a given activity is likely to be based as much on your fantasies as on any objective evidence. How well a child succeeds in the activity and how much he or she benefits from it depend largely on motivation from within. I think children are helped more when we give them a strong incentive to get very involved in *something* but also give them as much choice as possible about what that something is.

Rules about priorities are generally of the type that you would apply to all the children in a certain age group. If you make one teenager give a higher priority to schoolwork than to sports, be sure you give all your teenagers the same message. I was intrigued recently when I heard a baseball star talking about his aspirations for his children. He said he hopes that his son can follow him into major-league baseball and that his daughter can become a doctor. If that meant that he were to show no concern for his son's grades as long as the son excelled in sports but not allow his daughter the same choice, it would be unfair to both children.

I am not suggesting that both children should be expected to get equally good grades or be equally good athletes. That obviously depends upon their individual talents. But whatever is expected to come first—schoolwork or sports or other activities —should be the same for both children.

Respecting others' rights and feelings	Consequences
No swearing (words on Mom's list), especially at someone in family	$1 per swear word used
	$2 per word
No insulting names	25 cents
No borrowing without permission	Person wronged will deal with it—but ask parent's help if needed—both parties may be punished
No punching or hitting	
Quiet down when asked	Sent to separate rooms
Telephone: leave message on fridge	No message taken for you, forty-eight hours. If culprit unknown, *all* kids take consequence
No arguments about phone	Children's phone unplugged for one week
Billy & Laurie have priority on TV, electronic games, etc., after dinner until bath or bed	

Mom has a list to which she can add any new word that she or Dad finds objectionable. They do not have to tell the children in advance all the swear words they can think of. Of course, each word is only added to the list the first time they hear it; the consequence starts the next time.

The "quiet down" rule is worth noting, because it illustrates how you can write a rule in general terms and then be specific about it on the spot. "Be quiet" would not, in itself, be an enforceable rule. "Be as quiet as you are asked to be" is perfectly enforceable. The same level of noise that is acceptable now may be unacceptable an hour from now, if someone is trying to nap.

With teenagers, you almost certainly need rules about the telephone. A separate phone number for the kids is a boon for parents, not only because it keeps your line free, but also because the privilege can be withheld to good effect. Suspension of phone privileges is a logical consequence for many rules involving communication, courtesy, or priorities.

For example, loss of telephone privileges for one night might have been a logical punishment, in place of a fine, for swearing or name-calling: "If you can't talk decently to your own family, you can't talk to others." (That would not work in this family, because the younger children don't use the phone much and the parents want a consequence that will apply to all four kids.)

Rules about motor vehicles	Consequences
Karen—replenish gas used, let no one else drive our car	Loss of car privileges, duration to be determined
Not allowed in *any* car if driver has had *any* intoxicating substance	Loss of license for one year

It is too bad when the automobile becomes a focus of contention between parents and sixteen- to eighteen-year-olds. Admittedly, it is a nuisance to have to share something that has previously been all yours. Under the right conditions, though, the day your teenager gets a driver's license can be the greatest relief for you, as a parent, since nursery school. Consider these wonderful facts:

- It marks the end, or at least, the beginning of the end, of your career as a chauffeur.

- The rules you make about care, maintenance, and responsible handling of your automobile are your first real opportunities to treat the adolescent as an adult. When you hand over your car keys, you are conferring the full respect and the same awesome responsibility—the power of life and death—that any adult driver has. You do not even need to say it; adolescents know it and, in most cases, are eager to prove themselves worthy of that trust.

- The privilege of borrowing your car and possession of a driver's license are probably the two most desired freedoms that you can restrict. Most states grant licenses to sixteen-year-olds only with parental permission and with the provision that *parents can revoke them*.

The rules may state explicitly when and how the car is to be used. Some parents find it convenient to limit the number of miles driven per week or the number of hours the car is away from the house. Alternatively, you can get an itinerary and time of promised return every time you lend the car, and make a rule about what will happen if those commitments are not kept. If you decide *not* to make a rule about such things, then don't complain about the miles or the hours.

Suspension of driving privileges, besides being the obvious

logical consequence for abusing the privileges themselves, is an appropriate consequence for all kinds of life-threatening irresponsibility—for example, being in someone else's car when that person has been drinking. The seriousness of that kind of behavior calls for a severe consequence, which you can be clear about before the occasion ever occurs. It is an exception to our general principles about not writing a rule until after something becomes a problem and starting with a small consequence that you can increase if necessary. The child who once drives while intoxicated, or rides in a car with an intoxicated driver, may not live to get a second chance.

Other rules	Consequences
No bikes left out—close garage door.	Bike impounded for one week
If you want to be picked up somewhere at a certain time, you have to ask in advance. Last-minute calls are okay only if it's an emergency (if we're convinced there was no other safe way for you to get home) & if it's not just an attempt to avoid consequence of being late.	
You are responsible for friends' conduct when in our house.	
No more than two friends (total, not per child) in the house when parents aren't home.	No friends can visit, duration to be determined
Each child may have one party per year, planned together with parents, and parents will be here during the party	

You can make rules about anything that you and your spouse agree is important enough for you to be willing to follow through with consequences. As a family counselor, I never answer "should" questions, such as "Should children be required to. . . ?" The question is whether it is important to you. If not, stop hassling the children; if the bicycle is left out in the rain, let it rust. If it *is* important to you, then instead of nagging, make a rule you know you can enforce: "If a bicycle is left outside, it will be confiscated for two days."

Parties, like cars, raise major issues for parents of teenagers. We shall discuss those issues in detail in Part II.

Rules are not always the answer. Before closing this chapter, I had better say that making rules is not the best way to deal with every issue. Here is an example where the parents try to make a rule and fail, because they threaten the child with a punishment they are not really willing to follow through on.

> EXAMPLE: The Ryans have attended church as a family every Sunday since their children were little. Catherine, seventeen, announces that she does not share her parents' convictions and refuses to go to church with them any longer.

> MISTAKE: Her parents make a rule: If we don't pray together, then we don't stay together. If Catherine will not attend church with the family, she had better find somewhere else to live. Catherine finds a family that is willing to provide room and board in exchange for child care. She has called her parents' bluff. Now they back down but remain angry and hurt, and the issue is unresolved.

> BETTER: There is nothing wrong with making a rule about church, but only to the extent you would really follow through. In this family's case, a two-way exchange of feelings would be more constructive than a firm rule, since the parents do care strongly about church, but not so strongly as to reject their daughter. In my experience, battles over ideology—whether political or religious—are better waged through active listening than through parents' insistence on having their own views accepted.

CHAPTER FIVE

Enforcing the Rules

The best way to be sure that your family rules will work is to avoid making rules that you cannot enforce. In order to be enforceable,

- A rule must be clear and specific.
- A rule must deal with observable events that will come to the parents' attention whenever a child decides to test the rule.
- A rule must have a legitimate purpose.
- A rule must have a consequence with which the parent is prepared to follow through.
- A rule must offer a choice: responsibility or restriction.

A rule must be clear and specific. Forcing yourself to put every rule in writing helps you think about whether it is going to be clear enough to all concerned. However, the mere fact that something is written down is no guarantee that it won't be vague or ambiguous.

> NOT ENFORCEABLE: "Get plenty of vitamins."
> BETTER: "Swallow one tablet from this jar every morning."

The Scout Oath is not a set of enforceable rules. Of the Ten

Commandments, only two can be expressed as enforceable rules.*

Your children will take upon themselves the job of finding loopholes in your list, flushing out every rule that is not specific enough. If the rule does not cover a particular action that a child tries, thank him or her for helping you with the system. Don't apply any punishment, but change the rule to make it clear for next time.

Of course, you are not going to write down a *temporary* rule (for example, "We're not leaving for the beach until everything in the playroom is put away"). However, once you have mastered the art of writing and enforcing your standing rules, you will find yourself automatically growing much more clear and specific about single-occasion rules as well.

A rule must deal with observable events. You are not a detective. For a rule to be enforceable, it must come to your attention when it has been violated. You cannot enforce a rule against truancy if the school does not report it to you. You cannot enforce a rule against drinking, but you can enforce rules against drunken behavior at home or being arrested for drunkenness. You cannot enforce a rule about using birth control in premarital sex—or about having sex in the first place—but you can let your teenagers know in advance the likely natural consequences of irresponsible sexual behavior.

In the previous chapter, we distinguished between *at-home* rules and *elsewhere* rules. Most of the at-home rules are the type that you make for the comfort and convenience of the household: chores that need to be done; rules about mealtimes, neatness, privacy, and TV. In general, one does not have to make such rules about the child's behavior outside or in other people's houses. Children who learn to respect at-home rules generally respect the rules of society at large. Their friends' parents are likely to be more restrictive than you about some things and less restrictive about others; but this never leads to confusion. Even two- to three-year-olds quickly learn to behave differently in different places, so long as each place has its own clear set of rules.

---

* The rules against murder and theft would seem to me specific enough, if earthly consequences were added. The other commandments are either too vague to be enforced—honoring one's parents, for example—or concern misbehavior that is unlikely to leave evidence—committing adultery, coveting, and so forth.

Those few elsewhere rules that you do make will usually be for the sake of the children's welfare or safety. These rules present bigger problems of detection and enforcement than do the at-home rules. "I can prevent him from smoking grass at home, but how do I know if he's smoking it elsewhere?" One thing you can do, after expressing your opinion about the dangers of marijuana, is to make a contract based on the child's honor-bound promise.*
But do not list the behavior itself (for example, smoking a joint in secrecy) as one of your explicit prohibitions. Do not have a rule against anything that you would probably not know about when it happened.

How can you translate a concern about something that might be done in secret into an enforceable rule? You may feel very strongly about drugs or teenage sex. With a younger child, you might have strong feelings about lying or eating too much candy. First ask yourself whether you would know when these things were going on. If not, then figure out what it is that really concerns you. We are generally worried about possible specific *effects* of immature behavior.

For example, make a list of the possible bad results of marijuana use. From that list choose the ones that will be clearly visible to you if they occur. Marijuana might lead your son to neglect his schoolwork, or to be late for school, or to get in trouble with the law.

> NOT ENFORCEABLE: "If you go to school stoned, we will ground you the next weekend."
> BETTER: "If the school reports any truancy or lateness, we will. . . ."

I am not going to tell you to stop worrying about things your children might do secretly, such as experimenting with pills. These are realistic fears, and you should share them with the child, but not in the form of rules. For the purpose of effective rules, focus only upon *observable* behaviors. This is where so many parents go wrong: By dwelling upon their worst fears, they distract themselves from setting any enforceable rules at all.

> EXAMPLE: The mother of eight-year-old Maria worries about candy and other snacks between meals. Her own

* Honor and trust are discussed in Part II.

sister is a compulsive eater, and she has read that this problem can begin in childhood.

MISTAKE: She constantly tells Maria how bad it is to stuff herself with snacks after school, keeps asking her if she has been snacking, and tells her that she will wind up obese and unhappy like Aunt Matilda.

BETTER: If Mother and Father would sit down and list their real concerns about between-meal snacks, they would include several observable facts: Maria's weight, for example, or her lack of appetite at mealtimes. They can tell her that meals are the only time Mother can ensure a balanced diet and that Maria is therefore expected to be hungry when she comes to the table. Her parents can ask the pediatrician what her normal weight range should be. If she goes above that range, she can only eat at mealtimes. So long as she is within the healthy range, however, and has a good appetite at mealtimes, she should be allowed to decide for herself whether she is hungry at other times, such as after school.*

Since so many children today have parents in two different households, I ought to point out that each parent's at-home rules apply to his or her own home, and only their elsewhere rules apply when the child is in the other parent's charge. You can enforce a rule about Johnny making his bed each morning or turning off the TV at 9:00 in your house, but it is up to the other parent and his or her current spouse to make and enforce the rules pertaining to their house. (See chapters 18 and 19.)

Rules must have a legitimate purpose: To ensure children's safety or welfare, to benefit the family, or to promote harmony. Children normally understand their parents' responsibility to be concerned about their behavior. What you are trying to get through to your children above all else is that you care about them and what happens to them. They may think you are old-fashioned, overly concerned, or just plain silly, but they will appreciate your rules anyway, so long as they respect your role as parents and household managers.

---

* An obese child needs therapy (chapter 21), but harping at any child about the evils of food is only likely to create a lifelong problem.

NOT ENFORCEABLE: "If I hear one peep out of either of you on the rest of this trip, I am going to stop the car."

BETTER: "If the noise level becomes a distraction to my driving, I will have to stop the car."

This system is not a way of getting your children to fulfill all your hopes for them—to become straight-A students, star athletes, or virtuoso musicians, and never bother you with any problems. Many children unfortunately get the message "If you have any negative feelings, any failures, any deviation from our standards, then our love and respect for you will end." That sort of message does not bring out the best in anyone.

When parents use their power for legitimate ends, the children soon grow more comfortable with rules than without. And as long as you yourself know that your rules are fair, you will feel comfortable in enforcing them.

Resolve not to break the rule. It is not quite enough that you have specified the rule in terms of an observable event. Equally important is your determination to follow through with the consequence.

NOT ENFORCEABLE: "If you ever take money from my purse again, I'll break your arm."

BETTER: "If you ever take money again without asking, you'll pay back double out of your allowance."

In the first case, the parent would end up breaking the rule instead of the arm, thereby losing credibility not only for the rule about taking money but for all other family rules as well. Never make a rule in the hope that it will not be put to the test. Assume that it *will* be tested at least once, and make sure that you and your spouse are prepared to carry out the consequence.

Notice that I use the word "break" for what parents can do to a rule, not for anything children do. Only parents have the ability to break a rule, because each rule says, "If you do X, we will do Y." If the child does X, is the rule broken? No. It is being tested. The rule will be confirmed if the parents do indeed follow through with consequence Y. If X does *not* lead to Y, then the parents have broken the rule.

EXAMPLE: John is supposed to lose part of his allowance if the lawn is not mowed by noon on Saturday. One day he sleeps until eleven-thirty, then tells his mother that he has a commitment to go bowling with some friends. He promises to mow the lawn when he gets back.

MISTAKE: His mother gives him the full allowance. Later, he comes home too tired to do anything but eat. The next day it rains.

BETTER: The first time this happens, of course you are going to give the child the benefit of the doubt. He is proud of his bowling trophies, and so are you. You would rather have an amicable relationship than run your family like the Marine Corps. I agree with you. But if it happens again and you break the rule by not following through with the consequence, you might as well cross it off your list. Once the child knows you do not really mean what you say, the credibility of every other rule you try to make will diminish.

MISTAKE: Christine is caught shoplifting, and her parents tell her that if it happens again, they will ground her for six months. It does happen again. Christine is grounded for a week. Again she is told, "Now listen, we mean it: There better not be a next time, or you will be grounded for six months!"

BETTER: These parents should have thought more carefully about what their actual response would be. Having made the mistake once and realized it, they should tell Christine, "We made a mistake when we said we would ground you for six months. Now we realize that we were making an idle threat. We don't really want to put you under house arrest for that long. We just want to take you out of circulation for a while so that you can think about what kind of life you want to lead. You are grounded for one week. We're trying to change, as parents. We're using a system in which we tell you what the consequences are going to be and stick to them. If it happens again, we will encourage the store to have you booked, and we will ground you for *two* weeks."

In general, you should follow through with what you said the consequence would be. But if you realize that you have made a mistake, it is better to label it as a mistake than to pretend otherwise.

If you make a mistake in the other extreme, promising a consequence that you now think is too mild, you can announce a tougher consequence for the future, but it should not apply until the next time the problem occurs. In other words, as much as possible, children should be warned about consequences in advance.

A rule should offer the choice between responsibility and restriction. Violating the rule should lead the child backward, away from mature independence, toward the restricted, dependent life of a younger child.

> NOT ENFORCEABLE: "You must be home by eleven-thirty."
> BETTER: "If you don't come home by eleven-thirty, your curfew will be earlier tomorrow night."

Children, like adults, would rather have choices than be ordered around. The wise nursery-school teacher asks, "Would you like to put away the crayons first and then the paper, or the paper first and then the crayons?" She lets the three-year-old feel in control and gets satisfactory results either way. A high-pressure car salesman will use the same device: "Which model do you want?" When you make a rule with a consequence, you are giving your child a choice: Come home on time or be grounded; mow the lawn or lose your allowance; stay sober or lose your driver's license.

Can parents really be satisfied offering that kind of choice? Doesn't it represent a *failure* when the child takes the consequence instead of following the rule? It will not be a failure in the long run, if the consequence leads the child a step backward, toward less independence and greater restriction. You are really asking the question "How mature, responsible, and free do you want to be? These rules are the conditions of the freedom that you can have if you want it. You can always fall back to less freedom if you can't handle it responsibly."

Children cherish their freedom as much as you and I do, but at the same time it scares them. Remember when your daughter was a newborn, screaming her head off? You were able to quiet her by picking her up and holding her firmly against your body, supporting her arms, legs, head—and soul. Fifteen years later, believe it or not, she still wants that kind of security: maybe not to be physically held, but to know that home and family provide a firm resting place, a haven from the uncertainties and risks of growing up and out into the world.

Parents must continually readjust their rules to provide a child with the amount of freedom that is appropriate at each particular time in his life. In the ideal state—the mode of life I call Liberty—children can ask for independence, can show that they are ready to handle it responsibly, but they can also be pulled back into a more restrictive shelter when those responsibilities become too much for them. They are grounded, for example, whenever they choose to get themselves grounded. They go to summer school when they choose to fail algebra. They do without TV when they choose to postpone doing their chores. Fully aware of the rules of Liberty, they must choose whether to conform or take the consequences.

You need not harp on that message; it is implied by the rules themselves when the consequences involve reductions in freedom. When children get themselves punished, you will find it effective to emphasize that this is not something you did to them but something they chose after you presented the alternatives. It was their decision to suffer the consequence. Maybe next time they will decide to respect the rule instead.

One night recently, I pulled out of a parking place and did a quick U-turn. I judged, correctly, that I had time to make the turn and accelerate before the oncoming traffic reached me. I also judged, incorrectly, that the nearest headlights were unlikely to belong to a police car. In choosing to pull into traffic without due caution, I made a decision to accept the possible consequence. Now I have to make another decision: whether to pay fifty dollars and suffer a blot on my driving record or to lose a couple hours' work by appearing in traffic court for a reprimand. That's life. All the arguing in the world is not going to change the fact that the original decision to disregard the letter of the law, the current decision about which consequence to accept, and the future decision about U-turns into traffic rest with me. They are a part of my freedom as a citizen of Chicago.

Creating that kind of freedom for your children is not difficult. All you need are rules that are as explicitly stated and as consistently enforced as the best and most essential traffic laws. The fewer rules, the better. The more reliably their violation is detected and the more swiftly and decisively it is punished, the better. And the less preaching, nagging, and complaining, the better. When you enforce a few rules and stop hassling your children about everything else, you give them a precious form of freedom: the freedom from being nagged at.

≡Why not rewards instead of punishments?

All this emphasis on negative consequences makes many parents uneasy. "Shouldn't we be watching for good behavior to reward, rather than bad behavior to punish?" Some child-development experts strongly advocate doing just that. They say little or nothing about how to punish children effectively. They seem to find punishment a distasteful topic, with the result that you may feel guilty and incompetent when, inevitably, you do have to punish your children.

Am I saying that punishment is more effective than rewards? Emphatically, no! This system is really one of positive reward. Treat your children positively, by

- Acknowledging their maturity and giving them more autonomy as they grow into adolescents and then adults.
- Not nagging at, hassling, criticizing, yelling at, or complaining about them.
- Listening to them and building a relationship based on mutual respect.
- Praising them sincerely, every chance you get.
- Using *consequences*, when you have to punish them, that reduce their freedom without diminishing self-esteem.

Some kinds of punishment are abusive, but consequences are not. More children are abused mentally and emotionally than physically. Parents harp on things that bother them, without making any serious effort to produce a change. The scars of emotional abuse are often hidden beneath the surface, but they last a lifetime. In fact, they are passed on to the next generation. Some of this abuse takes the form of direct verbal disparagement of the child as a person. The rest masquerades under the name of punishment, not in the form of specific consequences for ignoring clearly stated rules, but inconsistent, impromptu punishment: the parents' revenge for being angered or disappointed. Because it is inconsistent, such mindless punishment leaves the child feeling vaguely guilty, without feeling capable of choosing a better way to behave.

Consequences, on the other hand, are punishments that are consistent and that the child is warned about in advance. They have nothing to do with revenge or with making the child suffer. Consequences based on restriction are part of a systematic effort to adjust children's freedom to just the amount they can handle.

Rewards alone don't work. Believing in accentuating the positive, you might wish you could rely entirely on rewards instead of negative consequences. Unfortunately, that means ignoring inappropriate behavior while waiting for an opportunity to give praise or a material reward. But inappropriate behavior will not simply go away if you ignore it. It is often its own reward.

For example, television is more rewarding than homework, in a child's short-range view. How do you induce him to choose homework over TV? You make TV the reward for finishing homework. You can only do that if you also restrict the child's freedom to watch TV until the homework has been done. There is no way around it: You cannot use TV as a reward unless you also impose a negative consequence (no TV for a week, for example) whenever the child turns on the TV before finishing his homework.

An all-positive-consequences approach is a bad idea for another reason. Many so-called rewards can be harmful. Sincere praise never hurts, of course, but many of the more tangible kinds of rewards—toys, candy, money—create worse problems than they solve.

For example, once the child has more toys than he has time to enjoy, you lose your leverage. You might run out of effective bribes with which to purchase his cooperation. This dilemma leads to the use of consumable rewards such as ice cream or candy. When that kind of reward is used on a regular basis, children often learn to associate junk food with parental love or appreciation. As they get older, food becomes a means of emotional rather than physical nourishment.

There is a good reason not to teach your children to expect

any material rewards for following routine rules. Paying children to obey the basic rules of Liberty within their families is as if society were to pay adults to obey the law. Imagine being given a dollar every time you go to the bank without robbing it, a candy bar every time you go to the supermarket without shoplifting, or a gold star every time you are sober when you get behind the wheel of your car. Is respect for the law some sort of exceptional personal service to the community?

Rewards should be given for things *beyond* the child's obligations as a family member. As an inducement to do something onerous or particularly time-consuming, like cleaning out the garage, it does no harm to pay children. Nor is there anything wrong with offering an incentive like a new bicycle if certain improvements are achieved on the next report card. But children should never be offered extra inducements for standard chores or for obeying rules. If they try to wheedle rewards out of you by citing their good behavior, you can reply, "These are the things you are expected to do as a matter of course. Their reward is that they enable us all to live together in health, harmony, and mutual respect."

Allowance. An allowance is a somewhat different matter. If you think an allowance is a way of giving the child increasing freedom and responsibility, then there is nothing wrong in withholding it as punishment for his failure to do the things he is expected to do routinely. Just watch out for a trap: If each chore or personal responsibility has a monetary price attached to it, the child can simply choose to forego that wage; then the chores don't get done.

A good way to avoid the allowance trap, if you are going to withhold it in connection with chores, is to dock your child's pay for each *period of time* in which the chore has not been done.

> EXAMPLE: Peter, fourteen, receives an allowance of five dollars a week during the summer. Every week he is expected to mow the lawn no later than Friday. The five dollars are withheld when he fails to do so.
>
> MISTAKE: One week the lawn is not mowed by Friday, so Dad tells Peter he will receive no allowance this week. The lawn, therefore, does not get mowed until the following week. Dad gets no consolation from the sweat pouring off

Peter as he pushes the mower through a two-week growth, much less from the fact that the lawn looked like a mess all week and now looks uneven because it was too high to mow properly. Everybody loses and everybody remains angry.

BETTER: Peter's parents offer him five dollars per week for mowing the lawn by Monday. He is to receive only four dollars if he mows it the following Tuesday, three dollars on Wednesday. If it is not done by Wednesday, one of his parents will cut the grass or they will hire someone else to do it. However, since it will not be done until the weekend, they will not need Peter to do it the following week, either. His net loss of income will be ten dollars.

It may be inconvenient for you to have to find someone to cut the grass whenever your child does not need the money. (Some children are eager money-grubbers, whereas others value their leisure too highly.) In that case, do what any employer would do with an unreliable employee. In the above example, Peter would also be told that if his parents have to find a replacement for him more than once this summer, he will lose his job.

If you really want to insist that each child do his or her chores, you may have to apply more severe consequences than withholding allowance—for example, prohibiting a child from having friends over or from going out until the chores are done.

If allowance is linked to several rules (for example, the parents in chapter 4 docked their children for not doing chores as well as fining them for swearing and name-calling), you run the risk of having to dock the child for more allowance than he gets. Once the child has lost his allowance for two or more weeks into the future, he might as well tell himself he simply gets no allowance—and forget about your rules.

≡Consequences

A consequence is the punishment part of a rule. Impromptu attempts to "get back at" children, "give them what they deserve," or "teach them a lesson," when they had not been warned in advance, do not qualify as proper consequences. Here are some principles to follow in imposing consequences.

Only punish violations of clear rules. Once you have adopted this system of written rules, children should never be punished for doing anything that is not clearly forbidden, nor for failing to do anything that is not clearly required. If their behavior calls for a new rule, tell them so and write it down for the future.

On the other hand, children should *always* be made to experience some consequences for infractions of any written rule. As much as possible, the consequence should be specified in the rule. But even if you leave yourself some flexibility as to what the consequence will be, your written rule still makes it clear that there will be one.

For one-time rules, which only apply on the day you state them and hence are not written down, you should only punish the child if you have been reasonably clear about the consequences in advance.

> EXAMPLE: Jack is taking two of his children and two of their friends to an amusement park. They are caught in slow traffic on a scorching day, and he has a severe headache. He asks the children to stop shouting. He tells them to keep their voices down. He begs them. He yells at them. Each time, they are quiet for less than a minute. Jack feels like calling the whole excursion off—but that is against the principles of this book. *First*, he should say, "If you can't talk quietly, I'm going to turn around and go home." *Now* the children have had fair warning.

Natural consequences are your first choice, when feasible. A natural consequence happens as a direct result of the child's actions. If the rule indicates that you won't do anything to protect the child from the natural consequence of a certain action, then it is up to him to assume the risk.

> EXAMPLE: Sarah has a reputation for carelessness, so when her parents buy her new skates, they say, "These skates should last you through two seasons. You're responsible for them; if you lose them, they won't be replaced."
>
> Sarah comes home one day in tears, reporting that her skates have been stolen. She left them on a bench for just a minute, and when she came back, they were gone. The police, and I, consider the skates *lost*, not stolen. No new

skates, unless she buys them with her own money. (If the skates had been snatched out of her hands by a bully, the police would treat it as robbery. In that case, Sarah's parents should replace the skates if they could afford to do so.)

Actually, there is always at least one natural consequence: Someone is upset about the child's action. Otherwise, there would be no rule. Even if the natural consequence has proved insufficient to change the child's behavior, and you have to add more tangible consequences, you should still be sure the child knows how his actions have affected others.

> EXAMPLE: "You called me from Ricky's house to ask permission to play over there, but you didn't tell your sister. She didn't know whether to keep looking for you at school or to come home. As a result, she missed her ballet lesson. The consequence for you is that we're changing the rule: You are not allowed to go anywhere after school without arranging it the day before." The child is told of the natural consequence (inconvenience to his sister) at the same time the logical consequence is imposed (restriction of flexibility).

In a study of children's social development and responsibility, Professor Martin Hoffman, a psychologist at the University of Michigan, found that parents who emphasized the effects of their children's behavior on other people increased their children's rates of helpful and considerate behavior. Make your children understand the natural consequences of their actions, even if you have to use extra consequences to get their attention.

Other logical consequences. What do you do if your feelings are the only natural consequence (for curfew violations, for example)? Or suppose the natural consequence would be too mild or too severe (drunken driving). In that case, try to devise a consequence that has a meaningful connection to the actions you are concerned about. If the child has abused some freedom, take that freedom away for a period of time. Take away TV privileges if homework is not done first. Set back a curfew if the normal curfew is not observed. If the child has not respected someone else's rights, then restrict his ability to impose upon others.

EXAMPLE: Stephanie sometimes fails to ask permission before borrowing clothes from her sister and mother. If she asks, they usually say yes. But if she borrows again without asking, Stephanie will lose all borrowing privileges for a month.

EXAMPLE: Eric, thirteen, has been slipping away after dinner without helping wash the dishes. He is told that whenever he does this, he will have to prepare his own dinner the next night, after which he will have to clean up the kitchen without help.

Only use arbitrary consequences if there is no feasible logical consequence. Even then, you may be able to present your arbitrary consequence as a logical one. With a little imagination, you can almost always rationalize a logical connection between the consequence and the behavior.

EXAMPLE: One of Robert's chores is to change his cat's litter once a week. The rule states, "If you don't change the kitty litter, then Mom will do it, and since that takes about the same amount of time as driving you to soccer practice, you will lose one ride that week."

The more immediate the consequence, the more effective it will be. Anyone who has ever housebroken a puppy knows that catching it once in the act is worth ten times dragging it back to the evidence of its crime. This is just as true of young children. Even a five-minute delay may wipe out most of the beneficial effect of a consequence for a two-year-old. (Then he feels attacked out of the blue, which is counterproductive.)

By the time he reaches school age, a child's learning abilities outstrip those of any other animal. Language allows us to bridge time. However, if it were easy to put the memory of what we did yesterday together with the consequences we are suffering today, one's first hangover would be one's last. It is hard even for us to learn from delayed consequences; we can appreciate, then, how impossible it is for the young child.

Unfortunately, natural consequences—the best, in other respects—are often the slowest to occur. Therefore, with young children, an immediate logical consequence or even an immediate arbitrary consequence will work better than one that is natural but delayed.

> MISTAKE: "If you make noise while Grandpa is having his nap, then he will be too tired later to take you to the park." This natural consequence is too abstract for a young child to take seriously.

> BETTER: "If you make noise while Grandpa is having his nap, your friend Jennifer will have to go home."

A consequence does not have to be severe to be effective. In fact, the opposite is true. Severe consequences are less effective in the long run, because they are likely to provoke more anger than cooperation. The more you hurt the child's feelings, burden him with guilt, or simply spoil his fun, the more he wants to hurt you back. He probably will not express his anger directly, because you are too powerful; it will be expressed indirectly through more misbehavior.

What is important about punishment is its consistency, not its intensity. The intensity would matter more if the consequences were intended to hurt the child, but that is not the case. Within Liberty (and also within Probation), most punishments are really only symbolic.* For example, a child who is docked twenty-five cents for name-calling does not suffer in any real sense. The twenty-five-cent fine is a token, a ritual performed in the family so that the child can be reminded of the rule. In paying the fine, the child expiates the offense and acknowledges the parents' right to make rules.

Most children would rather conform to their parents' rules than resist them. But they often need a face-saving excuse to comply. Children have difficulty sacrificing immediate personal pleasure for the sake of the group. Although their real reason for complying is their natural devotion to the family, they may have trouble admitting it to themselves. Incentives and consequences help them express their motives in basically selfish terms. They feel more comfortable with "Do X and you can have Y," or "If you don't do X, you can't have Y," than with "Please do X for me."

---

* In the Crisis mode (see chapter 20), you will have to use serious, not just symbolic, consequences.

Start with the smallest consequence you think might be effective. You can always increase it if necessary. As soon as they realize that their actions are causing the rules and consequences to become tougher, children normally lose interest in resisting. But you cannot escalate the consequences in that way unless you start with small ones and increase them very gradually. Otherwise, you are soon imposing massive punishments, which incite rebellion rather than quenching it.

> EXAMPLE: When Dorie first begins dating, her parents tell both her and her date that she is expected home by 11:00. She makes it the first time, but soon she begins stretching the time—ten minutes, twenty minutes, then nearly thirty minutes late.
>
> MISTAKE: Her parents ignore what they consider a reasonable amount of looseness about the curfew, but when she finally stays out past 11:30 they ground her for a week. "I was only a few minutes late," she protests.
>
> "You were over half an hour late," they reply.
>
> "Last Friday, I came home at nearly eleven-thirty and you didn't do anything. So now I'm just a couple of minutes late and you ground me. You're grounding me a whole week for just two minutes?!"

Dorie is right. Her parents made two mistakes. They didn't make their rule and consequence precise enough in advance. And they came down unnecessarily heavily when they finally responded. Of course they were aggravated, but they themselves had allowed Dorie's misbehavior to occur for so long.

When a child's actions cause physical damage, the consequence should include making good the damages. In this case, the punishment is more than just a symbolic token. You usually want the child to feel the full effects of his irresponsibility. If there was some monetary loss, let the child pay for it if possible. That might mean working for the person who suffered the loss, until the debt is paid off. Or perhaps he can repair the damages himself: replaster the wall, resod the lawn, recane the chair.

What do you do if there are no actual damages but there could have been?

EXAMPLE: Anthony throws a pillow at his sister in the living room, hitting the stereo, which stops working. There is a rule against throwing things in the house, for which the consequence is that the child will be held responsible for all damages. Anthony is expected to pay for the cost of repairing or, if necessary, replacing the stereo. However, it turns out to be merely a loose wire; there is no repair cost. Consequently, there is no punishment.

That is perfectly acceptable. The rule has been followed to the letter, and Anthony is aware that he would have been held responsible if there had been damages. It is just like the case of the child who leaves her ice skates on a bench but is lucky enough to recover them from the lost-and-found the next day.

Children should make restitution not only for intentional damage but also for accidental damage if it occurs while they are willfully doing something wrong.

Older teenagers, especially, should be made to bear the full consequences of what they do.

MISTAKE: After Bill, a high-school senior, takes the neighbor's car for a joyride and demolishes it, his parents ground him for a month and refuse to loan him the money for a new amplifier he needs for his guitar, which would have enabled him to get weekend jobs with a rock group. Bill certainly gets the message that his parents are angry, but he knew that already. The trouble is, he gets two other messages: "We do not want you to be accepted by your peers and to work at a job that excites you" (implying, "We don't like rock music and we don't like you") and "We are willing to pay for the damage you cause; you are not responsible for the consequences of your actions."

BETTER: "You can forget starting college next year, because I have to buy Mr. Jones a new car, and you have to get a job to pay me back." This is an enormous penalty, but a fair and logical one. Bill is lucky the neighbor declined to press criminal charges. He is not mature enough for college. The extra year at home will be good for him, and the message is a positive one: Growing up means becoming responsible for your actions.

It is all right to make children take the consequences for circumstances beyond their control. Once in a while, of course, a child will have a reasonable excuse for violating a rule. But you should only accept the excuse if this happens rarely. Most children, at certain periods in their lives, test out the possibility that rules mean, "Be sure you have an acceptable excuse." This is not what rules mean. They mean, "Leave enough time so that you can get this done no matter what happens."

Take curfews, for example. The message should be: "You are responsible for being home at this time." If the child is late for any reason (flat tire, friends failing to drive her home, losing her watch, lunar eclipse, etc.), you can sympathize while you impose the consequence. Before you call me cruel and heartless, consider:

- We adults expect to bear the consequences of being late, even when it is not our fault. If we get a flat tire on the way to the airport, we don't call the airline and say, "Please hold the flight; we got a flat." When our teenagers have similarly innocent reasons for missing their curfews, what we ought to say, to prepare them for real life, is "You had some bad luck. Through no fault of your own, you have to suffer the consequence of missing your curfew."

- Of course, if this sort of thing happens rarely, you would not be so strict and unyielding. When it happens frequently, however, there is no way you can sort out the legitimate from the illegitimate excuses. If you base your decisions about consequences on the child's ability to offer a plausible excuse, you may unwittingly encourage lying. If you accept flat tires as an excuse but not other kinds of reasons, your daughter's friends may begin to have a truly astounding number of flats.

- It cannot be called cruel or heartless to refuse to accept excuses, if the punishments themselves are mild and essentially symbolic. Is it "cruel" to change her curfew from 1:00 A.M. to midnight for a week?

≡Spanking doesn't work

Sparing the rod does not spoil the child. The fact is that spankings and other physical punishments are less effective than natural consequences, restrictions, or penalties; and they are often worse than ineffective, in that they may actually set back your cause.

No one is in favor of physically abusing children. But spanking doesn't fall into the category of child abuse. It is obviously not the same as slapping in the face, punching, beating, or "whooping" with a belt. Most of us have resorted to an open-handed swat on the backside now and then. (In fact, I have even recommended it in the case of the two-year-old running into the street.) Nonetheless, it is best to avoid spanking. Although it is neither illegal nor immoral, there are many arguments against it:

- If you never hit your child, period, then you won't have to worry about where to draw the line. Severe spankings do hurt. They are done in anger. The angrier you are, the harder you hit. There is no clear boundary between serious corporal punishment and physical abuse.

- If parents spank with the intention of not really hurting the child—the "pat on the butt" many parents use with preschoolers—then the child soon realizes that the spankings are not serious. You want the child to know you *are* serious.

- A spanking is almost never a logical consequence of the child's actions.* Parents who resort to spanking often do so as their first option, without looking for alternative punishments in the form of natural or logical consequences of the child's own actions.

- To be most effective, a punishment has to be increaseable in the future. Once you have hit a child as hard as you can or as hard as your conscience will let you, you have no further options. When, instead, you use restrictions, you can always add more minutes or days, or take away more nickels or dollars.

- The older the child and the more serious the misbehavior, the less feasible it is to administer a spanking. It is easy to take a two-year-old over your knee—not so easy with a fourteen-year-old. So we have to admit that if we do spank a young child, we are taking unfair advantage of our vastly superior size.

* An exception might be, "If you hit your sister, I will hit you." But that ignores all of the other arguments against corporal punishments.

• Corporal punishment demeans the child, by implying that he is not worthy of the respect you accord to other human beings.

• Corporal punishment also demeans the parent. If I hit my son, it signifies my utter failure to communicate with him as a human being. As with other kinds of violent punishment, the parent who resorts to spanking ultimately *loses*. *Winning* your children's respect means convincing them to behave as civilized human beings without yourself behaving like a brute.

• Corporal punishment gives the child a model for violence as a method of solving interpersonal problems. Many parents worry about toy guns and violent TV shows yet routinely use violence themselves, instead of reason, when disciplining their children. Your own behavior has more effect on your children than a thousand TV programs.

• Any form of punishment that makes the parents feel guilty is less likely to be used consistently. Punishments are an inevitable part of making and enforcing rules for children. If you rely on a form of punishment that leaves you feeling guilty, you may hold yourself back from following through with your rules.

• Spanking upsets the child partly because of the humiliation and partly because it raises the possibility in his mind, at least unconsciously, that you may stop loving, feeding, watching over, and protecting him. You gain nothing, certainly not the child's loyalty, by sending that message, which has to do with love versus rejection. I have been advocating consequences in an entirely different dimension: freedom versus restriction.

The more you try to mitigate spankings, giving the child a rationalization, trying to convince him that it doesn't hurt or that he should not let it hurt, the lower your credibility goes. No child truly believes that his spanking is for his own good or that it hurts the parent anywhere near as much as it hurts him.

Some parents go to ridiculous extremes to try to avoid being bullies about spankings, without eliminating the spankings themselves. I have heard of fathers who make the child return blow for blow, so that the child can feel avenged for the hurt. This upsets him more, because no child is satisfied by hurting his parent (even if he felt like doing so, he would worry about what the further consequences of *that* were going to be).

Another technique is to make a boy hold out his hand for a slap and "take it like a man," without flinching. I am in favor of children learning to take their punishments maturely—girls as well as boys. But children who are bullied into "voluntarily" holding out their hands (or bending over to be paddled, in the English boarding-school tradition) are certainly not being allowed to be men or women. They are doubly demeaned: physically hurt and, at the same time, humiliated by the mixed message "You are taking this voluntarily. You can run away or flinch if you want to; but of course, then you get two for flinching."

Humiliation equals abuse

Television actor/producer Michael Landon, who began his career as a track star, says that he learned to run fast when his mother punished him for wetting his bed by hanging the sheets out the window. He had to dash home from school every day to remove the sheets before any of the other kids saw them. I am not sure this is a reliable way to make your child a track star, but I am very sure it is *not* an effective way to deal with bed-wetting. Humiliation is never a good consequence to employ. Humiliation has much in common with corporal punishment: It is degrading, it takes unfair advantage of your superior position, and it presents a poor role model. To be embarrassed in front of friends is devastating to children's self-esteem. Yet their self-esteem is your most valuable ally as they go out into the world; it is never in your interest to undermine it.

In fact, humiliation is the *worst* type of punishment. Spanking is short and quick. Humiliation continues indefinitely into the future. The child whose mother advertises his bed-wetting can be teased about it weeks, months, or years later. A child whose father calls him a "mental cripple" for leaving the lawnmower out in the rain may be crippled by that self-image for life (unless previous humiliation has long since rendered him insensitive). You can, of course, apologize and explain that you didn't mean what you said. But you have no control over the after-effects, particularly with public humiliation. The child goes on being punished even after his behavior has improved.

If, instead, you stick to *restrictions* for your consequences, you can put an end to the punishment when it has achieved its purpose.

> BETTER: Mr. and Mrs. Wilson take turns waking up at 4:00 A.M. to check nine-year-old Jack's bed. If it is wet, they wake him up and make him change his pajamas and sheets before going back to bed. If the bed is dry when inspected, but Jack wets it later, then the inspection time is postponed a half hour on subsequent nights; if the bed is usually wet, then the inspection time can be made earlier. The object is to apply the consequence as soon as possible after Jack wets the bed.
>
> The system is instituted along with a reward system. Jack gets a gold star each morning his bed is dry; ten gold stars are redeemable for a predetermined reward. Thus, when his parents wake him up, they are being a nuisance, but at the same time they are helping Jack to earn a reward.
>
> The system continues until Jack's bed is dry seven mornings in a row. Then he is congratulated warmly and given back his freedom to sleep all night without intrusion. The system can be reinstituted if the bed-wetting problem returns. The parents' inconvenience for a week or two is more than compensated for by the benefits of ending the problem, for them as well as for Jack.

≡Just desserts

Food has acquired mixed-up meanings in our society, beyond just nourishment and good taste. For some people, it is the way they try to cheer themselves up. For others, it is a way to punish themselves, either by self-denial or by making themselves fat. Susan Orbach, a therapist specializing in women's emotional problems, pointed out in her excellent book *Fat Is a Feminist Issue* that many women alternate between bingeing and starving all their lives. They feel bad about themselves when they overeat but just as bad when they deprive themselves.

Ambiguous messages concerning food begin in childhood. If children are repeatedly deprived of food when their parents are angry at them, they can suffer lifelong emotional scars in the form of eating disorders. Using food treats as a customary reward for "being good" can be equally destructive. The child is conditioned that eating a treat—hungry or not—means he is "good." Therefore, *never reward children with food, and never punish them by depriving them of food.*

MISTAKE: Terry, eight, is at the dinner table with his two sisters and their parents. He gazes longingly as four plates of strawberry shortcake are served, topped with globs of whipped cream. "Thanks for not making your bed this morning, Terry," coos his younger sister, Christine. "There's more for us." Watching his sisters lick their lips, Terry is not reminding himself to make his bed every morning. He is reminding himself to thrash Christine. He is also likely, without being conscious of the reason, to stuff himself with sweets at the next opportunity.

WORSE MISTAKE: "No, Christine," Mother says. "I saved Terry's portion for him. He can have it tomorrow morning after he makes his bed." The more she tries to offset the deprivation, the more the strawberry shortcake looms in importance and the more inconsistent is the message to the children about making their beds. At best, the consequence was arbitrary; now it seems to be halfhearted as well.

BETTER: Terry's mother should find a logical consequence for not making the bed or an arbitrary consequence not involving food.

A trip to a favorite restaurant *can* be used as a reward, because the treat is the occasion, the setting, the chance to choose from a menu—not the food itself. Conversely, you can refuse to stop at a favorite restaurant if the children have been fighting in the backseat. You are not depriving them of food; they will still get a nutritious meal at home.

You can refuse to serve a hot meal to your teenager who shows up late for dinner. But he should be allowed to help himself to a cold supper if he is hungry. Never use hunger as a punishment.

On the other hand, no child was ever abused by a rule stating, "If you don't finish what you take on your plate, you get no dessert." But that is the *only* rule for which "no dessert" should be the consequence. It is a rule about not wasting food. It stresses the importance of nutritious foods as opposed to sweets. But it does not make the dessert a reward for anything other than eating a balanced meal.*

≡What if you are really angry?

Don't hide your anger. Telling children how their actions have made you feel is an important part of any punishment. They need to know the direct effects of their actions, including their effects upon your feelings.

MISTAKE: "Go to your room."

BETTER: "I'm so furious, I'm trembling! Go to your room."

MISTAKE: "Your curfew is one hour earlier for the next week."

BETTER: "For the last hour we've been worried and upset. We feel taken advantage of—insulted. Your curfew is one hour earlier for the next week."

Punish the behavior, not the person. Unfortunately, many parents do not know how to make their children sensitive to the parents' feelings without inducing *guilt*. There is a simple difference. A guilt-inducing parent is one who treats the objectionable behavior as a constant aspect of the child as a person, thereby attacking the child's self-esteem.

MISTAKE: "You are an inconsiderate person. You did *X*."

BETTER: "When you did *X*, you weren't considering your sister's rights."

MISTAKE: "Why must you *always* do *Y*?"

BETTER: "That is the fifth time this week you did *Y*, and it is beginning to drive me crazy."

* The problem of getting children to eat certain foods is discussed in chapter 12.

MISTAKE: "If you cared about your mother, you would do Z."

BETTER: "How can I convince you to do Z?"

Guilt is a poor way of motivating children. It induces them to feel bad about themselves. That is exactly the opposite of your real goal, which is to make your children feel so good about themselves that they reject all opportunities to be bad. When you refer to the effects of certain actions, rather than to the child's worth as a person, you give the child an opportunity to increase self-esteem by behaving differently.* Assume that the *person* does care about you, wants to live within the rules of Liberty, and usually does so. It is the specific *act*, on a specific occasion, that you need to punish, treating it as if it were a surprising departure from the child's true personality.

Children do not want their parents to be unhappy. In fact, psychologists who study the whole family system have learned that children's aggravating behavior frequently serves to "rescue" their parents by distracting the parents' attention away from other problems. The children are sacrificing themselves, unconsciously, to try to cheer their parents up! Your child cares about your feelings, though he or she may sometimes conceal that fact. So the most effective message you can get across with any punishment is to make clear what the child can do so that life is less difficult for everyone in the future.

It is fine to confirm the fact that you are angry. What the child needs to know most of all, however, is how to be himself without making you angry. He can learn to do that through the clarity, fairness, and constructiveness of your rules. He cannot succeed if you give vent to character assassination.

≡ The complaining syndrome

If a rule is being ignored and you are frustrated, then you are not doing your job. Merely complaining about your child's be-

---

* To help parents focus on the behavior rather than on the child, Dr. Haim Ginott, author of *Between Parent and Child*, insisted that no parental complaint should have the child as the subject of the sentence. For example, "It is your sister's right not to be hit" is better than "Don't [you] hit your sister." Or "I am being driven crazy by all those dirty clothes that are left on the floor." This may be the easiest way for parents to remember not to attack the child.

havior, without enforcing the rule, is worse than having no rule in the first place. Criticism and complaints are a waste of the energy you should have invested in prompt enforcement and in modifying your rules so they work.

We have all known or heard about parents who don't know the difference between discipline and authoritarianism or even abusiveness. It is easy to understand, therefore, why most of us have mixed feelings about punishing children directly and decisively. Yet the fact remains that complaining and criticizing—like their inevitable associates nagging, pleading, and empty threats—always make the problem worse. When rules are clearly presented, consistent punishments do not upset children much. Having a choice between following the rule and taking the consequence gives children security, shows them you care about them, and puts them in control of their lives.

Complaining, nagging, and character assassination are more likely to drive children to rebellion. The hassling inevitably overflows into areas that really ought to be the child's own business. An example is Al's gratuitous remark about his daughter's friends, in chapter 1, when he referred to her "driving around with those scuzzy friends of yours." This sort of complaining about things there are no rules against stiffens children's resistance to all of the parents' preferences, as well as to the legitimate rules.

When you feel like complaining, think *rules* instead.

EXAMPLE: Danielle's parents have a rule that she has to show them her completed homework or she may not watch TV. This rule gives her a choice, and the parents have to be prepared to live with it. It is not fair to complain if she chooses to spend the evening playing with the cat. She is observing their rule. Suppose they change it to "homework must be completed before any recreation after dinner." The next evening, Danielle decides to test the rule by turning on the TV. Should her parents launch into a diatribe? Why aggravate themselves? They can simply ask to see her homework and, if it is not done, turn off the TV. She may come back after the homework is done. If the same thing happens the next night, she may watch no TV for the whole evening—then no TV for two days, three days, and so forth.

≡If you ask twice, you're nagging

When it comes to bedtimes, chores, homework, piano practicing—even just getting out of bed in time for school—how many things do you find yourself reminding your children about, again and again?

Eventually, "reminding" leads to mutual aggravation. If you ask twice, you are nagging. Children hate to be nagged; you hate to nag; they resent you; you resent them. Yet they refuse to move until you go to your limit, losing patience entirely, and either demean yourself by yelling at them or finally substitute a specific enforceable consequence for the meaningless "or else."

There must be a better way. The better way is to have an explicit rule in the first place, with a known consequence, and not to do any nagging at all. If the conditions specified in the rule are not met, apply the consequence.

Think about which of your rules should be *no-reminder* rules and which should be *one-reminder* rules. I cannot think why any rule should involve more than one reminder. You might feel that it is unfair to expect an eight-year-old to do her practicing every day without being reminded. In that case, the rule should state that you will remind her once. By the early teens, it is reasonable to expect practicing and chores to be done without any reminders at all. Say so in the rule. Bite your tongue when you see the children forgetting. Apply the consequence as promised.

Of course, chores and routines are not the only things that catch parents in the nagging trap. We also fall into it when we ask a child, for example, to turn down the stereo. Instead of asking a second time, put it in the form of a temporary rule.

> EXAMPLE: Not feeling well, you lie down, asking the kids to please play quietly. They proceed to chase each other up and down the stairs, screaming with delight. Don't yell; don't complain; don't nag. Don't punish them either; you are not allowed to punish them for anything that you have not previously made an explicit rule about. Say, "I'm going to have to make a rule, just for today because I don't feel well. If anyone wakes me from my nap before 5:00, we'll all go to bed an hour earlier tonight."

EXAMPLE: Your sixteen-year-old and his friends come in at 9:00 on a Saturday night with a take-out pizza. They supplement this from your refrigerator, leave the kitchen full of dirty dishes and glasses, and are ready to go out somewhere an hour later. You say to your son, "Please leave the kitchen as you found it." He says, "I'll take care of it later. We're in a hurry." You can accept this if you want to, but if you do not accept it, *do not yell and do not argue about it.* Merely say, with quiet authority, "If you don't leave the kitchen as you found it, right now, the next time you want to bring friends into the house, the answer will be no."

The two above examples will only work if the child already knows, from your actions in the past, that you mean what you say and that you will do what you promise to do if your instructions are ignored.

This is probably the nicest benefit of clear family rules. You will never have to nag your children, about anything, ever again!

≡ The "nothing works" syndrome

"What can we do? Nothing works." "The only consequence he understands is my belt." "The only thing she cares about is the phone, and we've taken her phone privileges away indefinitely, so there's nothing else we can do."

I hear these cries of helplessness from parents who are otherwise intelligent, imaginative, and effective people. Something happens to their effectiveness under the stress of trying to cope with their children. The question is: Are they helpless because their children are so troublesome or are the children troublesome because their parents act so helpless?

Here is something you can do to get out of that "nothing works" syndrome. Make a list of everything you now do for your children. Include every cent you spent on them in the last month, every time you helped any of them with anything, every minute you devoted to their needs and desires at the expense of your own. Now cross out the following items:

- Bought food for them.
- Clothed them.

- Kept a roof over their heads.
- Provided health care.
- Praised them for worthwhile achievements or efforts.

Everything else that you do for your children is something that you can stop doing if they are uncooperative, inconsiderate, or abusive. Different parents have to choose for themselves, from their own list, which services they are prepared to withdraw and in what order. You can easily refuse to vacuum your son's room if he is leaving it a mess. It would probably take more serious misbehavior before you would refuse to drive him anywhere or before you would make him cook all his own meals.

> EXAMPLE: The Gilberts have found that "nothing works." For ignoring his curfew, fifteen-year-old Danny has been grounded time and again. They also ground him for calling his brother names, refusing to do chores when asked, and getting in trouble at school. When he ignores the grounding, he gets a double grounding. "It doesn't have any effect," they say. "He comes and goes when he wants. What are we supposed to do—tie him up?"

The Gilberts' counselor asks them to make a list of all the things they do for Danny, excluding the essential food, clothing, shelter, health care, and praise. With her help, they come up with the following ranked list. At the top of the list are the things they are most willing to stop doing for Danny. Toward the bottom of the list are the things they are least willing to stop:

1. Drive him to school.
2. Give him money for things he says he needs.
3. Allow him to play the stereo without earphones.
4. Do his laundry.
5. Let him watch TV in their bedroom if outvoted on choice of program in living room.
6. Vacuum his room.
7. Take messages for him.
8. Clean the bathroom he shares with younger brother and sister.
9. Let him use telephone.
10. Give him equal voice in choice of programs when the family is watching TV.

11. Cook meals for him when he deigns to be home.
12. Drive him to hockey practice and games.
13. Pay for his hockey equipment.
14. Allow his friends to come over.
15. Allow him to play the stereo with earphones.

With this list, the task of making and enforcing rules no longer seems impossible to the Gilberts. They would hate to have to stop doing some of the things at the bottom of the list. (For example, they want to encourage—not oppose—Danny's enthusiasm for hockey and his relationships with friends.) But they now see, in the items at the top of the list, several privileges they can take away that will be more effective than grounding, less trouble for them, and more logically related to the different kinds of behavior they are concerned about.

You can surely list a dozen or more services you now perform routinely for your children. In addition to the kinds of things listed in the example, think about help you give them with schoolwork (especially with typing, preparing posters, and other projects), trips and excursions you take them on, parties you help them arrange, clothing and accessories you lend them, lessons you pay for. I am not suggesting that you stop doing those particular things. My experience indicates, however, that once you have made a complete list and ranked all the items in terms of your willingness to withhold them as consequences, you will no longer feel so helpless.

Something works; you just have to find it!

≡The "whodunit" syndrome

What do you do when you know that a rule has been ignored but you do not know by whom? Who spilled the popcorn on the floor in the family room? Who let the dog out? Who borrowed your tennis racket without asking?

The "who started it?" syndrome is a variation on the "whodunit." Who called whom "stupid" first? Who threw the first punch? Who took whose ski poles?

There is an easy, effective way to deal with both problems. Word your rules in such a way that if you don't know whom to punish, you can punish everyone who might have been involved. This saves you from playing detective, and it also does something even more important: It forces the kids to work things out as much as possible among themselves.

EXAMPLE: The Turners' three children share a bathroom. Two of the three frequently complain about each other leaving it a mess, and the third, the youngest, uses her parents' bathroom whenever possible. All three children deny responsibility for the mess, and all three try to get their mother to make the others clean it up—or to clean it herself.

Instead, Mr. and Mrs. Turner make some rules: "No children are allowed in our bathroom; we are not cleaning your bathroom; and you can work out your own system of keeping it clean with your own standards."

In a family meeting, the Turners help their children work out a plan for policing each other whenever specific criteria are not met. The kids' bathroom soon becomes cleaner than the parents' bathroom. Mrs. Turner would like to get her husband to agree to the same system.

EXAMPLE: "If the lawn work is not done by noon every Saturday, none of you get your allowance that week." Children who are old enough to take care of the lawn are also old enough to divide up the responsibilities and make sure the job gets done.

EXAMPLE: "When fighting gets too loud and we tell you to stop it, if it doesn't stop within thirty seconds, you both get punished."

With fighting, I think it is a good idea to set forth conditions under which you are willing to ignore it and let the children solve their own problems, and conditions under which you are going to intervene. As the foregoing example suggests, you have a right to respond when the noise bothers you, or when the furniture is in danger of being destroyed. You may also be concerned about protecting one child from another; but let the more vulnerable child tell you when your help is needed.

There are several ways to deal with children's altercations with each other. Some parents hold the oldest child responsible for preventing any physical fights. Others punish both children, no questions asked. In some homes, the one who enters the other one's room is always punished if a fight ensues. Other parents manage to ignore their children's fighting unless something gets broken.

Your rule will depend upon the particular circumstances of your family. But don't worry too much about whether the rule will always do justice in every situation. The important thing is to let all the children know in advance how you are going to deal with their fighting. Any consequence is fair if you gave all parties fair warning.

≡Don't punish yourselves

One final point about enforcing rules: Often, the punishments you impose will inconvenience you as much as the children. There is no way to avoid that, and you ought to be willing to make some sacrifices in order to get your family functioning well. But do not carry it too far.

Ask yourselves whether the long-term gain is likely to be worth the short-term cost. It is certainly worth skipping a night of bridge or a day of golf in order to show a teenager how much you care. But it may not be worth canceling a long-deserved vacation during which Grandma has agreed to stay with the kids. You can say, "We're not letting you spoil the trip that we've been looking forward to for so long. Your punishment will be postponed until we get back." Write it on your calendar so you don't forget.

CHAPTER SIX

Escalating the Consequences

A system of family rules is dynamic; it changes continually as children's needs and responsibilities change. In fact, the way you deal with any particular behavior problem in Liberty may move through three different phases:

1. Ask for cooperation without formal rules.
2. If problem persists, make formal rules.
3. If problem persists, escalate consequences.

In the first phase, you simply ask a child to modify certain actions. If this request gets results, then those actions don't need to be put in the form of written rules.

Some behavior problems, however, do require you to insist upon rules. That is the second phase, which is often effective with no more than an occasional need to apply consequences.

This chapter is about what to do if you have tried rules but the rules are being disregarded. You are following through by enforcing consequences, and the child is enduring the consequences but not changing the behavior. You need to deal with that behavior through a third phase of problem solving, still within the mode of life I call Liberty.

Moving into this third phase—escalating the consequences—does not mean that the system isn't working. It only means that you have not yet succeeded in adequately restricting the child's freedom. Various paths are open to you:

• You can merely *increase* the consequence. If your son is being fined ten cents every time he calls his sister a name and the name-calling doesn't stop, try raising the fine to fifteen cents, then twenty cents, and so on. This only works if you were right in thinking that the type of consequence you tried (in this case, a fine) would be effective. Then it is just a question of finding the right magnitude, by trial and error.

• You can change to a different consequence. For example, the consequence for your daughter's leaving clothes, papers, and books strewn all over her bedroom floor is that you refuse to vacuum the room. Suppose she doesn't care. If you don't want to put up with the dust gathering in her room, you can change the consequence. Would she straighten her room every week if she knew that otherwise you were going to pile everything on the bed on vacuuming day? If that would not work, could you dock her allowance? Or perhaps you could make the rule "If your room is picked up, I'll vacuum it; if not, you'll be required to clean it up *and* vacuum it before you can go out on the weekend." Knowing your daughter, what kind of consequence could you impose that would persuade her?

• You can tighten up the rule itself. For example, if the children are not allowed to watch TV until all homework is done, and you find out that one child has been handing in incomplete homework, you can prohibit that child from watching any TV at all on school nights.

• If none of the above work, you can put the child on Probation, which I shall explain in chapter 9.

All these alternatives give children a very important message: By ignoring my parents' rule, I have made things tougher for myself.

Before comparing the alternatives of increasing the consequence, changing the consequence, or tightening the rule, we need to discuss some general questions. *When* should you escalate? When should you *not* escalate? *By how much* should you escalate? And when should you *de*-escalate?

≡When you don't need to escalate: Misbehavior has a reason

If you only have to apply consequences once in a while, there is no need to escalate them. A child who occasionally ignores your rule may only be testing to see whether you are still serious about it. It is better not to move into the escalation phase until you have to. You can gather valuable information about the reasons for the child's misbehavior more easily in the *second* phase of Liberty than in the third. The second phase consists of:

- Written rules.
- Following through on the same consequence each time a rule is tested.
- Finding out what valid needs the child is trying to meet by disobeying the rule.
- Teaching the child appropriate ways of fulfilling those needs.

Suppose a child blatantly defies one of your rules and you cannot see why. It does not seem to be merely a contest of wills; the child seems to have some reason for thinking it worthwhile to ignore your rule despite the consequences. You should be more interested in finding out what that reason is than in waging a power struggle. In this situation, if you were to escalate the consequences, you would eventually "win" the power struggle, and the child would lose—which is no real victory for you. If you can discover the child's reason, you may be able to solve the problem in a way that makes you both winners.

EXAMPLE: Nine-year-old Donald plays in the backyard of his apartment building. He has a key to the front door but not to the back door. After coming home from school, he often goes out the back door and leaves it ajar so that he will be able to get back in. There is a rule against this, because many people use the back stairs and might be tempted to enter the apartment.

Although Donald's mother grounds him each time, she continues to find the door open about once a week. In fact, the only days she does not find it ajar when she gets home from work are the days when he has already come back in from playing. Should she increase the grounding from one evening to two evenings per offense?

No. Donald's mother needs to find out what he is accomplishing by leaving the door ajar. He says, "I just forget to close it." That might account for doing it once, but not for persisting in the face of consequences.

There are a number of commonly used, but inept, ways of demanding explanations in such situations:

MISTAKE 1: Paranoid. "Why must you deliberately defy me?"

MISTAKE 2: Sarcastic. "Are you too stupid to remember a simple thing like closing the door?"

MISTAKE 3: Ridiculous. "Do you want our whole apartment to be emptied out?"

BETTER: The best way to encourage anyone—child or adult—to feel comfortable about telling you why he did something is to ask him to imagine what would have happened if he had not done it. Donald's mother asks, "What do you think might happen if you closed the door when you went out?"

"I'd have to go all the way around the building to get back in."

"But you run around a lot farther than that while you're playing. You can afford the extra minute that it takes to go around front."

"Not when I have to go to the bathroom!"

It turns out that Donald once wet his pants by waiting too long and then running up the back stairs before he remembered that the door was closed. Since the back door locks automatically when it is closed, Donald is given a key to that door and the entire rule becomes unnecessary.

This example illustrates the fact that firm rules are no substitute for communicating with children patiently and nonthreateningly (see chapter 11). It may require several attempts before you understand the reason behind the child's actions; he may not be aware of the reason himself. If so, continue following through with your consequences each time. But don't escalate the consequences, because that only makes communication harder.

In some cases the child may *want* the consequence. For example, he might be getting himself grounded in order to avoid certain activities with peers. In other cases, the child feels that following your rule would be *worse* than the consequence—in Donald's case, he is afraid he may wet his pants. If his mother were to escalate the consequence without finding out the reason for his disobedience, she might eventually succeed in convincing Donald to follow her rule even if it means wetting his pants. But neither she nor Donald would be happy with that result.

Most behavior problems can be dealt with in this second phase, by finding out what physical, social, or emotional needs the child is trying to meet. The second phase—the rule-enforcement phase—is a better time to try to discover those needs than the first phase. In the first phase, when you merely say, "Please remember . . . ," the child can only follow your preference if it does not conflict with any other vital needs. It might create a conflict that the child cannot explain to you, either because he does not understand it himself or because he is afraid that you won't understand. You have to go to the second phase, making a rule, just to clarify your position and encourage the child to confront the real problem.

So it is important not to think that making rules signifies a failure of understanding. The best possible outcome of enforcing a rule is that you and the child come to a *better* understanding. Once that has been achieved, as in the example above, you may not need the rule anymore.

≡When to escalate

When you feel sure that the child knows the appropriate way to meet his valid needs, yet he continues to challenge your rule, *then* you escalate. Assuming that his continued defiance is nothing but a test, you are less concerned now about *why* the child is giving you so much trouble. You are ready to say, in effect, "You're not going to get what you want by ignoring our basic rules. You'll have to find a more mature way to tell us about the difficulties you're having. It's your choice, but as long as you continue these actions, we're going to get stricter and stricter."

EXAMPLE: Every time she acts aggressively toward the

new baby, three-year-old Sophie is sent to her room, which she does not like. Realizing that the aggression probably comes from normal sibling rivalry, Sophie's parents have begun to spend more time alone with her and go out of their way to praise her whenever she is helpful and considerate. Nonetheless, she continues to ignore the rule about being gentle with the baby.

MISTAKE: Her mother is strongly tempted to raise a welt on Sophie's backside. It would do no good, not only because a spanking is rarely effective but also because it is a form of attention, and Sophie should get attention for appropriate, not inappropriate behavior.

BETTER: Sophie's mother tells her how angry she is — but controls that anger — and increases the "time out" in her room by one minute each time. If it was five minutes to begin with, Sophie's mother lets her know that it will be six the next time, then seven, and so on. Numbers of minutes mean almost nothing to a three-year-old, but she will soon realize that the banishment time is increasing significantly. If Sophie does not like being sent to her room, she will decide to start respecting the rule.

EXAMPLE: Seth, sixteen, is rebelling against his curfew. His parents need to have him home by 10:30 on Sunday through Thursday nights, because that is when they go to bed. They have made a rule that the next night's curfew will be earlier by the number of minutes Seth was late the previous night. Although they enforce this, it does not bring Seth home on time. At least once a week, he fails to get home by 10:30, greeting his parents with a cavalier "I know, I know, curfew tomorrow night is 10:06 because I'm twenty-four minutes late."

They increase the consequence to two minutes earlier per minute late, and Seth starts getting home closer to 10:30 when he is late. But he is still late too frequently. When they make the penalty three minutes earlier per minute late, he starts to take the rule seriously. From then on he is rarely late in getting home, and if so, only by a few minutes. The parents are satisfied with that, and do not need to escalate any further.

EXAMPLE: Alex's father drives him to school on his way to work, so Alex gets there about twenty minutes early. After dawdling and making his father late for work a couple of times, Alex is told, "The car is leaving at 7:45 whether you're in it or not." Often he is not ready and so has to walk to school, getting there late. Unfortunately, Alex's school does nothing except notify his parents if he is late. So Alex's parents need a different consequence. Alex is told that if he is not in the car by 7:45, he will have to go to bed a half hour earlier that evening.

≡Escalate by small steps

You started with the smallest punishment that you thought might be effective so that you would have room to increase it if necessary. For the same reason, you should increase it by the smallest difference that the child is likely to notice.

Do not double the consequence. You cannot double a number more than three or four times before it becomes ridiculously large. In the above example with the three-year-old, after increasing the banishment by one minute each time, the fifth time she was sent to her room she would have had to stay there ten minutes. If her mother had doubled the punishment each time, the fifth time it would have been nearly three hours. Similarly, if you are taking fifty cents off someone's allowance, you can increase the fine by a nickel each time; if instead you were to double it each time, after ten increases the fine would be $512!

EXAMPLE: Scott, eight, is a classic bedtime dawdler. His mother, divorced and holding down a full-time job, decides that she needs to be serious about having Scott in bed by 8:00 P.M., for the sake of his sleep as well as her own serenity. She writes the simple rule "Any night when you are not in bed with the light off by bedtime, the number of minutes late will be subtracted from your bedtime for the next night." For the next week, Scott goes to bed at the following times:

Night	Bedtime	In bed	Late by:
1	8:00	8:15	15 min
2	7:45	8:15	30 min

Night	Bedtime	In bed	Late by:
3	7:15	7:30	15 min
4	7:00	7:00	ON TIME
5	8:00	8:20	20 min
6	7:40	7:40	ON TIME
7	8:00		

Notice that when Scott goes to bed on time, he is rewarded by getting his eight o'clock bedtime back the next night. Within a few days, he makes up his mind to conform to the eight o'clock bedtime. His mother can still expect occasional tests of the rule in the future, in which case she can enforce the penalty the next night.

Suppose, however, that Scott were to dig in his heels. His mother would have to resort to more persuasive consequences. The next step might be to say, "Only after you have observed the special bedtime three nights in a row will you return to your eight o'clock bedtime."

If Scott's mother does not consider it practical to set the punishment bedtime earlier than 7:00, she can make that the earliest it ever goes, still requiring three perfect nights before it changes back to 8:00. She can express the situation in terms of his voluntary choices: "You're keeping yourself on an earlier bedtime. Maybe you don't feel old enough yet to be allowed to stay up until 8:00."

≡De-escalate at every opportunity

Since it is to your advantage to have the punishments stay small—you are trying to convey a message, not devastate the child—it is a good idea to have a built-in *de*-escalation clause.

De-escalation means that the consequence will return to the original level if a designated time passes without a repeat incident. This rewards the child for respecting the rule.

Choose a time period a little longer than the amount of time that usually passes between violations. For example, if your five-year-old averages at least one tantrum per day, two days without a tantrum could be considered a sign of progress. If a teenager skips school about once every two or three weeks, a month without missing school would be a sign of progress.

EXAMPLE: Let's reconsider Seth, the sixteen-year-old whose curfew is moved up three minutes for every minute he is late. That might create a problem. If Seth has no plans to go out on Monday night, he has nothing to lose by being an hour or two late on Sunday. His parents decide, instead, on the following rule: Seth's normal curfew Sunday through Thursday will be 10:30 P.M. If Seth is late, then the curfew will be changed to one minute earlier per minute late, for a week. (If Seth comes in at 11:00 one night—thirty minutes late—his curfew becomes 10:00—thirty minutes earlier—for a week.) If Seth comes in later than the new curfew time, the curfew becomes earlier by another minute per minute late, and the week starts again. After keeping to the revised curfew time for one straight week, Seth will be restored to his 10:30 curfew.

EXAMPLE: Sarah's parents do not allow her or her friends to smoke in the house. When they find ashes or smell cigarette smoke (or incense, usually burned to conceal other fragrances), Sarah is grounded for one weekend evening. This has been happening so regularly that her parents decide to increase the consequence to two evenings; but it will go back to one if a week goes by without an incident.

The fact that the child begins to observe a rule does not mean you no longer need it; it may be quite a while before you drop the rule from your list. But you want to treat the occasional slip as a relatively minor matter. By de-escalating the consequence, you give recognition to the fact that the child has been making an effort.

EXAMPLE: In the list of rules in chapter 4, eight-year-old Billy and ten-year-old Laurie are required to check in with their parents before going from one place to another. For example, if they are at the playground and want to go to a friend's house, they have to come home first or telephone for permission, mainly to be sure that Mom and Dad know their whereabouts. Their older brother Bob has more freedom. "I'm going to be out riding around on my bike," he may say. "I'll be back by dinnertime."

Suppose Dad learns that Bob and his friend, contrary to

the rule, were playing in the railroad yards. Suppose also that Bob has been grounded for doing this once before. Dad's first impulse is to do what his own father would have done: whack the daylights out of Bob. He can do something more effective than that. He can simply cross out Bob's rule and add Bob's name to the rule for Billy and Laurie.

"When can it change back?" asks Bob. This means he understands what his parents are doing.

"Talk to us in a month," Dad says calmly. "We'll take a look at how responsible you have been."

Mom adds, "I'm writing it on the kitchen calendar. A month from today: Review Bob's freedom of movement."

When you put a child under a stricter rule, no other punishment is needed.

MISTAKE: You have told your fifteen-year-old that if she ever gets drunk, she cannot get her driver's license until she is eighteen. After she does get drunk, you will have to think of something more severe; the driver's license threat cannot be used twice.

BETTER: You can make the consequence one that can be escalated, rather than a one-shot disaster. "Because of this incident, you may not get your license until you are sixteen plus one month. If there is another incident, we'll add two months on to that, then three extra months, and so on. But for every month that goes by between now and then without any drinking problems, we'll take off a month. So you can, if you want, get back the privilege of getting your license at sixteen."

≡Summary

Escalate when a child continues ignoring a rule, for no apparent reason other than to test your resolve.

Escalate by small steps, whether you increase the consequence, change the consequence, or tighten the rule.

De-escalate whenever you can justify doing so as a reward for behaving responsibly.

CHAPTER SEVEN

The Art of Paying Attention

Good parents, as everyone knows, give their children plenty of attention. They play with them, attend soccer games and class plays, read homework assignments, praise every achievement, and are always available for a talk.

On the other hand, those same children are working hard to grow out from under their parents' surveillance. They don't always want attention; sometimes they want to be left alone. They want and need responsibility, which means that their parents gradually have to stop monitoring all their activities. All children need increasing autonomy as they develop.

How much attention is enough? How much is too much? Can you leave it up to the individual child to tell you when to pay attention? Unfortunately, you can't. Your child's behavior may indicate a need for more attention, but the behavior itself may be inappropriate. If you attend to the child at that moment, you will be rewarding the wrong kind of behavior.

As the following chart shows, there are two situations when children should be given *less* attention: One is when they are misbehaving in order to win attention, and the other is when they are behaving appropriately and want autonomy.

	Child wants more attention	Child wants less attention
Child's behavior is appropriate	Give MORE attention	Give LESS attention
Child's behavior is inappropriate	Give LESS attention	Give MORE attention

The chart also shows that there are times when children should be given attention they do not want. For example, suppose your child's math homework is habitually sloppy and incomplete. The child needs supervision but may not like you to get involved in going over homework assignments. Your unwanted attention is then an excellent logical consequence; if grades do not improve, you will supervise the homework more closely.

In short, sometimes attention is a reward and sometimes it is a form of restriction. When children's behavior is appropriate, give them more attention if they want it, or more freedom from your attention if that is what they want. On the other hand, when their behavior is *not* appropriate but seems to be an attempt to win your attention, give them *less* attention; if the inappropriate behavior seems to be an attempt to escape supervision, that is when you need to attend to it more.

EXAMPLE: Meghan, age four, frequently disappears when her mother sends her outside to play. She goes across the street, which is against a rule. As a consequence, she has to come back inside; but that seems to be just what Meghan wants. She is misbehaving as a way of competing with her baby brother for Mother's attention. The consequence is changed so that the misbehavior gets Meghan less attention, rather than more. If she crosses the street, she has to spend time in her room alone. At the same time, Meghan's mother starts giving her more attention for positive behavior—such as helping with the baby—instead of for negative behavior. The problem vanishes.

EXAMPLE: Barbara, a single parent, is upset about her nine- and eleven-year-old girls' frequent fighting. When Barbara is getting ready to go out, the girls create an uproar, the younger daughter starts crying, and Barbara winds up late for her date as she tries to console the younger one and rebuke the older. It soon becomes clear that the girls' fighting serves to attract her attention and that she has been unwittingly rewarding them for fighting.

Barbara does two things. She begins to set aside more time to spend with the girls, on a regular basis, *except* when they have been fighting. She makes a rule that if they fight, she will refuse to intervene unless the younger one asks for help, in which case both girls will be sent to their rooms.

The girls learn that when they have a dispute, they can come to her calmly and have a family meeting about it, but screaming at each other will no longer get her attention, nor will she cancel her own plans because of it.

EXAMPLE: Fifteen-year-old Alexandra's mother and stepfather have an active social life, so they are happy that she goes out nearly every Friday and Saturday. The problem is that she does not come home at the established hour.

MISTAKE: Her parents make a rule about curfew, the consequence for each failure being that Alexandra is grounded the next Friday or Saturday night. Unfortunately, she seems to like this consequence. She is consistently late on Fridays and stays home with her parents on Saturday nights. She has elected a standoff. As long as it continues, Alexandra is earning more attention by ignoring the curfew.

BETTER: These parents have gained some important information: Alexandra has been asking for more time with them! It would be better to give her that attention as a reward for appropriate behavior than for inappropriate behavior. Even if the standoff were acceptable to her parents, they would be rewarding Alexandra for violating their own rule. If they want her to take the curfew seriously, they will have to find an effective punishment. Perhaps setting the curfew earlier by the number of minutes late would be more effective than grounding her. As long as she follows their rules, they should make an effort to invite Alexandra to join them in activities that she likes (sports, making a gourmet dinner, or going to the movies, for example). They should refuse to do those things, or do them without Alexandra, when she has ignored their rules.

The following are examples of children who act as though they want little attention but show by their inappropriate behavior that they need less privacy and *more* attention:

EXAMPLE: Thirteen-year-old Dave is going through a period of antagonism toward his whole family. He has nothing to say to his parents at all, makes nothing but hostile remarks to his younger brothers. He never eats with the family, and the only time he spends in the house is in his own room with the door closed. Furthermore, he develops the habit of coming in the front door without acknowledging anyone else's presence, going straight to his room, and slamming the door. One day his mother intercepts him before he gets there. "From now on, if you don't say a friendly hello to everyone in the house when you come home, before disappearing into your room, and a friendly good-bye before you leave, we are going to take your door off its hinges so we can feel as close to you as we want to be."

"Sure, you do that," he replies, slamming his door. The next evening he comes home to find no door on his room. His family is at the dinner table. "Very funny," he says, trying to muster a contemptuous tone. "If I say hello to you, will you put my door back?"

"No, but I'll help *you* put it back," his father says.

"Hello, Dad. Hello, Mother. Hello, Billy. Hello, Mike." All of this is delivered in a sarcastic tone, but it is a step in the right direction. Dave has got the message that he will not be allowed to have the privacy he wants unless he acts like a normal member of the family. "Well, where's the door?"

"We're eating dinner right now," his mother says. "Would you like to join us?"

EXAMPLE: Lisa, seventeen, appears to be nurturing a drinking problem. She comes home late from parties, either silly-drunk or sick-drunk, and she wakes up the next morning with a hangover. Although she angrily denies that she has a problem, her parents are right to be worried.

After consulting a counselor, Lisa's parents make a firm curfew rule and a special rule about drunkenness. If Lisa comes home on time and solidly on her feet, how much she has had to drink will be her own business. If she is late, or if she is brought home drunk, or if she has to sleep it off the next day, she is to be grounded.

The idea is to say to Lisa, "Okay, if you don't have a problem, show us that you can drink moderately and responsibly." An alcoholic cannot do that. One drink has to lead to another, and another. The more Lisa acts like an alcoholic, the more she will be treated as an alcoholic. If she continues to get drunk despite the rule, Lisa will be required to attend open meetings of Alcoholics Anonymous (AA) with her parents. Once the diagnosis is clear, Lisa may require rehabilitation in a medical setting and continued involvement with AA.

Look for appropriate behavior and comment on it. There is one form of attention that is never an intrusion, always a form of positive reinforcement. Parents' approval—a short, sweet comment—is so important that I have to mention it here, though it is discussed at length in Part II.

One mistake that inexperienced teachers, and too many parents, make is commenting only on behavior they don't like. This has a terrible effect. In one classroom study, a good teacher was observed giving her normal proportion of comments—more approvals than disapprovals. The amount of disruptive behavior in the class was recorded. Then the teacher was asked to omit any approving comments, only mentioning the behavior she disapproved of ("Arthur, get back in your seat"). The rate of disruptive behavior more than doubled!

Parents, therefore, as well as teachers, have to do two things. We have to pay as little attention as possible to inappropriate behavior. But since we cannot always ignore such behavior, we have to make up for our disapproving comments by giving plenty of praise for appropriate actions ("I like the way Arthur is working quietly in his seat!").

≡Other reasons for disobedience

The criticism "She's only doing that to get attention" is applied more often than it is true. There are many other reasons for misbehavior. Generally, when children persistently disobey their parents' rules, they are trying to solve a problem. One of their needs is not being met, and they don't know an appropriate way of getting their parents to meet it.

In addition to setting up consequences that will change the unacceptable behavior, you have to discover what those unmet needs are. Then you can teach your child how to meet his needs without violating your rules.

How do you find out what the child's real need is, what he is feeling insecure about, or what he fears might happen if he were to follow your rules? A good place to start is asking yourself what *effect* the disobedience has been having. If it usually wins extra attention, that may be the reason the child has been persisting in this behavior. As illustrated above, you need to find a way of paying attention as a reward for more appropriate behavior.

The same principle applies to other effects of disobedience. Perhaps a child's nagging usually results in distracting you and your spouse from fighting. If so, it is a good bet that the child will persist. In order to stop the nagging, you need to do two things: Enforce a consistent rule about it, and do your fighting on your own time, away from the child.

Some children misbehave in order to get a relatively uninvolved parent more involved in the family. They secretly—perhaps unconsciously—fear that the parents may be drifting apart. Other children's fears have more to do with playmates or activities they feel pressured to do.

> EXAMPLE: Bruce, eight, is supposed to ask permission before going more than one block from his house. He keeps violating this rule, which results in his being grounded. As a result, he is unable to play football with the children down the street. When his parents realize that Bruce has been deliberately getting himself grounded, they make grounding less attractive (no TV while grounded), and they stop pressuring him to be part of the football game. Bruce learns that he can

avoid football without disobeying any rules. His parents help him find a different group of playmates (see chapter 13).

As I pointed out earlier, there is no point in escalating the consequences until you are sure you have given your child ways of meeting his needs—for attention, security, friends, competence, or growing independence—within your rules. Children generally do not persist in disobeying their parents' rules without a reason. Once you have made your rules clear, you can stop the disobedience most effectively by eliminating that reason—in other words, by showing them appropriate ways of getting what they need. Attention is one of those needs, but only one.

What do you do if you cannot discover your child's motive for continuing to defy your rules? That is a good time to seek professional advice (see chapter 21).

CHAPTER EIGHT

The Art of Grounding

Grounding seems to be the punishment chosen most often by American parents. But grounding is less likely to be effective if your child believes it is the only recourse you have. He has to know that more severe consequences would be applied if he were to defy the grounding. So parents who can never think of any other consequence than grounding are in trouble. They are only one step away from the "Nothing works" syndrome, discussed in chapter 5.

On the other hand, there is one good reason for the popularity of grounding: It is often a perfectly logical consequence. Children's growing up means growing out of their parents' homes; so the logical thing to do when they do *not* demonstrate maturity is to keep them at home. The parents' job is to relinquish control only when the children show themselves mature enough to handle it.

Grounding means *restricting a child's freedom of movement, for a specific period of time or until certain conditions are satisfied.* Sending children to their rooms is one way of grounding them. So is making them do their homework after school before they are allowed to play. This type of punishment is much harder to enforce than, for example, withholding allowance or refusing a teenager the keys to your car. These latter consequences involve only your own actions, whereas grounding involves controlling and monitoring the child's whereabouts.

A further difficulty is that one type of grounding will not do for all situations. How you go about grounding the child depends upon the problem you are trying to solve. Grounding is an art.

≡Difficulties with grounding

Let's take care of three difficulties that you may have already had with grounding. "What if our child doesn't mind being grounded?" "What happens if our child goes out in defiance of our grounding?" "What if we don't want to stay home to monitor the grounding?"

What if the child doesn't mind being grounded? The child might *like* to stay home or to be alone in his room. In that case, grounding is no punishment. You have to find something else. Try taking away whatever privileges the child enjoys while grounded: use of telephone, television, or stereo, for instance. Or try the opposite of grounding: Make the child go outside for a time.

> EXAMPLE: Kelly, age seven, has developed a habit of screaming when she does not get her way. Usually her younger sister or her mother is on the receiving end of Kelly's tantrums. Her parents try sending her to her room, but it is her sister's room, too, and Kelly is happy to have it to herself for a while. They change the consequence: When Kelly screams, she gets one warning; if it happens again, she has to go outside in the backyard for fifteen minutes. Her sister then enjoys sole possession of their room, the rest of the house, and Mother's attention.

What should you do if a child violates the grounding? If that has never occurred in your family, don't worry about it. Children can usually be trusted even while they are "on punishment," especially if they have not been dishonest or defiant in the past. On the other hand, the honor system will not work with a teenager who is grounded for a substantial period of time as a consequence of serious misbehavior; a parent will have to stay home to enforce the grounding. (The following suggestions do not apply to teenagers who have a history of violence or who are capable of physically abusing their parents. I do not recommend using grounding at all with such children; in this case, see chapter 20.)

If your child does defy a grounding, the consequence must be a longer grounding. However, it is not in your interest to escalate the grounding too much, because that might provoke further defiance. The secret, as with any consequence, is to start small. Grounding should be in units of minutes, hours, or days, not weeks or months. If you increase the grounding, you only need to do so in small steps, not by doubling it.

EXAMPLE: Compare three possible schedules for escalating a teenager's grounding:

	Doubling	Adding original unit	Adding small unit
Normal consequence	1 week	1 week	1 week
First escalation	2 weeks	2 weeks	8 days
Second escalation	4 weeks	3 weeks	9 days
Third escalation	8 weeks	4 weeks	10 days

Since you are likely to need three or four escalations in order to get your message across, the third column is the only feasible choice.

EXAMPLE: Thirteen-year-old Jennifer comes home late for dinner and is grounded for the evening. Later that week she is late again and gets grounded for two evenings. On the second evening, Jennifer says she does not feel well and is going to bed early, whereupon she slips out her bedroom window. She is immediately collared by her father, who was not born yesterday.

MISTAKE: Jennifer's father decides this is a power struggle that he has to *win*. He grounds her for a month, nails her window shut, and suspends her allowance.

BETTER: If the original punishment was two consecutive evenings' grounding, then Jennifer still has to stay home for two consecutive evenings. She violated the grounding on the first evening, so essentially she has to start all over again the following evening. I would not add any extra grounding for sneaking out the window. Having to start over on a punishment she had already partly taken might be extra punishment enough. (Remember: Intense punishments work against you. Simply make it clear to the disobedient child that she is digging a deeper and deeper hole for herself the more she resists.) If the pattern were repeated, however, the parents would have to add another day to the punishment each time, or switch to Probation mode.

Now suppose Jennifer manages to take her full punishment, lets a week go by without incident, and then once again comes home late for dinner. Her parents feel a sense of despair. They imagine themselves saying a few weeks hence, "Jennifer, you're now grounded for three months." But that need not happen. They can just as well go back to the minimal punishment again, thereby rewarding the week of obedience. The message is: "You took your punishment for what happened in the past, and you were fully restored to our normal rules. However, don't forget that the rules still apply. If you want to get into another round of escalating punishments, you can. But you also have the power to cut off the cycle right here by getting home on time as a matter of routine."

Even with small increments, a grounding can soon become unenforceable. So it is important to get it over with. Don't allow the child, by failing to take the grounding, to build it up to so many consecutive days that he knows you won't enforce it. If necessary, *force* the child to stay home. (Physically taking hold of a child and carrying or pulling him into the house is not child abuse.) Add an extra consequence for forcing you to use force. This means that a child who goes out when grounded one night will wind up being forced to stay home two nights; but at least after those two nights the incident is over.

EXAMPLE: Your fifteen-year-old daughter is supposed to be grounded on Friday evening. Arriving home from work at 6:00, you find this note: "Dear Mom, I know you're angry at me but I can't be grounded tonight, this party was planned for a long time, it's for a girl whose parents were burned to death in a . . ." (you skip ahead) ". . . I love you, Kathy."

One way of looking at Kathy's machinations is that the party is simply more important to her than your rules, let alone your feelings. Another way of looking at it is that she has decided to pay the price for tonight's defiance by staying home on subsequent nights, when no party is planned. Both these perspectives may be valid, but what matters more is that you see Kathy's action as a crucial test of your resolve.

With a few phone calls to parents of Kathy's friends, you can find out where the party is. Go get her. (She and you will be embarrassed, but this is not an unfair "humiliation." You are not revealing anything that Kathy's friends do not already know.) Take her home, enforce the grounding, and ground her on Saturday night as well, her consequence for not staying home as she was supposed to on Friday.

What if grounding inconveniences the rest of the family? There will be times when your own plans will have to be canceled in order to enforce a grounding. You might have been looking forward to doing something with the whole family—a barbecue at your sister's, for example—and you hate to leave one child home.

As soon as parents think seriously about all the extra time and trouble grounding is going to cost them, they begin to have doubts about it. They say things like "Our Friday bowling night is the only regular time we have for being with our friends. Besides, it is a commitment to the other couples in the club. We can't let our children's misbehavior ruin our lives."

My response to that would be to ask these parents which is more important, their children or their friends. It is a matter of needing to make some *short-term sacrifices* for the sake of putting an end to a potentially *long-term problem*. If your son were ill with a violent intestinal flu, you would stay home and nurse him back to health. Psychological ills deserve the same concern. Your family is temporarily unwell. It can get better with the right kind of treatment, but not without some extra care on your part.

When you need to use grounding, then, think of it as a temporary set of emergency measures. Be prepared to alter your own routine, not just the child's, and remind yourself and your spouse that the changes you are going to achieve will more than compensate for whatever social or recreational opportunities you pass up in the meantime. However, those sacrifices are only worth making if the child finds them even more undesirable than you do. If your son wants you to stay home with him, or your daughter would rather stay home than go to her aunt's barbecue, then to ground them in that way would be to reward, rather than punish, their misbehavior.

These obstacles can be avoided. Schedule the grounding for a day when you have no plans. Don't take the child's plans into account one way or the other. Don't skip a day when you know his friends are having a party, but don't deliberately choose such a day, either. Take the next day when (1) he could have gone out (a Friday or Saturday, if he doesn't go out on school nights), (2) you have no plans, and (3) the child has no plans that you would want to support, such as choir rehearsal or a track meet.

Once you have scheduled the grounding, at least one parent should be committed to staying home to monitor it. Treat it as an iron-clad date. Only a real emergency should cause you to change it.

> EXAMPLE: Richard, thirteen, is grounded for the weekend. His best friend calls with a last-minute invitation: They have two extra tickets for the football game. Can Richard and his father go?
>
> MISTAKE: Richard's parents say yes, hoping that if Richard sees how nice they are, he'll be grateful and decide to shape up. Maybe they can buy his future cooperation by giving him a break on his penalties for what happened in the past.
>
> But that is *poor psychology*. If ignoring family rules leads to a free ticket to the football game, Richard will continue to ignore them.
>
> BETTER: A fast and firm, though sympathetic, "No!" This is an opportunity for Richard's parents to show their resolve. "It's a shame that you grounded yourself. But grounded you are."

≡Grounding for what purpose?

If grounding is to be a logical consequence, it has to be adapted to the particular behavior that has been a problem with your child.

Often the reason for grounding a child is to convey the message "You are not using your freedom responsibly, so we must restrict your freedom somewhat." In this case, your goal is to apply just enough restriction so that the child feels punished but to restore the freedom after a short time so that the child has an opportunity to demonstrate an improvement.

EXAMPLE: Don comes home fifteen minutes late for dinner. He is grounded that evening. The next day after school, he has his freedom back—to see whether he can manage it responsibly.

Sometimes your reason for grounding is to provide extra supervision. In this case, you have to specify what is to be done during the grounding.

EXAMPLE: Sharon is grounded on school nights until her grades show a significant improvement. She is not only to stay home but also to do her homework at the kitchen table and to have it checked by one of her parents before she is allowed to watch TV or talk on the telephone.

Sometimes your reason is to ostracize the child, to make him realize that certain actions are incompatible with being a member of the family. In this case, being grounded means being alone.

EXAMPLE: Tory has been warned that if he punches his younger brother or sister, he will be grounded for the rest of the day. The important part of this punishment is that Tory get no attention from the family, so he is grounded in his own room, meals included.

Sometimes your purpose is to separate the child from particular friends whose behavior you disapprove of, or from a particular event. There is nothing wrong with doing this if you warn the child about the consequence in advance.

EXAMPLE: Sue has bought a ticket to a rock concert that will be held next month. There have been some incidents of marijuana smoking, and Sue's parents now make a rule: If Sue or any of her friends are found with any drugs between now and the date of the concert, Sue will be grounded on that night.

≡ Summary

Grounding is not always the best punishment. If you use it only because you can't think of anything else, you're just a step away from the "Nothing works" syndrome.

When you do choose grounding as a consequence, choose it for a reason. Then *use* the time when the child is grounded, either to provide extra supervision (if the problem is the child's irresponsibility) or to block the child from getting attention through misbehavior.

CHAPTER NINE

Probation

There is a limit to how long you can go on escalating the consequences. If you feel that Liberty is not working, you may need to shift the child to a different mode of life. I call that temporary mode Probation, which comes from the same root as the word *prove*. The children now have to *prove* themselves reliable enough to be trusted with Liberty.

The concept of Probation is readily understood by children. Teenagers, in fact, already know what the word means. They know that athletes with failing grades are put on Probation—suspended from the team until they bring their grades up. Parents do the same thing when they put a child on Probation: They set forth one or more special conditions that have to be met for a particular period of time, after which the child can return to the ordinary rules of Liberty.

Probation versus Liberty

The rules of Liberty provide a structure for everyday life in your family. They specify clearly what freedoms your children have and do not have. They protect the children from being nagged at, yelled at, or criticized. When your rules are tested, the Liberty mode allows you to insist upon them. You can increase the consequences just enough to accomplish their purpose. You can add or cancel rules or change their wording as needed. Liberty is a flexible mode of life.

In Liberty, you do not expect *perfect* performance. So long as the child follows the rule most of the time, you will not be too concerned about occasional slips. You will merely follow through with the prescribed consequence. In Probation, however, there is a standing restriction that will not be lifted until your rule has been respected perfectly for a prescribed period of time.

The difference between Liberty and Probation is that the consequences in Liberty don't necessarily require children to *prove* themselves. In fact, the consequences often take away, for a time, their chance to show that they are capable of following the rule. A Probation is specifically designed to get proof of responsibility *before* the child's freedom is restored.

> LIBERTY: Your daughter is grounded for staying out past her curfew. This punishment takes away her opportunities to observe the curfew. Not until the grounding is over, and she has her freedom back, can she prove herself capable of coming home on time.

> PROBATION: Instead of grounding your daughter, you set the curfew earlier and will only restore it if she observes this new curfew perfectly for two weeks. This gives her an opportunity to prove herself.

When should you take a child out of the Liberty mode and into Probation? That depends on the child, the problem, how long you have been trying to deal with it, and your own patience. Don't hesitate to use Probation *whenever Liberty is not working and you don't consider it practical to increase your consequences further.* Use Probation also whenever you find that you no longer trust the child; the burden of proof is now on the child to win back your trust.

A relatively short Probation is better than a long one. The duration has to be long enough, though, so that you can be sure you are really seeing a change. To correct a problem that occurs once or twice a month, the Probation would have to be a couple of months. If the problem has to do with grades, the Probation would have to be at least one grading period. If you are dealing with a problem that recurs daily—a bedtime problem, for example —a week might be a long enough Probation.

The time it actually takes the child to serve out the Probation will often be longer than the period you prescribe. This is because the calendar restarts if the rule is violated.

LIBERTY: After sneaking out of the house at midnight, Paula is grounded for three consecutive weekends. This consequence gives her no opportunity to prove herself.

BETTER (PROBATION): Paula is grounded every Saturday until she has observed the curfew on three consecutive Fridays. This means the Probation will last at least fifteen days: If she is on time Friday the 1st, Friday the 8th, and Friday the 15th, she can go out Saturday the 16th. But it could conceivably last for months, because it starts over if Paula ignores the rule on any of those Fridays.

EXAMPLE: Patrick gets a ticket for going through a stop sign. The judge lets him off with a warning; however, his parents had made a rule that he would "lose driving privileges for a suitable period of time" if he was ever cited for a moving violation.

MISTAKE: Patrick's parents prohibit him from driving the car for a month. This is a fairly severe punishment, but it is not a Probation, because it does not give Patrick a chance to prove himself a safe driver.

BETTER: During the period of Probation, Patrick is only allowed to drive with his mother or father in the car. In fact, he is *required* to drive whenever they go anywhere together, until he has logged one hundred consecutive miles without a driving error. (This Probation is measured in miles rather than days.)

EXAMPLE: Cheryl gets a D in math, and the teacher reports that her homework was frequently incomplete. Despite a rule that requires "homework before phone," Cheryl has been talking to her friends for at least an hour every night, having told her parents that her homework was done.

MISTAKE: Angry about having been lied to, the parents feel like punishing her by taking away telephone privileges entirely. But that would not be a Probation.

BETTER: Cheryl's parents put her on Probation with respect to homework. They demand to see Cheryl's com-

pleted homework assignments each evening before she uses
the telephone. In addition, she has to bring home a card
signed by the teacher every Friday, reporting on the work she
has handed in, or she loses phone privileges until the following Friday. The Probation continues at least until the next
report card. If the homework record is good and her grade is
C or better, she will return to the honor system. If the homework record is good but the grade is still a D, she will get
special tutoring in math. If her homework completion has
been sporadic so that she has lost phone privileges for two or
more weeks during this period, the Probation will continue
through the following term as well.

≡Probation with a capital *P*

Any of the consequences in the foregoing examples could be
applied without explicitly using the special term *Probation*. It is
the *principle* of probation—an extra restriction until the child
gives evidence of observing your rules—that matters, more than
the word *Probation* with a capital *P*.

There are some advantages, however, to making a big deal
out of Probation. You can say, "We've tried to deal with this
problem within our normal rules. We've seen no progress. You're
on Probation until you prove to us that you respect our rules."
Take the attitude that Probation is unusual and regrettable, a
whole different mode of life. You don't enjoy it a bit; you are sur-
prised and chagrined that it has become necessary. Here are some
ways to help emphasize its significance:

• The time period specified should always be consecutive, not cumulative. Any violation restarts the penalty.
Paula, in the example above, has to observe the curfew three
consecutive Fridays, not a total of any three Fridays.

• During Probation, life should be less flexible for the
child than was the case in Liberty. Avoid making exceptions,
especially to the rule whose violation put the child on Probation in the first place. Whether you want to say that *all* rules
have to be followed perfectly during a Probation is up to
you. In any case, make it clear what the terms are.

• If the reason for the Probation has anything to do

with rude or inconsiderate behavior, or with things that the child has been refusing to do for you, it is logical to stop doing favors for the child. Continue to be friendly and supportive, of course, but don't go out of your way during a Probation to drive the child places, invite his friends to dinner, or take him to the movies. Make the child prove himself considerate first. (This advice does not apply if the child is on Probation for other reasons, such as school grades or bedtimes.)

• Consider that the child who is on Probation has lost credibility. He has to earn back your trust. In the meantime, his word isn't good enough. The kind of promises you might accept in Liberty ("Let me watch this one program and I'll immediately do my homework, I promise") should not be accepted. In Probation, systematically *confirm* everything important that the child tells you. Do *not* give him the benefit of the doubt. When in doubt, call to check that he is where he is supposed to be. Make him show you his homework; check that every item has been completed. Teachers are usually happy to cooperate by sending home signed and dated assignment sheets.

MISTAKE: As a consequence of frequent truancy, Robert's parents have put him on Probation, taking away various privileges. Robert is told that there must be four consecutive weeks without a truancy before he can go off Probation. The school social worker has agreed to telephone on Fridays to report any unexcused absences for the week. Thus a whole week can go by without his parents' knowing how he is doing.

BETTER: Call the social worker and the principal. Explain that you take the problem very seriously, mention this book, and say that Robert is on Probation. Ask if they would mind your calling the school office every day at some convenient time, for a couple of weeks or until the problem has been corrected. They will not mind. They will admire your resolution and be glad to cooperate.

EVEN BETTER: A friend of mine, a former social worker, knew where the high-school kids usually went when they "ditched" school. She made an arrangement with the teacher whose class her son was most often skipping. The teacher promised to send an immediate message to the school office the next time the boy was absent. When the office secretary phoned her, my friend went out and rounded up her son, drove him back to school (leaving his friends standing there open-mouthed), and personally escorted him to the classroom before the end of the period.* Never underestimate the power of astonishment in bringing about changes in children's behavior.

The child won't like not being trusted. You do not want him to like it. Emphasize over and over, "You are on Probation. You have to prove to us that you can respect our rules, and then we'll go back to normal. Right now we don't trust you. We want to trust you again."

Remember to act as though you assume that the child is only *temporarily* untrustworthy. Children need to be put on Probation just as, at other times, they need to be kept home in bed; it is not a part of their permanent character.

≡The art of the standoff

A standoff occurs if a child chooses to stay on Probation indefinitely, not fulfilling the terms and therefore not being restored to liberty. A well-constructed Probation offers a choice; whenever you offer your child a choice, you should be sure that you will be satisfied either way.

> EXAMPLE: Nicholas, fifteen, is on Probation for repeated curfew violations. His weekend curfew is to be 11:00 until he has observed it perfectly for a month. Then it will return to midnight. In the meantime, whenever he is late by a number of minutes, he suffers an equal number of minutes off the next night's curfew—and the one-month Probation starts over. To his parents' surprise, this results in a standoff for nearly a year. Nicholas seems to prefer an 11:00 curfew with occasional violations to the extra freedom and responsibility of a midnight curfew.

* This was not humiliation, because the mother did not reveal anything her son's friends did not already know about him—except that he had a mother who cared.

EXAMPLE: Shortly before his sixteenth birthday, Barry began seeing me in family therapy, along with his mother and two younger brothers. Hurt and confused by a divorce that had occurred more than five years ago, Barry was taking a "tough guy" stance toward his mother and brothers. Along with rudeness, constant arguments, and picking on the youngest brother, a big issue was chores. When it was his turn to do the dishes, Barry would let them pile up in the sink and let his mother's nagging build up to the screaming point.

The therapy was not just a matter of changing Barry. His mother had to be put in charge of her family, a role she had never felt comfortable about. When it came time to take Barry for his driver's license exam, I helped her make a rule: She would not do that or any other favor for him until he had taken his turns with the dishes, without being nagged, for a month. Instead of nagging at him, she would simply do the dishes when he failed to.

This led to a standoff for six months. When the other boys complained that Barry was getting away without doing the dishes, their mother and I pointed out all the things she did for them that she was no longer doing for Barry—not driving him anywhere, not doing his laundry, and so forth.

His mother was amazed that Barry let this happen, even though he complained vociferously about not having his license. But then his reasons became clear; having a driver's license would subject him to certain norms in his peer group, with respect to dating, that he was not yet ready for. He was actually *choosing* to stay on Probation as a way of not gaining too much freedom too fast.

In both examples, the standoff was mutually accepted by the children and their parents. You never have to accept a standoff—you can change your family rules whenever they are not achieving the results you want to insist upon—but there is nothing necessarily wrong in acquiescing to a standoff. Remember that your rule is not broken unless you fail to follow through with the consequence. If you have said, "You can't have Y until you do X," and your daughter considers the price too high, there is no honor lost on either side. She does not do X, and you do not give her Y.

If you don't want to accept a standoff. Like grounding, Probation is likely to require some sacrifice on the part of the parents. It can be an inconvenience to you, for example, to supervise your teenager's driving for a month, or to check your fifth-grader's homework every night.

Obviously, if such a Probation becomes a standoff, it becomes even more inconvenient. The ways to minimize that inconvenience are:

- If possible, design the Probation so that you wouldn't mind if it turned into a standoff (if Barry's mother had needed him to get his driver's license, that standoff would not have been acceptable).
- If a Probation does turn into a standoff and you aren't willing to accept it, escalate the Probation.
- If a Probation is satisfied but the problem returns, escalate the next Probation.

You can escalate Probations like any other consequence. If you start with a short Probation and the child fulfills its terms but then returns to old habits, the next Probation should be more restrictive, or longer, or both.

≡Back to Liberty

When a child fulfills the terms of Probation and returns to Liberty, you may want to reassess your rules. If it looks as though some of the rules were not working as intended, you should change them. In doing so, there are a couple of strategic points to think about.

Tightening rules: If you decide that the old rule was too liberal, you can make it stricter. Then the child will return from Probation to a Liberty that offers somewhat less freedom than he previously enjoyed. It would be better to tell the child that this is going to be the case when you impose the Probation, rather than after it is over. Otherwise, while he is meeting the terms of the Probation, he will be looking forward to returning to the old rules. He is likely to feel betrayed if he learns at that point that Liberty is not what it used to be.

EXAMPLE: Curfew time is midnight. You change it to

10:00 as a Probation, but at the same time you realize that midnight is too late a curfew for this child at this age. At the *beginning* of the Probation, you tell him that after the terms of the Probation are fulfilled, his curfew will be changed to 11:00.

Loosening rules: When returning from Probation to Liberty, the Liberty rules should be no looser than they were before Probation, or they might have the effect of rewarding the child for the misbehavior that earned the Probation. ("I ignored the rule," the child thinks, "and I had to put up with Probation for a while, but it was worth it because now they have relaxed the rule.") If you do feel the old rule was too strict, return first from Probation to the old rule, and then tell the child that you are planning to liberalize that rule after it has been observed for a certain period of time.

EXAMPLE: Curfew time is 10:00. You change it to 9:00 as a Probation, but at the same time you realize that most of the child's friends have a curfew of 10:30. At the end of the Probation, therefore, you tell the child that his curfew is back to 10:00, and that after a month, if there are no problems, it will be changed to 10:30.

EXAMPLE: After repeated curfew violations, Cindy has been on Probation for three weeks. She fulfills the terms of the Probation. The next time she is about to go out, she comes to her parents and says sweetly, "I took my punishment, so I'm back in your good graces, right?"

"You were never out of our good graces," her father replies. "But if you mean that you're back on your normal curfew, that's correct."

"I was wondering if you would consider changing it to midnight, because then it would be the same as most of my friends, and I wouldn't have any trouble keeping to it."

MISTAKE: Having Cindy approach them reasonably is such a rare pleasure that her parents cannot resist saying yes. They think they are rewarding her for the way she asked them, but what is really happening? They are being manipulated by their daughter.

The problem is that in Cindy's mind, consciously or unconsciously, violating the original curfew was part of what persuaded her parents to change it. Despite the Probation, she has learned that it may be worth defying rules if you want to get them changed.

BETTER: The parents can say, "That sounds possible, but you picked the wrong time to ask. We'll think about it and talk about it with each other, and we'll be seeing how responsible you are about following our rules for the next month. Then you can ask us again."

≡ Summary

Probation consists of one or more temporary restrictions that a child must adhere to before his or her regular rules are reinstated. The special restrictions should be designed so that the child can *prove* himself capable of meeting the parents' expectations. For example, if there was a problem of unsafe driving, the Probation should involve driving under supervision, rather than a suspension of driving privileges.

Although the principle is a good one to apply with all consequences whenever possible, there can be advantages in reserving use of the word Probation for an advanced phase of dealing with behavior problems, emphasizing that the situation is serious, unusual, and regrettable. Part of the goal is to make the child appreciate Liberty.

CHAPTER TEN

You Have the Power

Our society seems to be suffering from an illusion of helplessness, particularly among parents, in the face of increasingly out-of-control behavior by children.

It is ironic that parents so often feel powerless, when in truth we parents have virtually *all the power!* Of course, if you *feel* powerless, you tend to *become* powerless. If you expect to be a victim of chaotic, inconsiderate, irresponsible, or even abusive behavior, you will become a victim.

On the other hand, parents who are too afraid of losing power over their children's lives may err in the other direction. They are in danger of exercising that power too heavily—inflexibly, insensitively, antagonistically. When parents are authoritarian, their children have only two alternatives: Either they must capitulate and fail to become mature, independent adults; or they must oppose the parents in a power struggle that both sides will lose.

The danger that parents will overreact and use their power destructively is just as great as the danger that they won't be powerful enough. Therefore, after the preceding chapters on methods of parental control, I aim to do two things in this chapter: to assure you that you do have the power to implement a system of rules for your family, and to help you avoid overexercising that power.

≡We're OK, you're OK— But we're parents and you're not

Parents have to give their children three equally important messages:

1. We're in charge; you're still a kid.
2. We like you.
3. We're happy you're growing up.

These messages meet the three basic needs I mentioned in Chapter 1: limits, attention, and autonomy, respectively. Giving all three messages requires a subtle balance, because they seem to contradict each other.

The first message makes it clear that the parents are responsible for the family until the children grow up. It emphasizes the necessary hierarchy and makes it clear that with respect to certain decisions children do not have equal rights.

Since that unfortunately can be experienced as a put-down, the second message reassures children that it is okay to be a child. "You are all right; we like you the way you are." This has to be *unconditional:* not "We like you but . . ." or "We would like you if . . ." Our children need to know that we continue to like them even when we are also mad at them, tired of them, worried about them, and even when we don't like some of their actions.

That message, too, has a possibly upsetting implication. If we like them as they are, does that mean we don't want them to grow up and gain their independence? The third message reassures them on that score: "It gives us joy to see you developing into a more mature, competent person."

Finally, the third message has to be tempered with the first message. Although the child is growing up, growing up takes time, and in the meantime the parents remain in charge. Even when children are physically larger than their parents, even when they think they are wiser or saner, as long as they are living in their parents' home, they are subject to the parents' rules.

The true basis of your power is the child's dependence. In criticizing corporal punishment, I made a point that bears repeating here. Your control over your children is not based on their physical or mental inferiority. It is based on the fact that they depend on you for nurturance, protection, love, and, more materially, time and money.

You would probably meet your children's basic needs regardless of their behavior. No matter how angry or frustrated you may become, you plan to go on providing food, shelter, medical care, and other basic needs. Children should never be made to doubt that. (Even in Crisis mode, if you are forced to put the child out of your house, you will make every effort to find someplace he can stay.) But above and beyond those basic needs, they depend on you for all kinds of things that are not essential to life or growth. I mentioned some examples of those things in connection with the "Nothing works" syndrome in chapter 5: transportation, space in which to entertain friends, laundry and other household services, new clothes, coins for the arcade, sports equipment, help in fixing things. In order to go on receiving those things, the child depends on your good graces and on his own appropriate behavior.

When you withhold nonessentials, you will not undermine any of the three crucial messages. You will show that you are in charge of the family's resources. You will continue to provide life's essentials, including affection and praise whenever you can do so with sincerity. And you will encourage the child to grow toward maturity and independence.

On the other hand, it is also true that you are bigger than they are. Even when your children grow taller or broader than you, they still have memories of being two feet tall, looking way up at you. When it comes to a showdown, there are a couple of ways you can use your body and your voice to carry more weight.

It doesn't really help to raise your voice, because children can scream as loud as you can—perhaps louder. *Deepening your voice* will impress them more than sheer volume. The lower the pitch, the more ominous the message. Whether you are a baritone or a soprano, you can sound intimidating when you reach down to the bottom of your range.

Another good way to make a strong impression is to move closer to the child. It is psychologically easier to defy you from across the room than when you are just a foot or two away. If you send your son to his room or tell your daughter to pick up her clothes, and they ignore you, move closer to them before repeating the order. When you cut the distance between you and the child in half, you appear four times as big. The area of your image on the child's retina increases with the inverse square of the distance separating you. For example, when you move from four yards to only one yard away (one-quarter the distance), you fill $4 \times 4 = 16$ times as much space in the child's visual field.

This is true regardless of the child's size. However, it is also true that the child's size on *your* retina becomes sixteen times as large at one yard as at four yards. So if your teenager is taller than you, you may have to remind yourself not to be intimidated when you move closer!

I like these techniques because they are effective without being abusive. Compare them with a derogatory remark about the child, no matter how softly spoken. Perhaps the child overhears one parent using the word "stupid" in describing him to the other parent. That is a form of child abuse. Walking up to the child and firmly giving a straight order in as persuasive a tone as you can muster is a way of clarifying the family hierarchy without attacking the child's self-esteem. It says, "I am in charge," without saying "I don't like you" or "Don't grow up."

Warning: These techniques only work if you feel truly decisive about what you are saying. If the child senses that you lack the conviction to follow through, it makes no difference how ominous you appear.

≡Pleas for exemptions and revisions

You may have wondered why I have left the children out of the rule-making process. In this system, it is the parents who draw up the set of rules. You might have family meetings for other reasons—for example, to allocate chores or to deal with conflicts—but not to make the major decisions about what rules are needed and what the consequences should be for disobeying them.

The reason I insist *you* make up the rules is that a family is not a democracy. In a family meeting, the children may feel that some sort of injustice has been done if they do not get an equal vote. They begin to think of rule-making as a negotiation: "We won't accept *this* unless you give way on *that*." They may even try to insist that the rules have to apply to the parents as well: "If we don't get to watch TV after dinner, neither do you."

Who makes rules for adults? Society does: a great many rules, even in a relatively free society. If you violate them, you may have to pay a fine; or go to jail; or suffer public humiliation; or lose your license, your house, even your children. In other words, the rules we are bound by as adults work very much like the rules that we should impose upon our children. But it is not up to the children to make rules for us. A family cannot work democratically.*

However, it is fine to be liberal *after* you have established a set of family rules. When one or more children come to you requesting temporary exemptions or permanent revisions of particular rules or consequences, it is a *very good idea* to discuss such requests and grant them whenever they are reasonable. If you follow certain principles, you and your children both have a lot to gain by giving them a large role in the process of revising the family rules.

In general, children have a greater stake in observing rules if you accommodate their reasonable requests for modifications. They know that if the new rule doesn't work, you will change back to the rule they didn't like. If you make an exception to a rule and it is abused, you won't make such exceptions in the future. Your children get the message that Liberty can become tougher or easier as a result of their actions.

When should you yield to a child's request? Assuming that the child's request is "reasonable"—by which I mean that it is just as likely as the original rule to accomplish your purpose—which of the following situations is an appropriate time to make a rule less strict or a consequence less severe, or to make a temporary exception to a rule?

> 1. When the rule has not been working, because the child has been resisting or defying it. You hope to win his or her cooperation by being softer.
>
> 2. When the child has been following all your rules pretty well, though complaining about them.

The correct answer, obviously, is 2. You want to reward children for following the family rules, by responding favorably to all

---

* I think the best political structure for a family is a *benevolent constitutional monarchy* with certain sacred rights, including the child's freedom to express opposing views, the right to a fair and speedy hearing, and the right to make personal decisions about matters not specified in the "constitution," which is the list of family rules.

reasonable requests. The message is, "You have shown us that you are responsible, so we think you can handle more freedom."

If the child ignores or defies a rule, and soon afterward you liberalize *any* rule, even a different one than was disobeyed, you are rewarding the disobedience. The reward could easily outweigh the negative consequence for the disobedience.

> EXAMPLE: Seven-year-old John has been sent to his room for teasing his sister. As his mother passes his door, he call out amiably, "Mom, can I be allowed to ride my bike to school?"
>
> His mother replies, "This is the wrong time to ask. I wouldn't even consider changing any rules right now."

Here are some other principles to follow when you respond to pleas for changes and exceptions:

- The child must make the request in advance, not after already having violated the rule. (For example, he may not ask permission to stay up late after his bedtime has already passed.) If a rule is violated, you should respond as you said you would; *then* you'll consider changes for the future.

- When you make a change or an exception, be explicit. Which child or children does this apply to? When? What part of the rule still holds? If it is a temporary exemption for a special occasion, you do not need to change the written rule. But whenever you do want to make a lasting change in a rule, cross out the old rule and write down the new one.

- The child should be allowed to make his best case and should be made to feel that you have heard all his arguments. He will not feel that way unless you really listen. You may need to use active listening techniques, repeating what you heard him say and checking your understanding: "You feel that 10:00 is too early on school nights because several of your friends are allowed to stay out later and it embarrasses you to have to come home earlier than they do. Is that right?" Then you make your decision. Case closed. If you have been convinced, then try to live with the new rule, just as if you yourself had thought of the change. (Don't act like a martyr about it; after all, you have the power to change back to the earlier curfew if necessary.) If you have not been convinced, say, "We know how you feel, but we're not convinced. Try us again in two months."

What happens when the child keeps badgering you about the rules? Use the system. If badgering gets to be a problem, make a rule against it. Write it down. Enforce it.

The fact that you have the power to make and enforce rules means that you have no need to complain, and no right to complain, if your children ignore those rules. Simply apply the consequences. (The energy that you waste complaining only perpetuates the problem, instead of being used to solve it.) However, because your children do not have the power to make rules, they ought to be allowed to express frustration about specific responsibilities or prohibitions that they find particularly onerous. And you have to allow them to plead for changes. But you can make rules about what form their complaints should take.

> EXAMPLE: "We will listen to your complaints about any rule, provided that you have something new to say and you're not merely harping on the subject. Once we have heard you make your case, if we make a decision to keep the rule in effect for a certain period of time, we may stop you when you start to harangue us. If you are asked to stop, further complaining that day will receive the same consequences as if you had violated the rule you are complaining about."

It will help if you realize that your children's complaints are really questions: "What do these rules mean? What do these punishments mean? Do they mean you don't like us? Do they mean you don't see that we're growing up, or you see it and you don't like it?" You can listen to their complaints and reassure your children about the answers to those implied questions while remaining steadfastly at the helm.

≡Your greatest power: The power to shape the child's self-esteem

Although teenagers sometimes pretend otherwise, children at all ages are extremely sensitive to what their parents think of them. They form their sense of identity (*who* they are) and their self-esteem (how *satisfied* with themselves they are) from only three sources of information:

1. What they are told about themselves directly.
2. What they are told indirectly by the way people act toward them.
3. The models they see in the people they identify with and care most about.

Obviously, parents are more powerful than anyone else in all three processes of building a child's identity and self-esteem. Your direct statements carry far more weight than other people's. Your indirectly conveyed attitudes about the child also carry more weight, start at an earlier age, and build up over a much greater number of interactions with the child than those of anyone else. And the parents are the child's most salient adult models.

You have learned to use some of your power in helping your children become rule-abiding citizens, respect others' rights and contribute toward the smooth functioning of the household. However, just as those traits are only a small part of the competent, self-confident, happy, mature, adaptable persons you hope your children will become, so, too, the *restrictive* use of your power is only a small part of your task. We are now ready to take up the *constructive* side of the job.

SUGGESTED BOOKS: Clear Rules and Consequences

Balter, Lawrence and Shreve, Anita. *Who's in Control? Dr. Balter's Guide to Discipline without Combat.* New York: Poseidon, 1989.

Brenner, Barbara. *Love and Discipline.* New York: Ballantine, 1983.

Dinkmeyer, Don, and McKay, Gary. *The Parent's Handbook: Systematic Training for Effective Parenting (STEP).* New York: Random House, 1982.

Dobson, James. *Dare to Discipline.* New York: Bantam, 1977.

Dodson, Fitzhugh. *How to Discipline With Love.* New York: Signet, 1978.

Dorr, Darwin, et al. *The Psychology of Discipline.* New York: International Universities Press, 1983.

Dreikurs, Rudolf. *Discipline without Tears.* New York: Dutton, 1974.

Eimers, Robert, and Aitchison, Robert. *Effective Parents, Responsible Children.* New York: McGraw-Hill, 1977.

Gordon, Thomas. *Teaching Children Self-Discipline at Home and at School.* New York: Times Books, 1989.

Lundell, Keith. *Levels of Discipline: A Complete System for Behavior Management in the Schools.* Springfield, IL: Thomas, 1982.

PART II.

How to Construct a Person

Part II deals with the other half of being a parent: the job of constructing a person. In chapter 11, general techniques are discussed, for building self-esteem and self-confidence in children of all ages. The skills of active listening and positive communication are explained. In chapters 12 through 16, I deal with specific problems that arise in the preschool years, in the elementary-school years, and in adolescence.

CHAPTER ELEVEN

Building Self-Esteem and Competence

The things we parents are most concerned about cannot be dealt with in our family rules. Our ultimate concerns have to do with decisions our children are going to make when they are alone or with their peers, outside our knowledge and supervision. We are concerned about their motivation to do their best; about their compassion and consideration for others; and about their ability to negotiate the obstacle course of adolescence, with its peer pressures and its mood swings from grandiosity to despair.

Our best hope to affect those decisions comes through building strength within our children. We do that by supporting their emotional vitality and competence in many different areas: academic skills, physical skills, social skills, and creativity.

Negative consequences for violating rules, though necessary, do not make children more competent and do not build up their self-esteem. Pruning a rosebush may be necessary for its health or appearance, but what really makes it grow is good soil, sunlight, and water. Our goal is not to manage our children but to give them the resources they need in order to manage their own lives.

The "fertile soil" for children consists of the lifestyle and values with which their parents surround them. More than the material comforts of life, it is the personal comforts of family life —mutual respect, affection, and honesty—that form a good foundation. This includes relationships with grandparents, cousins, and others who share the children's heritage. And it includes the values of the communities in which they are raised.

The "sunlight" is the stimulation children get from exposure —at home as well as at school—to music, art, history, and literature; from exploring how things work, like magnets, cars, and computers; from family trips; from sports and games; and from being encouraged to develop and pursue their own interests and talents.

The "water" is praise and acceptance. Pour it on. One shouldn't drown children in praise, but, like plants, they can survive an occasional excess better than they can survive a drought. By acceptance, I don't mean accepting everything they do, but I *do* mean accepting their weaknesses, their fears, their bad feelings as well as their strengths and talents.

This chapter discusses principles for providing these essential resources to children. The following chapters apply those principles to specific issues that arise at different ages.

≡Praise the child

The most direct way to build children's confidence and self-esteem is to praise them frequently. However, praise only works when it is specific, sincere, and unadulterated.

How frequently? There is no such thing as too much praise for a child. There is such a thing as too much *nonspecific* praise—or too much *adulterated* praise, as I shall explain shortly. But what child was ever harmed by too many sincere, specific, straightforward compliments?

> EXAMPLES: "You did a terrific job of setting the table."
>
> "Your hair looks great."
>
> "Okay! You took a good swing at the ball."
>
> "Wow! You used every crayon in the box!" Or "That's quite a drawing—and all with one crayon!"
>
> "Ninety percent correct on the test? I'm impressed!" Or, "Sixty percent—three points higher than last time! Well done!"

"You looked so graceful out there on the ice!" Or "That was great the way you picked yourself up and went on skating."

"Congratulations on winning." Or "You played well—you can't win them all." Or "Well, we all have bad days—but you were good losers."

How often do you say things like that to each of your children? Try to count the times over a period of several hours. Perhaps you and your spouse can keep records on each other. At the same time, count the number of reprimands, criticisms, and negative consequences you give out. What is the ratio of positives to negatives?

Roughly speaking, if your ratio is 3:1 or better, you deserve a gold star. If it is less than 2:1 (less than two positives for every negative), you get no praise from me. Less than 1:1 means more criticism than praise, which is counterproductive.

Contrary to what you might guess, the *worse* your child is behaving, the more you need to *increase* the positive-to-negative ratio. That is hard to do. As a child becomes more difficult, it becomes harder to find anything to praise him for, as well as harder to contain one's criticism. Yet it becomes more and more important to do that.

For example, a child who frequently whines and clamors for attention should be ignored as much as possible during those episodes. It is obvious that he should receive no positive attention, but neither should parents attend to him with complaints and criticisms. Instead, he needs to be heavily rewarded with praise and attention for all kinds of appropriate behavior that might be taken for granted in the average child. If he is reproached or punished ten times in a day, the best strategy is to find forty or fifty occasions for complimenting him. That is how psychologists treat severely disturbed children in hospital behavior-modification programs. You have to reward appropriate actions if you want them to replace the inappropriate ones. In contrast, a child who rarely has to be chastised for anything can thrive on one or two compliments a day.

Don't wait for children to "earn" compliments. Get in the habit of looking for any opportunity to give meaningful praise. Sometimes your children's greatest achievements may be in areas for which you yourself have little enthusiasm: performing rock music, building go-carts, or playing billiards. Who is to say that those activities are less worthwhile for children than classical music, science projects, or tennis?

It is a mistake to only praise your children for doing things *you* value. Their self-esteem depends just as much—perhaps more —on being complimented for the way they pursue goals they themselves have chosen. There is a better chance of their channeling those same energies into productive activities later in life if you support them now in pursuing *anything* with dedication. Don't disparage the one thing they happen to be interested in at this age.

> MISTAKE: "You took piano for a year and dropped it; then you took guitar and dropped it right after we bought you the guitar; then it was soccer—after one season you quit —and now it's the same with Scouts. You never stick with anything."

> BETTER: "You really are incredibly good at Nintendo, Michael. I'm impressed with how you stuck with it until you had mastered the game."

I agree with you that the same amount of persistence and energy invested in the piano or Scouts would do more for a child in the long run than Nintendo. But you are not given that choice. The reality is that this child did not find those particular activities as interesting as Nintendo, at this point in his life. So your choice is either to build up his confidence in the area in which he *has* shown persistence and energy, or to tear it down because of your own disappointments.

Be specific. Try to make the child feel good about specific things that he has control over. Self-esteem can only be built up one brick at a time. The child may have missed the ball and struck out, but he took a good swing at it. When you specifically mention his swing, you are doing two constructive things. You are calling the child's attention to a specific aspect of his skill that should be maintained (building *competence*), and you are making him feel better about himself (building *confidence*). He was not rewarded by hitting the ball, but your positive response will help him get a hit next time.

Earlier I pointed out that specific criticisms of actions are better than generalized criticism of the child as a person. Now I am saying that specific compliments are better than general ones. Generalized flattery can actually be harmful. Compare "You're brilliant" to "That composition was brilliant." The former may create anxiety in the child: Can he live up to your superlatives? The latter, on the other hand, refers to the specific thing he *has* accomplished, which *was* excellent. It does not imply that you will be disappointed if he is sometimes less than brilliant.

Don't say it unless you mean it. As I tried to show in the examples above, you can almost always find some honest way of complimenting a child. It is not necessary to be insincere. In fact, it is a mistake.

> MISTAKE: Claire has had her first permanent, which her Aunt Marge admires in glowing terms. Later, thinking that Claire is out of earshot, her mother asks Marge, "How could you tell Claire you like her hair? Isn't it awful?"
>
> "Ghastly!" Marge agrees, unaware that Claire is in the next room. "But what could I say? She seems to think it looks good."
>
> Insincerity leads to inconsistency, which destroys credibility. It also says that the person making the compliment doesn't really care about the recipient at all. One or two incidents like this are enough to render Aunt Marge emotionally worthless to Claire.
>
> BETTER: Aunt Marge could have told Claire, "I think it's going to be hard for me to get used to the change. But how daring of you to try it!"

> MISTAKE: George, sixteen, has been studying the clarinet for about four years. His father tries to compliment him: "You're the next Benny Goodman!" He assumes his son knows it is meant as a supreme, though exaggerated, compliment. But for children in a certain frame of mind, it can be more discouraging than encouraging.
>
> George knows that he is *nowhere near* Benny Goodman. He is skilled enough to have fun with the clarinet and eventually to play jazz or chamber music with friends, but not to become a virtuoso. The implied message from his father is,

"Benny Goodman is my standard of good clarinet playing."
In that case, why not quit right now?

BETTER: "You're the Benny Goodman of Elmwood
Avenue!"

But-less praise. The final criterion of worthwhile praise is that it
should be "but-less," by which I mean unadulterated with buts.

MISTAKES: "It's a good picture, but why didn't you
use more crayons?"

"Great swing, but why didn't you hit the ball?"

"Sixty percent correct is an improvement, but what
about the other forty percent?"

"Congratulations on winning, but if you can't score
more than two goals a game, you're not going to win often."

"Dear Granddaughter, Congratulations on your acceptance at Northwestern. Mrs. McGillicuddy's granddaughter
is going to Harvard."

"I'm proud to have a daughter with a Ph.D., but
couldn't you have studied something that would be more
useful in the job market than medieval Italian poetry?"

"A Nobel Prize! Good for you; did you know that
Marie Curie won *two* Nobel Prizes?"

Comments like these should be counted in the *negative* column when estimating your positive-to-negative ratio. Don't count
the part leading up to the "but" as praise, because it is *wiped out*
by what follows.

When children show real ability in some area—sports, music,
academics, a job—it is natural to encourage them to strive their
utmost for ever-higher levels of achievement. Yet the more talented they are, the more they already know what the higher levels
of achievement are, and the more the push has to come from
within themselves. Reminding them how limited their present accomplishment is, and how much greater they can be if they work
at it, is not telling them anything they don't already know. This is
*dis*couragement, not encouragement.

This unnecessary suggestion of "room for improvement" is
the mistake I most often make as a parent. It takes a serious effort
to keep it to a minimum. I shall have some suggestions in chapter

13 for motivating children to do their best. Adulterated praise is not a way to do it.

Praise in connection with rules. Mr. and Mrs. Green were working hard in family counseling to agree on a set of rules and back each other up in enforcing them. They found that it went against their grain to impose negative consequences, until they hit upon the idea of a "Family Newsletter" to go on the refrigerator each week, below the rules. The results were so good that they contributed the first issue for me to share with readers:

GREEN FAMILY NEWSLETTER

Good work, Ben!! Fines being paid up on time. No food, glasses, or pop bottles have been left in your room. We also liked the way you took the time to look over Sarah's science books.

Good work, Sarah!! Lunch dishes have been put in sink and soaked. All dirty clothes were put in basket three times this week. We have also noticed your effort to be in PJ's by 8:30. Don't be discouraged about missing it a few times and having to go to bed early the next night. The normal bedtime will soon be "routine."

Dad: Thanks for taking more active role. Love, Mom.
Mom: Thanks for this good newsletter. Love, Dad.

What had actually happened was that Ben's name-calling showed no improvement the first week, and Sarah tested the bedtime rule several times. But the parents were able to express some compliments about other things, including the fact that Ben had paid the twenty-five-cent fines every time he called his sister a name.

Over the course of several weeks, the Greens had more opportunities to congratulate Ben and Sarah in their family newsletter and fewer occasions to apply the negative consequences in their list of rules.

≡Stimulation

It is not enough to water your plants. You also have to give them the right amount of sunlight. With children, you look for ways to stimulate them. You take them places, you read to them when they are young and suggest books when they are older, you urge them to pursue activities offered at school or church, and you pay for all kinds of lessons.

But a plant can wither from too much sun, just as it can from too little.

Children benefit more from pursuing one or two activities in which they are truly interested than from being pushed to dabble in many. Parents should provide lessons and other opportunities to get started with new interests. The child *might* choose to pursue them. After providing an opportunity, you have to ask whether the motivation for the child to continue with that activity is coming from him or from you. If it is only coming from you, you can probably find a more productive use of his energy, as well as your money.

> EXAMPLE: Laurie's parents pay for her piano lessons, remind her to practice, and praise her profusely whenever she plays. She also takes figure-skating lessons. In neither activity does she show much talent. But she loves the skating and pursues it without being urged. Although she verbalizes an interest in piano, the enthusiasm is obviously not there.
>
> Her parents say, "We've noticed how enthusiastic you are about skating, but there's only so much time to devote to it. Would you be interested in stopping piano for a while, in order to work more on your skating?"

The child might decline the offer. Nonetheless, you have conveyed a certain attitude. You can also make a rule about how much time she must spend practicing if you continue to finance the lessons.

The various enrichments you offer should be items on a menu, not a whole program. The child is bound to pass up some of the items on the menu.

≡ "Fertile soil":
Communication and active listening

As vital as praising children and providing them with enriching activities is creating a foundation of personal comfort and security within the family. Children's self-esteem depends upon feeling heard and understood, especially by their parents.

Dr. Haim Ginott, author of *Between Parent and Child* and other books, taught us what an enormous difference open dialogues can make. Parents can learn to use one of the principal techniques professional counselors use, reflecting back what the child has said. This shows the child that you have listened and implies that you care about his feelings. At the same time, you can stand firm if necessary, without alienating the child. Ginott developed a whole style of discourse for doing this, by making the child's actions, rather than the child himself, the subject of the sentence.

You may also have heard of Thomas Gordon's Parent Effectiveness Training (P.E.T.) courses. If you have taken the course or read one of Dr. Gordon's books, then you have had thorough instruction in the four listening skills of *passive listening* (paying attention without interrupting), *acknowledgment* (nodding, smiling, saying "uh huh," etc.), *invitations* ("I'd like to hear your feelings about that"), and *reflecting back* (what you have understood).* I think a fifth skill is an important part of the package: *formally requesting the floor before replying*. I shall try to teach you these "active listening" skills in a simpler way than Gordon does. But the idea is really the same.

Marriage Encounter and other relationship-improving seminars similarly emphasize active listening and communication skills. So do management-training courses. And this is an important part of every professional counselor's training. Whether one is a counselor, a manager, a friend, a spouse, a parent, or a child, the goals of active listening are:

1. To understand clearly what other people are saying, including the motives and feelings behind their words.

2. To make them feel that they have been fully heard and clearly understood, and that whether you agree with them or not, you respect their point of view.

3. To increase the likelihood that they will do (1) and (2) for you, in return.

* Dr. Gordon calls the fourth skill "active listening," but I want to use that phrase for the whole package. All five components are really active, not passive.

In actual daily life, good communicators use their active listening skills informally and unobtrusively. This is easiest, however, after you have first learned a strict, formal routine. The formal routine is also the one that works best under conditions of stress, to prevent a disagreement from turning into a fight.

The formal rules of active listening. Suppose a father and daughter are arguing about her lackadaisical attitude. Without some rules to govern the conversation, it might get out of hand, like this:

MISTAKE: *Father*: Why don't you go somewhere instead of moping around the house?

Daughter: All my friends have summer jobs. And I can't do anything because you won't give me an allowance anymore.

Father: Why don't you get a job?

Daughter: All the jobs were taken.

Father: Well, you didn't look around.

Daughter: I did too! Dad, the only jobs are lifeguarding and fast food, and they weren't hiring any more kids.

Father: They must have been hiring when your friends applied.

Daughter: They applied months ago! And the only reason Sandra got hired at the pool was because her brother works there.

Father: People don't ring the doorbell and offer you a job—you have to pound the pavement. You have to ask people.

Daughter: Dad, get off my back, will you? I asked plenty of people.

Father: How many of the fast-food places did you try?

Daughter: I wanted to work at Bigger Burger, but how can I get there without a car? If you'd let me take the car every day, I could work there.

Father (exasperated): Why don't you just tell the truth? You don't want a job; you just want to complain.

This father is not going to convince his daughter of anything. All that will come of the conversation is more mutual irritation. And because the daughter never wins a point, she winds up more defeated and unmotivated than she was in the first place. Dad has logic, conversational experience, and greater knowledge of the world on his side. His daughter has nothing but fifteen years' experience of being in the wrong.

BETTER: Now suppose, instead, this father and daughter take turns holding the floor. One will be the speaker and one the listener. They will exchange roles several times, with an important difference from the dialogue above: The listener has to request permission to take the floor; the speaker only consents when he is sure he has been heard.

Rules for the Speaker:

1. Can say anything he wants.
2. Must not yield the floor until he feels listened to.
3. Should not ask a question until he is prepared to change roles and listen to the answer.

Rules for the Listener:

1. Must not reply, express any opinion, or signal disagreement with any of speaker's statements.
2. Must reflect back what he is understanding (for parents, it is especially important to acknowledge and accept any and all negative feelings that the child expresses).
3. Must ask questions to clarify anything he does not understand.
4. When he feels sure he has understood, and wants to reply, must check his understanding and then get permission to be the new speaker.

So the discussion would go something like this:

Father: Why don't you go somewhere instead of moping around the house?

Daughter (speaker): All my friends have summer jobs.

Father (listener): Oh. So you're feeling bored?

Daughter (speaker): Yeah, I'm bored and also broke, since you won't give me any allowance.

Father (listener): Is that creating a problem for you?

Daughter (speaker): What do you think? I can't go anywhere, because I don't have any money.

Father (listener): Could you get a job?

Daughter (speaker): No.

Father (listener): If you could get one, would you want one?

Daughter (speaker): Sure.

Father (listener): Do you need any advice on getting a job?

Daughter (speaker): No.

Father (listener—after a pause): Well, I hear you saying that you're frustrated because you're bored and broke. I can understand how frustrating that must be. It also sounds like you're angry with us for deciding that you were too old to be given an allowance.

Daughter (speaker): No, that would be okay if I could get a job, but there aren't any.

Father (listener): And I also hear you saying that you'd really like to have a job like some of your friends.

Daughter (speaker): *All* my friends.

Father (listener): Like all your friends, but you're pretty sure you can't find a job. (Pause) And I also understand you to be saying you don't want my advice.

Daughter (speaker): Right.

Here, if the two had formally agreed to take turns actively listening to each other, Dad would ask, "Can I have a turn?"' and his daughter, if she felt she had been heard, would become the listener. In a spontaneous conversation, Dad would probably just ask:

Father (listener): Well, can I tell you how I'm feeling?

Daughter (speaker): I know what you think.

Father: I know you think you know what I think. But I listened to you, and I'd like a turn.

Daughter (still with a sour tone): Fine.

Father (speaker): First of all, since I contributed to this problem by stopping your allowance, I'm sorry. I think you're justified in being a little angry or hurt about that. (Daughter shakes her head.) Secondly, I'm feeling real frustrated because you're frustrated, and I'd like to help. But all my experience tells me the ones who get the jobs are the ones who really hustle and check out every fast-food franchise within bicycling distance. I just don't have any better advice to give.

Daughter (listener): How many fast-food places do you think there are?

Father (speaker): Let's see. About seven, within a mile of here. About another half dozen that you could get to by bus.

Daughter: They don't have any "Help Wanted" signs.

Father (speaker): Wait. (Refuses to respond to the last remark, because daughter has stepped outside the role of listener.) Hear me out, okay? You said you didn't want advice, so let me just talk about what *I'm* feeling. It wouldn't really bother me if you just took the summer off and didn't work. It's the combination of your complaining and yet not doing anything about the problem that I find exasperating. When I hear complaints and yet I'm told to keep my advice to myself, it drives me crazy. And I guess it makes me irritated with you, which probably hurts your feelings.

Daughter (listener): Do they ever hire people even when there's no "Help Wanted" sign?

Father (speaker): Yes, often. Or they take your name and call you in a week or two when somebody quits. Or they tell you to come back on a certain date when they expect to have an opening. Sometimes they'll say, "No, but the bakery next-door is looking for somebody."

Daughter: Okay, I get the idea. I'll try that.

Technically, the rules of active listening allow the speaker to say anything that is on his mind, even if it insults the listener. However, in practice, as in this example, when a parent is in a conversation with a touchy child, he is wise to put the added restriction on himself of staying with his own feelings and frustrations, referring to particular actions of his daughter that have made him uncomfortable, rather than impugning her motives or her personality. (Ginott, incidentally, would have carried this an extra step, suggesting statements like "when I hear moping and complaining" instead of "when you mope and complain.")

The reason this second conversation worked better than the first is that Dad carefully laid the groundwork for his own chance to be listened to, by making sure his daughter felt that her position was heard before he attempted to reply. This is *easy to do* if you keep reminding yourself that a listener may only ask clarifying questions:

> EXAMPLES: "Do you wish that you . . ."
> "Does it feel unfair because . . ."
> "Are you saying that . . ."
> "If I understand you, . . ."

You might catch yourself at first asking pseudoquestions that really express an opinion or imply disbelief.

> MISTAKES: "Can you really sit there and tell me . . ."
> "Don't you realize that's not why we have this rule?"
> "Haven't I told you a thousand times . . . ?"

You will learn not to make such mistakes after a few of them lead you back to the kind of exchange illustrated in the first dialogue above. If the child seems unable to listen to you without hostility, pause for a moment and reflect. Are you being aggressive (attacking) instead of assertive (expressing your own feelings)? Try again.

With practice, active listening will become more natural and successful. However, don't expect your kids to listen actively to you right away. After years of tense encounters, they won't trust you at first. I will guarantee an improvement in your dialogues with them, but only after they notice consistent active listening on your part, over a period of several weeks.

Dr. Ginott's and Dr. Gordon's books, along with others recommended in connection with this chapter, contain many examples of active listening by parents in different situations. But you can't learn to do it by reading about it. You learn by trying it. The best way is to have another family member observe your conversation. Have that person stop the listener every time he interrupts, stops paying attention actively, or expresses or implies a response. *Before responding, the listener must check whether the speaker feels understood and is ready to yield the floor.*

Making children listen. Can you insist that your children be active listeners, too? Of course you can. Just make a rule—for example,

"No changes or exceptions in rules will be made unless the requester engages in an active listening dialogue lasting until each side has had at least three turns to be heard."

I know of no better time to train children in the courtesies of adult conversation than when they come to you wanting something. It has to be clear that you *sometimes* modify rules when they have been discussed in an adult fashion, but *never* when the complaints take the form of harangues or other provocations.

> EXAMPLE: *Son*, age seventeen: I shouldn't have to be in by 10:30 on weeknights in the summer. I don't have school the next morning.
>
> *Single mother*: Do you want to discuss it?
>
> *Son*: No. Just change the rule.
>
> *Mother*: I'll discuss it, if you want to have a polite discussion where we take turns doing active listening.
>
> *Son*: Okay.
>
> *Mother*: I'm listening.
>
> *Son*: As I said, I shouldn't have to be in by 10:30 when I don't have school. It's stupid.
>
> *Mother*: Don't your friends have to be in by that time?
>
> *Son*: Only the ones that are in summer school. Kenny can stay out till midnight, same as weekends. Bruce doesn't have any curfew.
>
> *Mother*: I see. Well, I understand why it seems silly. From your point of view, weeknights are no different from weekends. Now, can I tell you the problem from my point of view?
>
> *Son*: Sure.
>
> *Mother*: I have to get up at 6:30, same as during the school year. My bedroom being right next to the door of the apartment, you wake me when you come in. The 10:30 curfew is for my benefit, not yours.
>
> *Son*: So I'll be quiet! I'll—
>
> *Mother*: Wait a minute, you don't have the floor.
>
> *Son*: I understand what you're saying. Is the only reason I have a 10:30 curfew so that I don't wake you up?
>
> *Mother*: Yes, that's the only reason. That's why I let you stay out till 1:00 on weekends—because I don't usually go to bed before then anyway.

Son: Are you saying that if I would come in without waking you, I could stay out as late as I want?

Mother: Let me think about that a minute. Well, yes, you've never given me any reason not to trust you.

Son: Would you be willing to drop the curfew if I carry a key to the back door and don't wake you?

Mother: I'm willing to try it. *But if you do* wake me, we'll reinstate your curfew. Or if *anything* happens to make me feel that I need to monitor what time you're coming in, we'll reinstate your curfew.

Son: It's a deal.

As I mentioned in chapter 10, you do not need to defend your policies continually. One good, full explanation is enough. You can make a rule about how frequently, and at what length, you are willing to discuss your decisions. When your child feels the need to protest a rule, one good dialogue in which you insist on both sides listening to each other before responding will satisfy the child better than twenty of the chaotic discussions you may have had in the past.

Understanding is a two-way affair. On the parents' side, it is a matter of listening and questioning children directly about their feelings, needs, and concerns. It is a matter of understanding them through their actions by tuning in to their implied messages: "I'm angry"; "I'm scared"; "I'm no good." This is where modern parents have the advantage of learning from the great students of children's play, including Anna Freud, Erik Erikson, and Selma Fraiberg, whose wonderful book is listed at the end of chapter 12. We realize, as our grandparents did not, that turbulent mixtures of conflicting emotions are acted out symbolically by perfectly normal children.

Parents' understanding is also a matter of analyzing, sometimes with the help of a family therapist, what function is being served by the misbehavior we are concerned about.

As I have said, however, it is at least as important to make your children understand you. I do not mean analyzing you or empathizing with you—after all, they are only children—but understanding exactly what reactions they can expect if they act in certain ways.

This kind of understanding does *not* come only from rules and consequences. When rules are enforced, questions are generated in children's minds. They need not only answers to the questions they ask but help in asking the ones they may not be able to express. That is the purpose of active listening dialogues between parent and child.

It is also the purpose of family meetings. Besides the mechanical details of who should do which chores when, the real purpose of meeting formally as a family is to have everyone feel listened to. Each member should also leave the meeting feeling pleased with himself for having understood everyone else. If you aren't anywhere near that ideal, then your meeting isn't ready to adjourn.

EXAMPLE: Betty, the mother whom we met in chapter 1, loses her temper when eleven-year-old Doug is mean to his younger brother. She drives the eight-year-old to school and makes Doug walk. Afterward, she recognizes her mistake: Her unusual firmness is experienced by Doug as "picking on him." Betty sits down with her husband to make a formal list of rules with consequences specified in advance.

When the list is ready, Al and Betty call a family meeting. Betty begins by talking with Doug about what happened: "You must have been angry with me for not waiting for you."

Once Doug has had a chance to express his feelings, the parents explain to all three kids that they realize they have sometimes been unfair in the past. "We are changing. Here are the rules. The things on this list are important to us. We're going to try not to hassle you about anything that's not on this list of rules. We're also going to try to stop nagging and complaining about things that *are* on the list; we'll just follow through with the consequences." The children have some things to say about the list of rules. Their feelings are acknowledged. They make several reasonable suggestions for simplifying and clarifying the rules. The amended list is posted on the refrigerator.

☰ Parents' communication with each other

In the realm of "fertile soil" for child development, nothing is more important than the quality of life demonstrated by the parents themselves. Not the material quality of our lives—possessions, recreation, and so on—but the emotional quality and the interpersonal quality.

Whatever your values are—whatever religion, whatever race and culture, whatever political stripe—the only effective way to pass them on to your children is to live them. In the long run, children do what we *do* more than they do what we *say*.

This does not mean parents should be perfect. We cannot prepare our children to be competent, self-confident adults in the real world by pretending to be more competent or more self-confident than we really are. Instead of worrying about how to produce "successful" children, perhaps we should prepare them to deal with success when it comes, and with disappointment when it comes, too. Do we do that by a training course? Or do we do it by sharing with them the vicissitudes of our own lives? Personally, I learned more from the ways my father handled his own successes and disappointments than from any lessons he consciously tried to teach me.

Our children learn much that will be of value to them when we acknowledge problems in every aspect of our lives and set the example of adults working to solve those problems rather than denying them or caving in before them.

Parents should not pretend to live in constant harmony when they don't, nor should they live in permanent disharmony. It does not depress children, upset them, or decrease their self-esteem to realize that their parents are in disagreement. It *does* depress and upset them—and greatly reduce their confidence in many areas of their lives—to feel that their parents have resigned themselves to permanent tension or depression. There may be issues in your marriage that you feel have nothing to do with raising your children. Yet resolving those issues, with professional help if necessary, will make an enormous improvement in the environment from which your children draw their most important resources for the future.

They are not the only ones who are growing. When the process of family development is working right, the growth of the children enhances their parents' continuing development, and vice versa. In fact, the great child psychologist Erik Erikson has revised the Golden Rule in a way that especially applies to parents: "Do to another what will advance the other's growth even as it advances your own."*

≡Advancing the growth of parent and child

The next five chapters discuss some of the specific issues that arise as children develop from infancy to young adulthood and as their parents grow from adulthood to maturity.

The course of childhood is divided into three main periods—preschool, primary school, and secondary school—because the parents' and child's agendas go through fundamental changes from each of those periods to another. The agenda for the years from age one to six is primarily *communication;* the child has to learn language and the basic rules of social relationships. From age six to about twelve, the agenda is *competence;* the child is busy acquiring hundreds of skills and evaluating himself in relation to other children. In adolescence, the agenda is forming an *identity,* asking "Who am I?" and balancing youthful ideals and aspirations against an increasing understanding of reality.

These fundamentally different concerns at different ages mean that, inevitably, parents will need to make different kinds of rules. For example, the parents of preschool children are most concerned with rules about control of aggression, destruction, and selfish impulses; children have to learn to subordinate their desires to the needs of others. In the next period, parents are more concerned about children working seriously in school and in outside activities. With adolescents, there are concerns about the influence of peers and about experimentation with drugs, sex, and other risky activities.

Although rules are needed at every age, as children develop, less can be accomplished with rules. Parents' concerns about their children depend more in the later years upon the self-esteem and

* Erik Erikson, *The Life Cycle Completed,* New York: Norton, 1982, p. 93.

competence that they have managed to build within their children during the early years. When the issues are learning to put toys away and not to crayon on the walls, rules are practically the whole story. But when the issues are motivation in school, responsibility about drugs, safe driving, and so forth, parents' rules are only an indirect (though necessary) aid. More important are children's feelings about themselves. They have to make an increasing number of decisions on their own, away from their parents' supervision; many of those decisions are of life-or-death significance, yet their parents will not even know when the decisions are being made. Therefore, the parents' influence has to have occurred earlier, through the attitudes and strengths they have managed to implant within their children.

SUGGESTED BOOKS: Building Self-Esteem and Competence

Brazelton, T. Berry. *To Listen to a Child.* Reading, MA: Addison-Wesley, 1986.

Briggs, Dorothy. *Your Child's Self-Esteem: The Key to Life.* New York: Doubleday, 1975.

Chess, Stella, et al. *Your Child is a Person: A Psychological Approach to Parenthood without Guilt.* New York: Penguin, 1977.

Faber, Adele, and Mazlish, Elaine. *How to Talk So Kids Will Listen and Listen So Kids Will Talk.* New York: Avon, 1980.

Gardner, Richard. *Understanding Children: A Parents' Guide to Child Rearing.* Cresskill, NJ: Creative Therapeutics, 1973.

Ginott, Haim. *Between Parent and Child.* New York: Avon, 1969.

Gordon, Thomas. *P.E.T. in Action.* New York: Bantam, 1976.

Harrison-Ross, Phyllis and Wyden, Barbara. *The Black Child: A Parent's Guide.* New York: Peter H. Wyden, 1973.

Nelsen, Jane. *Positive Discipline: Teaching Children Self-Discipline, Cooperation, and Problem-Solving Skills.* Fair Oaks, CA: Adlerian Consultants, 1981.

CHAPTER TWELVE

The Preschool Years

The child's agenda for the first five or six years of life is to learn his parents' language. Talking is only part of the task. In order to communicate with others, the child has to learn the basic concepts we take for granted in daily life: distinctions between edible/inedible, for example, or clean/dirty, safe/dangerous, inside/outside, mine/yours, past/future, girl/boy.

From one point of view, the child's parents' task is to transform a naive ape into a civilized human being. *Socialization* is the psychologist's word for that remarkable transformation. But socialization would not occur without the use of language and the basic concepts that languages refer to. Nor could the child learn to communicate without being socialized.

So your basic agenda and your young child's basic agenda are compatible. If there is a struggle, it isn't really between you and him. It is between the part of him that wants to be civilized like everyone else and the part of him that resents any restriction upon his impulses.

Those two conflicting desires are successfully resolved only when parents manage to instill *understanding* and *trust* as well as *self-control*. Socialization means more than conforming to rules. It is not just a matter of whether a two-year-old, for example, is toilet-trained or whether a four-year-old puts away his toys at the end of the day. The child has to understand the *reasons* for those rules. He also has to trust that his needs will be met even though he suppresses his impulsive desires. He has to feel in control of himself even while he submits to his parents' limits.

This chapter will discuss the special tasks that parents of preschool children face. After a reminder about the diversity among children, I shall make some generalizations about this age period—particularly about the problem of communicating with a not-yet-logical mind, the problem of trust, and the problem of organizing and controlling a young child's energy.

≡Individual differences

Part of the wonder and joy of parenthood is the discovery, in each child, of a unique person with unique talents, unique feelings, and unique interests. Nothing I say in this chapter, as I generalize about "the preschool child," can possibly be true of every child. Let's start by looking at some of the ways children differ from one another during these years.

Girls versus boys. Researchers have recently found evidence that boys' personalities and temperaments already begin to differ from girls' personalities and temperaments by age two, if not earlier. For example, girls tend to be more verbal, boys more aggressive and belligerent. On the other hand, preschool boys, on the average, are more creative in exploring new toys than girls are. These differences are the beginnings of lifelong inequalities between males and females. Women are more often superior in language tasks; men are more often superior in conceptualizing things spatially, imagining how they look from different angles. The difference in creativity, beginning at age two, may be closely related to this ability of males to see things from new perspectives more easily.

However, when we make such generalizations, we have to add that there are millions of perfectly normal boys who are *less* aggressive than the average girl, and millions of perfectly normal girls who are more mechanically creative than the average boy. Furthermore, innate differences between boys and girls in their "typical" characteristics are less significant than the differences imposed by our cultural expectations: We dress boys and girls differently, we give them different kinds of toys, and we react differently to them even when their behavior is the same. Small differences are there innately, but in every culture parents make the gender differences greater.

In fact, it is possible that *most* of the differences we see between our sons and daughters are differences of our own making. And most of the remaining differences—the inborn differences—are simply due to their individuality, not to their gender. When we think about our children or describe them to our friends, we tend to highlight the characteristics that are consistent with our image of a boy or a girl. If we can avoid *over*doing that, we can see them as individuals rather than as stereotypes. Thus we can free them to be themselves.

Active versus quiet. Regardless of gender, children differ enormously from one another in how long they can sit quietly engaged in one activity and in how much energy they can expend before needing to rest.

I am not discussing "hyperactivity"—leave that diagnosis to your pediatrician—but simply the normal range of differences among children. Observing your child's nursery school for a few minutes, you can see one child fidgeting constantly, a second child moving from one activity to another without sticking to anything long enough to complete it, a third absorbed in an activity and hardly aware of anyone else, a fourth passively watching the other children swirl around him. Each of these children's activity levels will rise and fall over the course of the day, yet the individual differences among them will remain fairly constant.

Is there anything parents should do to try to slow down the high-energy, low-patience child or to speed up the quiet, absorbed child? In truth, there is not much you can do, even if you want to. But it is worth keeping in mind that these children may have somewhat different needs. In order for the active child to get the satisfaction of finishing what he starts—for example, setting up a farm with his toy people—he may need to be protected from distractions across the room. At the same time, another child joining his game may not slow him down much. The quieter child is just the opposite. He may be less distracted by competing activities elsewhere in the room yet abandon his play if a more energetic child swoops in to dominate the scene. Rather than trying to change your child's temperament, you can provide him, for at least part of each day, with an environment to which his particular temperament is suited. This would mean a minimum of competing activities for the active child, a minimum of intimidating intrusions for the quiet child, so that both can explore the world, practice new skills, and enjoy attention from adults in their own ways.

Both the physically energetic, noisy child and the quiet child are actively learning and practicing their skills during all their waking hours. Both are watching, listening, exploring. One moves around more, but the other is picking up just as much information. The children to be concerned about are the ones who dash around the room without relating appropriately to the people and objects in it, even for a few minutes, or those who withdraw into themselves without watching the other people in the room. Any child might exhibit those extremes of activity or inactivity upon occasion; but if it seems to be a habitual pattern, alert your pediatrician.

Clingers versus explorers. Another dimension of the young child's personality is how secure he or she feels about leaving the parent's side to explore a new environment. Don't confuse clinging with "attachment"; the latter refers to the strength of the emotional bond between parent and child, and it is the *securely attached* toddler who has the confidence to move away from the parent or to be left by the parent for a while. Clinging shows insecurity rather than attachment.

How do you make a child feel more secure? Not by pushing him away. Nor by encouraging him to cling.

MISTAKE 1: Eva, two, refuses to leave her mother's lap when they visit friends. On one occasion, the host's children are one and four. Embarrassed by Eva's clinging, her mother pushes her toward the children: "Go on, stop hanging onto me. Play!" Eva sucks her thumb and buries her face in the couch by her mother's side.

MISTAKE 2: Eva's mother apologizes to her friends: "She's afraid of other children. She never leaves my lap when we're in a strange house." Mother strokes Eva's hair reassuringly. Eva continues to suck her thumb and bury her face by her mother's side.

BETTER: Eva's mother should let Eva cling to her until

the child feels ready to venture forth. But Eva's mother shouldn't label it as a personality attribute, as though she expects her to continue clinging throughout the visit. She should provide a comfortable haven from which the child can survey the new surroundings and to which she can return as often as she wishes. Otherwise, Mother should ignore her and let the attractions of the other children's toys lure her away. Each time Eva returns, Mother should welcome her with a friendly pat and express an interest in whatever Eva shows her.

On the other hand, there is such a thing as too much independence in a young child—defiance when it is time to go home, for example. At home as well as elsewhere, all children need to learn the acceptable bounds of exploration and play. As early as the third year of life, they can learn rules about what things may be played with, what they need to ask permission for, what kinds of play are unacceptable. These decisions are up to you, but you probably need some such rules. Children cannot feel good about themselves unless they know, first, that there are limits to their behavior and, second, that they are usually successful in staying within those limits.

Slobs versus compulsives. Like the rest of us, young children vary in their dedication to neatness. To some extent, they reflect their parents' attitudes about this, responding to rules about bathing, wearing clean clothes, putting things away, having their hair brushed. But they soon develop their own self-concepts, which have more effect on their devotion to order and cleanliness, or to chaos and dirt, than any rules their parents can hope to enforce.

It is good for parents to realize that no rules, no matter how clear or how consistently enforced, are capable of changing the natural slob into a dedicated cleaner-upper. We have to adjust our standards and expectations for each child. One child needs reassurance that it is all right to have dirty hands or to go to bed without lining up all the stuffed animals on their shelf. The next child is so much the opposite that you give up trying to impose any serious standards of cleanliness; you settle for "Before eating, hands must be clean at least up to the wrist" or "There must be a path to walk from the door to the bed without tripping over anything."

There are many other differences among young children. The

ones mentioned are probably sufficient to caution us that none of the generalizations I shall make in the rest of this chapter should be taken too literally with respect to your own particular children. No one knows them better than you do!

≡ The logic of rules

Parents' actions and statements toward children convey many messages about family hopes, expectations, and fears; about mutual respect; about the child's importance. Are young children sophisticated enough to grasp those messages?

Intelligence develops through four main periods of childhood. It begins in the year and a half (roughly) before the infant begins to learn the meanings of words. Then, up until age five or six, the child learns more and more language, but no logical thinking. The preschool child cannot draw inferences. For example, he cannot solve a problem like this (a syllogism):

> Jenny is bigger than Kenny.
> Kenny is bigger than Lenny.
> *Is Jenny bigger than Lenny?*

The young child (in that second period, from eighteen months old to five or six years) does not realize that he has been given enough information to answer the question. That is why formal schooling does not begin until age six. The first-grade curriculum requires basic logical inferences that most children do not make until about that age.

The third major period in mental development encompasses the elementary-school years, when the child can reason about concrete relationships, such as whether Jenny is older than Lenny. The fourth period, when abstract logical thinking becomes possible for the first time, begins in adolescence and continues into adulthood.

The question arises, therefore, whether adults' rules can be understood by one- to five-year-olds. Rules have a logic. If *X*, then *Y*: "If you throw the blocks, they will be taken away from you." Does this make sense to a preschool child?

The answer is yes. This is exactly the kind of logic the child *can* understand, and even thrives upon. Almost everything he

does, from birth onward, can be viewed as an attempt to ac-
cumulate "if-then" information about the world.

> If I cry, Mother comes.
>
> If I bite instead of sucking, she removes me from the breast.
>
> If I shake the rattle, it makes noise.
>
> If I pull up the daisies, Father yells.
>
> If I say "doggie" when I see this kind of animal, every-one smiles approvingly.
>
> If I cross the street without an adult, I have to stay in-side for a while.

So the preschooler can learn "if-then" rules, provided that they are simple contingencies rather than syllogisms.

Furthermore, he soon comes to respect *written* rules, even before he can read them. Just as he remembers the stories that go with the pictures in his books, he will remember that what you wrote down says, "If anyone throws blocks, the blocks will be taken away." He sees that big people are terribly interested in the written word. That motivates him to try to become part of the world of reading and writing as soon as he can.

What can you expect? Apart from the question of logic, there is the question of whether the young child is physically or mentally capable of meeting your expectations. Most child-development experts would agree that children should not be expected to do the following things before (approximately) the ages respectively in-dicated:

Feed self with spoon	1 year
Learn to obey "No, no"	1 year
Undress self	1–2 years
Pick up toys after use	2 years
Use bathroom alone	3 years
Share toys	3 years
Put on shirts, pants, socks	3 years
Button clothes	4 years
Tie shoes	4–5 years
Help care for pet	5 years
Brush teeth	5–6 years
Play games with rules	6 years

Such a list can only be a rough guide, of course, but these examples may help you evaluate your own expectations. If you thought most of these activities could be performed by children younger than I have indicated, perhaps you need to guard against unrealistic expectations; if you thought most of these items could not be performed by children this young, then perhaps you can be a little more challenging. In any case, you will have to be guided by your own children's individual rates of developing the various skills.

≡Self-esteem begins at one

In my book *The Mental and Social Life of Babies: How Parents Create Persons*, I suggested that the moment when the infant first shows self-consciousness is the moment when, just having learned to walk, he falls and looks around to see how people are going to react. If they laugh at him, he may cry; whereas if they smile reassuringly, he usually gets back on his feet.

Self-consciousness really means the consciousness of *others* seeing one and evaluating one as a person. Self-esteem comes to the child as soon as he realizes that other people are watching him and approve of him. Hence, at around the time he takes his first steps, if not earlier, he acquires the first bricks for that edifice of self-esteem he will be laboring all his life to construct.

It is important, therefore, even with the very young child, to do a lot of specific, sincere, unadulterated praising. Not just praise for being "good"—following rules—but even more for all the little achievements of preschool play. Drawing, stacking blocks, setting up toy people and animals, making a toy car go fast, singing, reciting the alphabet: All are major accomplishments deserving genuine praise.

You no doubt started on the right track with pat-a-cake, "How big are you?" and "Where's Mommy's nose?" You clapped your hands and made a big fuss when the infant performed the correct response. You urged him to repeat the feat for every relative and visitor. He felt successful, and important to the whole family!

After about age two, those kiddie catechisms lose their value. The child outgrows the joy of repeating simple things and wants to be more creative. Just find something nice (and true) to say about what he has done, and go on with him wherever his play may lead.

EXAMPLE: *Parent*: Oh, you're setting up a town. It's a good town.

Child: This is the fire station.

Parent: Oh, right, they need a fire station in case there's a fire.

Child: There's a big fire. (Makes noise and destruction.)

Parent: Oh my, you're making a *big* fire!

Child: Now they build a new skyscraper.

Parent: Uh huh. How high is it going to be?

Child: Up to the sky.

Parent: Oh, wow, that's a tall building. Eight blocks, nine blocks—

Child: Ten blocks.

Parent: *Ten* blocks, without falling down! That's incredible. (Implicit message: "I think you're quite a kid.")

≡Messing up and cleaning up

There are many ways of looking at children's development. One way is in terms of the amount of time parents have to spend cleaning up after them. "At first the infant," Shakespeare wrote, "mewling and puking in the nurse's arms." On this dimension, the milestones of childhood go something like this:

> Learns to eat without flinging mashed food all over self and kitchen.
>
> Toilet-trained for daytime.
>
> Helps put away toys.
>
> Dry at night.
>
> Responsible for own room and possessions.
>
> *   *   *
>
> Does own laundry.
>
> *   *   *
>
> Moves into own apartment.

The first few items on this list involve big issues for parents of preschool children: table manners, toilet-training, and putting toys away. You can make rules about all three. Keep in mind that they are all related:

• There is nothing wrong with making a mess if someone is willing to clean it up. Over time, from age two to about age six, parents become less willing to clean up their children's messes of all kinds; they make more demands on children to clean up after themselves.

• When young children make a mess with food, toys, sand, water, pots and pans, or anything else, their play is a metaphorical way of dealing with the major socialization task of toilet-training. To put this another way, toilet-training is one of several arenas in which the child has to resolve the conflict between sloppy pleasures and parents' standards.

Freudian psychologists may make too much of that insight, but others dismiss it too lightly. Children do need to be reassured that making a mess with food or toys is a natural, pleasant thing to do (just as moving their bowels is). Cleaning up is somewhat less natural. But the result is pleasant for everyone in the family.

So whether it is messy eating or going to the bathroom or pulling every toy out onto the floor, you don't have to give a negative message about the mess when you give a positive message about the clean-up. You can react positively to *both* the mess and the clean-up.

Toilet-training. About ten years ago, when my firstborn and all his playmates were two-year-olds, I suddenly acquired new respect in the other parents' eyes. My work as a researcher may have seemed rather abstract and theoretical, but I surely was an expert on one important subject: We trained our son to use the toilet in a couple of days, and, following my advice, so did all our friends.

The simple method, which I learned from Dr. T. Berry Brazelton, is based on the fact that two-year-olds *want* to go to the toilet like everyone else.

Wait until the child expresses a definite desire to use the toilet ("like a big boy/girl") instead of diapers (I promise this will happen!). You have nothing to gain by rushing it,* and a lot to lose. Before the child is interested, it is likely to be an aggravating power struggle, an unnecessary emotional stress, and an experience of failure for both of you.

---

* Some day-care centers do not accept toddlers in diapers. If your child is not ready to be trained, my advice is to find a different day-care center.

Dr. Brazelton is a distinguished Boston pediatrician who makes a strong point of discouraging his patients' parents from trying to toilet-train them before age two. Based on a study of nearly twelve hundred children who were trained at an average age of twenty-eight months, he reports that 80 percent of them started using the toilet perfectly with only a few days' transition period. They had significantly fewer soiling and bed-wetting problems in later years, compared with children whose parents pushed them for earlier "achievement" of this milestone. Brazelton asks, Why is earlier better? Why should using the toilet be something a child has to be coerced into doing?

Any time between the second birthday and the third birthday is fine. There is nothing "better" about early toilet-training. Having lived in England, where many children are "potty-trained" before their first birthday, I am inclined to agree with the comment that it's really the mothers who are trained. And not that well trained, either: Those babies spent inordinate portions of the day strapped onto their potty seats.

The fact is, toilet-trained toddlers are more trouble than those in diapers. When you are out in the car—or shopping, or in a restaurant—it is no treat to have a child who needs to be taken to the bathroom immediately. Only then does one appreciate the fact that the child carried his bathroom around with him for the first couple of years.

When your child thoroughly understands the whole process of how people use the toilet, and repeatedly indicates a willingness to do it that way, plan toward a significant day, no more than a week in the future. Tell the child that on that day he will get to wear training pants and "no more diapers." The day can also be celebrated with a new toy, such as a miniature car or a play-family set—anything the child can look forward to in advance.

In the meantime, buy or borrow a toddler's toilet seat and let the child play at putting it over the grown-ups' toilet. Forget about the kind of potty chair you have to empty and clean—that is more work than diapers! If you had started toilet-training at a younger age, you might have needed a potty chair because the toilet might be too big and frightening. But if you wait until the child is really ready, you can go right to the kind of seat that fits over your toilet seat.

During the last three or four days preceding the big day, watch for signs that the child is about to have a bowel movement. Say, "Okay, let's go to the bathroom," and take the child into the bathroom to finish the job. If he fills the diaper before you have time to get him on the seat, dump the contents into the toilet and mention that if he tells you when he has to go, he can sit on his seat "like a big boy [or girl]."

Get in the habit of leaving the toilet seat down all the time, with the child's seat in place whenever possible. It makes the toilet look much "friendlier." With the seat up, if you're only two feet tall, a toilet looks like a gaping chasm.

Use toilet paper to wipe the child, throw that into the toilet, and let the child flush it. (Sometimes children don't want to flush it; don't make an issue of it. They may even want to leave the room before you flush. You don't care who flushes it or when, so give the child the satisfaction of choice in the matter.)

On those occasions when you miss the signs, don't treat it as anything to be concerned about. Casually say, "Oh, you made a BM [or whatever word you want him to use for bowel movement]? Next time tell me or Mommy [or Daddy], and we'll help you do it in the bathroom." Lead the child to the bathroom for the diaper-dumping routine. About once a day (no more, unless the child brings it up), mention that when he wears training pants, he'll be able to do it right into the toilet, the way you do.

This period of practicing before you start with training pants can be longer than a few days if you want. The only reason I suggest keeping it short is that a two-year-old has little sense of the future beyond tomorrow.

The important part of toilet-training is that you decide the child is ready for training pants on the basis of what he tells you. *Don't* wait until he always, or even usually, makes it to the toilet. *Don't* refer to it as "having an accident" when he has a BM in his diaper. As long as he is wearing a diaper, the assumption should be that he may use it for its intended purpose. The practice period when you have introduced the potty seat but not yet put him in training pants should be a time when using the toilet is merely an enjoyable variation for the child.

When you make the switch to training pants, then a BM without asking to go on the seat will be labeled an "accident."

You won't go back to diapers just because there are occasional accidents. You will then make it clear that using the toilet is the right way and soiling the pants is the wrong way.

When the big day comes, put the child in training pants. Give him or her the promised toy. It is a ritual present, like a birthday gift, not a contingent reward (you won't take it back when the child has an accident). *Stop using diapers, except at night.* If you put the child in training pants some days but not all of the time, you are sure to drag out the toilet-training for months. Children are ambivalent about using the toilet, and if they get the message that you are ambivalent, too, they have no motive to change.

From now on, when you take the child to the bathroom, help him sit on his toilet seat (he will need a step of some kind for climbing up). If he does it in his pants without telling you, act disappointed, but not angry. Let him walk around with dirty, wet pants long enough to be uncomfortable, but not long enough to make a mess anywhere else. Then dump the contents into the toilet, and before flushing, let him sit on the toilet for a few minutes. The contingencies should be:

- If child does business in toilet: cheering and applause from everyone in the household.
- If child sits on toilet without doing anything: neither praise nor blame. If he wants to get down, fine.
- If child goes in pants: moderate disappointment, plus a natural consequence—the child's discomfort.
- But if child is upset about an accident: suppress your own disappointment and reassure him that it is no tragedy.

I can almost guarantee success within one to four days, if you stay with the training pants despite a few accidents. If you have no success, it means your child was not yet ready. Matter-of-factly say to the child, "It looks like you still need your diapers." Try the same method again in a few months. If the child is usually successful but continues to have accidents regularly, consult your pediatrician.*

---

* Children normally regress a bit when a younger baby enters the home. Try to avoid toilet-training within three or four months before and after the birth of the new baby. The same applies if there is a divorce or death in the family.

Urination comes under control pretty much by itself once the child is in training pants. Again, give enthusiastic praise for success, matter-of-fact acceptance or moderate disappointment for accidents.

You don't have to "train" the child to be dry overnight. It is just a matter of waiting until the child prefers it. (In Brazelton's study, the average age was three years, or eight months after daytime training.) Wait until the child has been dry in the morning every day for a week. Then you can switch to training pants for nighttime, too; and once again, don't go back to diapers just because the child has an accident or two.

Other clean-up issues. The same period of time, between the second and third birthday, is a good time to begin setting limits on messes at mealtimes and making rules about putting toys away at certain times. You can convey the attitude that no one is expected to stay neat and clean but that there are simple ways we clean up after ourselves.

═══Anger and control

Issues of messing and cleaning are sometimes exasperating with preschoolers, but they rarely make parents feel so helpless and infuriated as the other major group of problems do. These are the problems of controlling anger, aggression, wildness, and refusal to cooperate. You *must* teach the child to behave within the bounds of certain rules, even when he is angry. But at the same time, leave him with the understanding that *the angry feelings are okay and can be expressed in ways that don't hurt anybody.*

Using the system of rules and consequences, deal with the first instance of hitting anyone (including you) by making a clear rule to apply the next time. Don't hit the child back. (However, some children who pull hair or pinch get the message from one good simultaneous demonstration of what it feels like to be the victim.)

Removing the child from the scene (leaving the victim in possession of the spoils) is a good consequence for antisocial behavior. Five minutes' ostracism is long enough for any one- to three-year-old. After about the age of three, you may need to increase separations to six, seven, eight minutes, and so on, until you find what works. Never put a child in his crib as a punishment—unless you want him to hate his crib.

You can make similar rules about throwing toys, refusing to share, loud aggressive screaming, or whatever you feel should not be allowed. But in all these cases, it is not enough just to follow through with the negative consequence. While removing the child, or the toy, or yourself from the room, you should ideally give a verbal explanation, including:

1. Acknowledging the child's feelings.
2. Reminding him that this way of expressing them is unacceptable.
3. Pointing out that it did not get him what he wanted.
4. Suggesting how he might have been more effective.

EXAMPLE: Three-year-old Jacob yanks a toy away from his infant brother, who naturally screams. Their mother happens to be relaxed, in a good mood, and at the top of her form today. She is able to take care of all four of the points listed above:

"Jacob, I know that it makes you angry when Todd picks up the cars you are playing with. But the rule is, we don't yank anything away from him. If you do, he gets to play with the toy longer." She gives the toy back to Todd. "What can you do if you don't want Todd playing with one of your cars? Don't leave it where he can reach it."

Incidents like that happen many times each day. It is important not to look upon them as abnormal.* Jacob is not a "bad boy," nor is the fact that he behaves aggressively toward his baby brother any reflection on his parents. It is normal for young children to test all such rules time and again.

So you don't need to escalate consequences for normal transgressions like the one just described. Probably there is no reason to escalate at all before age three, and from three to six you should only escalate consequences for truly destructive or dangerous behavior. For less serious problems, just keep following through with the smallest consequences that seem to make an impression on the child, even if they do not completely eliminate the problem behavior.

* Habitual bullying is another matter, discussed in Chapter 21.

If you were to look upon these occurrences as abnormal behavior or think of the child as being "impossible," you could rapidly work yourself into a foul attitude that would permanently detract from your enjoyment of the preschool years. That attitude goes away once you realize that this is the young child's normal way of working out a kind of emotional balance.

On one side of the balance are the child's primitive feelings of anger and selfishness. On the other side are the standards of civilized behavior that you impose on him. After firmly but patiently correcting numerous unacceptable ways of expressing those feelings, civilization manages to worm its way into the child's brain. You might as well remain cheerful as you perform those corrections. They are a major part of the job you took on when you decided to have a child.

The energy problem: Organization versus disintegration. Dr. Brazelton has given us a sensitive picture of life with young children. In his books *Mothers and Infants* and *Toddlers and Parents*, he consistently calls attention to a problem the young child faces many times each day. It is the problem of harnessing enough energy to master new skills without "burning out" and crashing like a spent rocket.

Suppose, for example, that your daughter is concentrating intently on a set of blocks of graduated sizes. Suddenly and surprisingly, she hurls one of the blocks across the room and loses interest in carefully stacking them. Trying to impose some rational sense on the child's act, we might guess that she has become frustrated with the difficulty of the task she set herself and wants to express her anger at the blocks. Dr. Brazelton's observations teach us not to assume so much conscious thinking in the toddler's brain. The real explanation may lie at a lower level in the nervous system. It takes a lot of energy to focus on a challenging task and to coordinate the body's movements. When the child's emotional energy and concentration build up to a level greater than her nervous system can manage, she "disintegrates," as Brazelton puts it.

If you start watching toddlers with this idea in your mind—that their batteries alternately get overcharged and drained—you can avoid feeling as though something is terribly wrong with them. What you are seeing is not a temperamental child but a situation in which the child can't maintain just a moderate level of concentration. Realizing that, you can take the child out of the situation. Discipline is not necessary; just decrease the stimulation.

MISTAKE: Eighteen-month-old Meghan suddenly flings a toy aimlessly across the room. The response is, "Bad girl! We don't throw our toys!" Mother puts Meghan in her room and closes the door, ignoring her cries during five minutes of strict ostracism.

BETTER: That consequence might be appropriate for a child who habitually throws toys at people and is being trained not to. In this case, however, the problem is not misbehavior but "disintegration." Mother could put the blocks away and invite the toddler to look at a favorite book, a less taxing activity because it is so familiar to Meghan. After the quiet time with the book, her energy for more challenging play may build up again, unless it is getting toward naptime. (Try not to put a child to bed as a direct consequence of misbehavior; get her quiet and relaxed first.)

Tantrums. There are times when children seem so far out of control that they would sour the most perfect mother's or father's sweet disposition.

Actually, tantrum behavior is not necessarily "out of control." Sometimes it is a deliberate attempt to manipulate parents. Other tantrums come when a child is simply too tired to behave like a rational person. Those are a matter of disintegration, discussed above; getting them under control means reducing the energy demands upon the child.

In both cases, the child has gone beyond the bounds of civilized behavior. You do not have to be concerned about whether the tantrum is genuine disintegration or merely a performance. There are two absolute rules for parents dealing with tantrums:

1. Stop the tantrum, as described below.
2. Do not reward the child by responding positively to the tantrum in any way. On the contrary, show the child how the anger could have been expressed and how the result he

wanted could have been achieved if he had *not* thrown a tantrum.

Most parents have little trouble dealing with the occasional tantrum as with any unacceptable behavior. It is only if tantrums become a way of life for the child that the parents are likely to call their pediatrician for help. In that case, a systematic program is needed in order to eliminate the tantrums.

As with all rules at any age, it is important for the child to know in advance precisely what will happen if he has a tantrum. Therefore you need to develop a routine response:

1. When the tantrum comes, holding the child tightly is often enough to stop it. Try kneeling or sitting behind the child and holding both his arms stiffly at his sides, at arm's length from you. Squeeze his arms as hard as you can for five to ten seconds. Then, if he calms down, comfort him and try to get him to relax in your arms. The security of being in his mother's lap will sometimes help him recover control over his rage.

This cuddling must be offered in response to the child's *stopping*, not in response to the tantrum itself. (Be sure that the child can get a hug from you without going to the trouble of throwing a tantrum.)

You will have to experiment with different methods of stopping the tantrum. When you find what works, do it every time. Some parents find it effective to throw themselves to the floor and feign an even bigger tantrum than the child's. If you try that, overplay it, like a clown. Don't just outyell the child in an angry outburst of your own.

2. The next step, 2a or 2b, depends on whether you are successful in stopping the tantrum.

a. If the child does not calm down (I wouldn't expect step 1 to work the first time you try it), send him to his room just until he calms down. It may be necessary to station yourself outside the closed door of his room. Let him know that the price of freedom is sixty seconds of silence.

b. When the child is reasonably quiet, *whether or not he lets you hug him*, ask him calmly what you can do to help him. The problem may be as simple as a construction toy that isn't fitting together properly or the refusal of siblings to play with him. On the other hand, if the tantrum came after you denied him something, you can let him know that you understood what he wanted, and you can lay out the long-term prospect for getting it by *appropriate* behavior. "Now that I know you like chicken better when it is fried, I'll make it that way next time. But tonight I've cooked it this way, and this is all that's being served for dinner."

Now I hear you objecting, "Oh, I've tried that and it didn't work." The problem was that you didn't stick to the same series of consequences enough times to make them clear and consistent.

Here is how this will work. You will probably have to go to step 2a two or three times. Then, to your surprise and relief, the child will start responding to you at step 1, even accepting your offer of physical comfort. Gradually, the tantrums will decline in frequency.

Throughout the above procedure, try to say as little as possible about the tantrum behavior itself. I would not say, "Big boys don't cry" or "I can't stand those tantrums" or "There you go again." That kind of comment refers to the undesirable behavior as if it were becoming a permanent aspect of the child. What you really want to do is give him a better way to express his bad feelings. You are not looking for an excuse to punish him. You want to understand what is hurting him, and you want to do everything you can to make that hurt go away. The child has to learn that there are some effective ways of getting you to help (or at least to do your best) but that a tantrum will always lead to a firm, predictable, undesirable result.

Dawdling. With many children, crankiness and temper tantrums are less of a problem than their more passive cousins, dawdling and ignoring. Although the child who throws himself down in the sandbox kicking and screaming could hardly appear more different from the one who continues playing quietly while his mother calls him a dozen times, both reactions often have the same cause.

As children develop skills, they naturally acquire greater control over objects and events. Their growing mastery excites a desire for even more mastery and gives them their first taste of freedom of choice about their activities. This, of course, collides head-on with adults' understandable attempts to control and contain the young child's exuberance.

A certain amount of dawdling is normal. But it should not become a routine power struggle between parent and child. If he has no way of exerting control other than to be slow as molasses every time you tell him it is time to do something, then you are in for a perpetually frustrating struggle. Sensing your impatience and anger, the child will become even more resistant. The more irritated you seem to be at his slowness in eating, putting toys away, or walking home from the playground, the more he will dawdle—and the closer you'll get to your boiling point.

The cycle has to be broken in two ways. Neither way alone will do the trick. Half of the solution is to stop nagging at the child and to make simple rules about dawdling. They can include one-time rules as well as more permanent ones.

> EXAMPLE (permanent rule): Jason is in the "terrible twos." He would rather play with his food than eat it. His parents decide to stop nagging at him. They consider thirty minutes more than enough time for Jason to complete a meal. After twenty minutes, they give him a "ten-minute warning" by setting the kitchen timer. When it rings, all the food is removed from the table. Jason protests, but at the next meal he is hungrier and eats appropriately.

> EXAMPLE (one-time rule): Lev does not want to leave the corner Tot Lot with his father, probably because he has nothing to look forward to but bedtime when they get home. He stops to inspect every crack in the sidewalk and the hubcaps of every parked car. Some parents might start nagging in an irritated tone. Lev's father says, "Shall we read a book when you're in bed? Which book?" Lev names his favorite one. "Okay, but only if we have time. If you keep stopping like that, we won't have time for a book."

The second half of the solution is to give children more choices and more control over things that do not matter so much to you. Lev was allowed to choose which book he wanted. However, the trade-off does not have to be so immediate as in that example. If children are habitual dawdlers, they are calling for more choices and control *in general*, not just at the time they are dawdling. Even at this age, a child's self-esteem demands a sense of power over some part of his or her life.

Deciding what power you can give to the child requires a thoughtful examination of your priorities. What rules do you really need to insist upon, and what preferences can you yield in favor of more freedom of choice for the child? You might be a little bored by some of the child's choices, time after time, but it is a small price to pay for cooperation.

Battles over meals. Many parents ask what to do about finicky eaters. That is a question for your pediatrician, who knows the individual child's nutritional needs. My only advice is that food *types* (vegetables, fruit, protein, dairy products, etc.) are more important than insisting that the child must eat any specific food. There is nothing wrong with allowing children to decide that they do not like a particular vegetable—so long as they eat other vegetables—or that they do not like a particular dairy product, so long as they get the protein and the calcium from other products. No child was ever spoiled by being allowed to refuse to eat beets.

Once again, I am emphasizing the child's need for choices. Research has shown that most children will choose a balanced diet when presented with an array of foods. They may get too little calcium one day and too few carbohydrates another day, but over the course of a few days their appetites will guide them correctly.

Don't be afraid to put children in control of the amount they eat, as well as allowing them to choose specific foods. Even if you think they are under- or overeating, don't take action without consulting your pediatrician. If an overweight child is put on a diet, he may feel compelled to resist and defeat the diet just to regain a sense of control. He would rather be fat through his own voluntary eating than thin under others' control. Part of therapy with an obese child (though not the whole treatment) may involve providing *larger* meals than he wants, so that he can be in control of the amount he eats. Conversely, if your child refuses to eat as much as you and your pediatrician think he should eat, try giving him even *smaller* portions than he wants, so that he will be hungry and ask for more.

≡The electronic baby-sitter

TV was already an entrenched part of our society when you and I were children. The era of many more channels, home video, and video games has not really changed the issues parents have to deal with.

In early childhood, there are just two major issues. One has to do with the problem of overstimulation. The other has to do with TV as a baby-sitter—in other words, as a cheap substitute for parent-child interaction.

Audio/video overload. Dr. Brazelton makes special mention of TV in relation to his point about toddlers building up more intense levels of concentration than they can stand.

> The energy which it takes to control the input from such an attractive source is demonstrated by a child who sits mesmerized in front of a set, unable to be reached unless a parent shouts in his ear, or physically draws him away. The cost to him is easily seen as he disintegrates at the end of a program—screaming, whimpering, and "raw" after a period of such intense involvement.*

There are several things parents can do to make this situation easier for young children. One is to keep the volume fairly low—audible five to ten feet away from the TV but not all over the house, and not as loud as the child's own normal voice.

Another alternative is to have the TV on only at certain times of day, for certain programs. The choice of programs is up to you, depending on the ages of your children and on your tastes as well as theirs. You can be flexible, of course, but I strongly advise against the custom of leaving the TV on even when there is nothing that you consider worth watching. It creates a constant barrage of stimulation. The young child has to either absorb it to the bursting point or tune it out by dulling his senses in general.

A final choice is just to accept the fact that audio/video overstimulation is bound to occur at times. When your child "disintegrates" like the child in Brazelton's example, turn off the TV and invite him into your lap. Try to create a calm, quiet nest for a while. If the child continues to cry, you may have to treat it as a tantrum—especially if he is demanding something you aren't willing to give him at the moment. But not every irrational crying

* T. Berry Brazelton, *Toddlers and Their Parents*, p. 161.

episode is a tantrum; often, the child stops crying after a few minutes of comfort.

The TV as baby-sitter. When "Sesame Street" was conceived in the 1960s, one of its principal goals was to be visually and musically attractive to parents as well as to young children. The Children's Television Workshop producers designed the show to generate extra "cognitive" (mental) interaction between children and their caretakers. Research shows that they succeeded. If it is hard for you to walk past the TV when your three-year-old is watching "Sesame Street" without joining him for a few minutes, it doesn't mean you have immature tastes. The program has mature appeal.

Unfortunately, "Sesame Street" is almost alone in this respect, among programs for the young child. I can't stay awake through a whole "Mr. Rogers's Neighborhood," beloved as the show is by tots. Fred Rogers has the talent of sustaining a warm, comforting, slow-paced environment, which many young children are not able to get from their parents.

On the commercial stations, the cartoon shows are designed to deliver a specific audience to their advertisers: children and children alone. The commercials are designed to make the child ask for the sponsor's product. Hence there is no need—in fact, no desire—to get the parents to watch.

All programming for young children can be considered from this point of view. Whose attention does it capture, and how? Is it something that amuses you at the same time it interests your child, so that it brings the two of you together for some preschool enrichment? Does it provide something that might be valuable for your child, even if it doesn't interest you? Or is it merely calculated to keep the child occupied and tuned in to specific messages, creating a demand for cereals and toys? Your answers to those questions will help you make decisions about limiting hours and choosing programs.

I strongly feel that children's competence is enhanced by limiting their time in front of the TV, at every age. Even the best program is less valuable than reading a story with you or playing a game. The truth is, *your* children don't need television at all. Evidently, they have a parent who likes to read—and who cares.

≡A support system is a must

Much of the time, parents of preschool children feel like lion tamers. In fact, they are under more stress than a lion tamer, for several reasons. When the lion tamer is working with one lion, the others usually sit patiently on their platforms awaiting their turns, whereas your children are likely to turn on you all at once. Second, lions are *supposed* to be wild animals, so that it is remarkable when they submit to any discipline at all, whereas children are supposed to become reasonable, civilized, intelligent human beings, and when they are not, people blame their parents. Third, the lion tamer is admired and handsomely paid for his work. And when he is tired, he can lock the lions in their cages and walk away.

Even with all those advantages, the lion tamer still gets a staff of five or six helpers to handle the animals and to discuss whatever problems come up each day. You definitely need a support system, too. Researchers find that of all the factors leading to child abuse, one of the surest is a parent trying to manage alone, without enough other adults to talk with about the ordinary daily stress of parenthood.

Don't wait until you are at the end of your rope. Build a support network for yourself *before* you need it. It should include at least three of the following kinds of support:

1. Your spouse, or an intimate friend who meets your needs for adult companionship as well as helping to solve problems with your children.

2. The children's grandparents.

3. Other relatives who care about your children, especially your sisters, brothers, sisters-in-law, or cousins who have children of their own.

4. A paid sitter.

5. Friends with children the same age as yours, who live near enough to get together with you on a regular basis.

6. A formal, cooperative play group. Supermarket bulletin boards are a good way to get in touch with other interested parents.

7. A neighborhood drop-in center for parents of toddlers. Call any minister or pediatrician in your neighbor-

hood for suggestions, get a list of community services from your city or town hall, or try the Yellow Pages.

8. A parent stress hotline. There are many of these across the United States and Canada. They have the advantage of anonymity. If you are feeling guilty about having struck your child, or neglected him, or merely felt like doing so, a hotline is a way to talk with other, more experienced parents (volunteers) who won't be shocked. They have had the same feelings. To get the number of a hotline near you, try the same sources listed in the preceding paragraph.

EXAMPLE: Matthew, age five, is the only child of a single mother. Still mourning his father, who was killed a year ago by a drunk driver, Matthew tends to throw tantrums when he is tired and something frustrates him. At those times, he is liable to break toys, scream so loud that a neighbor once called the police, and recite every four-letter word he knows.

MISTAKE: His mother feels helpless and distraught when this happens. She has tried everything: spanking him, sending him to his room without dinner, pretending to ignore him (until he started throwing things), and once, at a friend's suggestion, she even poured a glass of cold water on Matthew. That stopped the tantrum, but a few days later there was another one. His mother collapsed on her bed, sobbing. Matthew's screaming stopped, but the next day he did it again.

BETTER: These two people are both suffering a lot, and they need help to deal with their loss: from a counselor, their extended family, and good friends who can spend a lot of time with them.

In chapter 21, we shall discuss when and how to get professional help for various kinds of problems. Not all tantrums are a cause for seeking therapy. But tantrums like Matthew's, which leave you feeling helpless and enraged, are definitely a sign that you need help. The ideas in this book are only the first approach. Drawing upon your support network is the second approach. A family counselor is the third.

≡Problems not to worry about with young children

Nature is kind to parents of toddlers and preschoolers in one way: Their problems don't last very long. Even if parents do the worst possible job of dealing with some problem—toilet-training, for example—chances are that the child will outgrow the difficulty. The process may take months instead of days, but the child will eventually use the toilet properly.

With certain common concerns during this period, it may even be counterproductive to worry about them. Some of these have to do with what might be called "normal obnoxiousness." Others are merely symptoms of moderate anxiety.

Terrible twos. I personally have never found two-year-olds to be terrible. It is an age of steady progress toward self-care and cooperation with family rules, and it is also an age of blossoming creativity. However, it is true that two-year-olds say "No" more often than "Yes," and resistance to suggestions often seems to be their preferred mode of operating.

This may drive you crazy, but other than that, it is not a real problem. Children have to assert their ability to say no before they can *choose* to say yes. That is what makes us human beings rather than robots. It is similar to the way adolescents need to reject adult society before they can voluntarily enter it. In fact, the pediatrician and writer Fitzhugh Dodson called the third year of life "first adolescence." But I think "terrible twos" is a good name because it helps to remind you that all you have to do is survive until the child is about three.

The "why" stage. Some, but not all, children pick up a nasty habit of incessant questioning. This may happen at two, three, four, or five. I would not treat it as nagging (which you can make a rule against) but as the only way the child knows of sustaining a conversation with you:

> *Three-year-old*: Why are fire engines red?
> *You*: So people can see them.
> *Three-year-old*: Why?
> *You*: So if we're driving our car, we'll see the fire

engines coming a long way off and we'll pull over to the side of the road.

> *Three-year-old*: Why?
>
> *You*: To let them pass.
>
> *Three-year-old*: Why do we let them pass?
>
> *You* (sigh): So they can get to the fire.
>
> *Three-year-old*: Why?
>
> *You*: You know why.
>
> *Three-year-old*: Why?
>
> *You*: Why do you ask?

These conversations usually degenerate when the parent tires of responding. (The story writer Ring Lardner captured it perfectly with his line " 'Shut up,' my father explained.") You can stop them at any point, simply by asking the child a question of your own.

Fears. It is normal for young children to have fears—of the dark, for example. There is no point trying to "get them over it" unless the fear is so intense and irrational that it inconveniences the rest of the family (like a fear of being left with baby-sitters). The best first approach to a young child's fear is to protect him from the thing he is afraid of. Put a night light in his room; keep dogs away from him; don't require him to go into the basement.

If you reassure the child that you can understand why at his age he may be afraid ("Yes, dogs are scary if you don't know them") and that you are confident he will feel more secure at a later age ("When you're bigger, you won't be afraid of dogs anymore"), your acceptance will usually help the child get over the fear sooner. Pushing him to overcome the fear—by insisting that he has to get used to sleeping in the dark, for example—is likely to make the problem worse.

EXAMPLE: One of my sons was nearly six years old when he became afraid of a circus poster of a lion that hung in a hallway of our home. He refused to go down that hall unless he could hold an adult's hand, and even then he always closed his eyes as he passed the poster. My first response was that this was ridiculous; he should not be indulged in such a silly fear. We would have to convince him that the picture could not hurt him, perhaps give him a series of "desensitization" trials as psychologists do to cure phobias. But a simpler solution suggested itself: We took down the poster. About a year later, with the child's permission, we put it back.

Undoubtedly, at that time, this child was working through some more significant feelings, which the fear of the lion merely expressed, and which exploratory therapy might have brought out. But why? That kind of effort would only have been worthwhile if the fear had been a real problem. Accepting the child's way of dealing with his feelings—even if neither he nor his parents ever fully understood what those feelings were—was easier, infinitely cheaper, and probably more effective.

If the thing the child fears cannot simply be removed or avoided—for example, if a two-year-old is afraid to go to sleep in her own room at night—you and the child can develop a magic ritual together that will often satisfy her. Don't lie down with her every night until she is asleep. But she may feel secure if her dolls have been placed in a certain way, if her bear has been tucked in and kissed good night, and if the door is exactly six inches ajar. Give her some choices. Why does this work? Does the child really believe the bear can protect her if the proper ritual is observed? Probably not. But in cooperating with her in observing the ritual, you give her the message that it is all right for little girls to be afraid, and that you care. And you take bedtime out of the realm of the unknown; if it is the same every night, no unexpected monsters will appear. (My suggestion for toilet-training above is also based on the use of a ritual to give the child security.)

Irrational fears persisting into the elementary-school years—or beginning then—should be treated as more serious. At that age, it becomes more important to ascertain the true cause of the child's anxiety; removing its superficial focus may only leave the anxiety to affect the child in some other way. But younger children outgrow most of their fears if parents simply acknowledge them and allow the children a measure of control over their environments.

Thumb-sucking, nail-biting, bed-wetting. Probably every young child manifests some such imperfection in behavior—and which of us adults is not defective in some way? All such nervous habits will be cause for concern, and possibly therapy, if they persist much into the school years. But again, with preschool children, the most helpful thing you can do is to reassure them that the habit is perfectly all right for now, that you are confident they will get over it, but that there is no hurry. Then ignore the behavior. There is a good chance it will go away; the odds are worse if you hassle the child about it.

Stuttering, lisping, repeat-repeat-repeating words, and other garblings of speech. These are very common in preschoolers. Don't worry about them until the school years, and then discuss the problem with the child's teacher. To some extent, it may help if you encourage the child to slow down, and show that you will listen without losing patience. But in general, criticizing young children's speech does not inspire them to improve it.

Lying. A serious problem in older children, lying is not a disciplinary issue before ages six to eight. Until then, don't moralize. Ask yourself instead what the child seems to be trying to avoid by telling untruths. Lying conceals fears, and your job is to understand the fears. Then you can deal with them directly, and the child can deal with you more directly and honestly.

≡Summary

In the years before children start school, their principal agenda is learning the language and rules of their parents. They don't need many written rules, but they greatly need consistency, clarity, and a secure structure from which they can begin to explore the world, and to which they can return after each exploration.

The show-offable achievements of the preschool years—reciting the alphabet, counting to twenty, and so forth—are less important than the self-esteem parents begin to instill by conveying their delight in those achievements. The early years are for play, not work—play within a secure social environment (basic trust comes from basic rules) and with ample praise for every act of creativity, cooperation, or appropriate expression of feeling.

SUGGESTED BOOKS: The Preschool Years

Ames, Louise, and Chase, Joan. *Don't Push Your Preschooler*. New York: Harper and Row, 1981.

Beck, Joan. *Best Beginnings: Giving Your Child a Head Start in Life*. New York: Putnam's, 1983.

Brazelton, T. Berry. *Infants and Mothers* (revised edition). New York: Delacorte, 1983.

Brazelton, T. Berry. *Toddlers and Parents*. New York: Doubleday, 1989.

Donaldson, Margaret. *Children's Minds*. New York: Norton, 1979.

Fraiberg, Selma. *The Magic Years*. New York: Scribner, 1968. (This is the best book ever written about early childhood.)

Kaye, Kenneth. *The Mental and Social Life of Babies: How Parents Create Persons*. University of Chicago Press, 1982. (Requires some background in psychology.)

Sutton-Smith, Brian, and Sutton-Smith, Shirley. *How to Play With Your Children (and When Not To)*. New York: Hawthorn, 1974.

CHAPTER THIRTEEN

The Elementary Years

Having learned the basic language, the child's main agenda from age six to about twelve is *competence*. Besides reading, writing, and arithmetic, there is a profusion of other skills to be mastered. Physical competence extends to competitive sports, ballet, gymnastics, bicycling, boating, skating, skiing, and now video games. Learning to whistle may be a major occupation for months—and learning to play an instrument for years. There are the hand-eye skills of drawing, sculpting, constructing models. The rules of games have to be mastered, not just for playing correctly but also for trying to beat someone else. There is also the perpetual task of remembering and identifying vast details from stories, movies, songs, television commercials, as well as real life. In all of those domains, children increasingly match their knowledge against adults as well as against other children.

Perhaps most important, the child has to master social skills: how to talk to other children in different situations, how to negotiate a decision about what to play, how to make a suggestion, how to respond to suggestions, how to ask adults for things, and how to say no gracefully.

Younger children are also concerned with mastery, of course. So are adolescents and adults. But there is no period of time when these concerns are so intense and occupy so much energy as during the elementary-school years.

Judging from the conversations of parents with one another,

during this period, and also from the questions they ask teachers, pediatricians, and psychologists, children's competence is as big an issue for parents as it is for the children themselves. Two questions come up again and again: how to *motivate* children to try harder rather than giving up when they get frustrated, and how to *direct* their interests in the directions parents consider most worthwhile. A related question is how to help them *feel* competent in the face of so many messages implying they are not competent enough.

These three questions will occupy most of this chapter, with respect to school, extracurricular activities, and relationships with other children. At the end of the chapter I shall add some suggestions for instilling two other vital qualities before adolescence begins: *responsibility* and *honesty*.

≡Individual differences

All children are unique individuals. Although we try to discuss them in general terms, we cannot reduce all boys to one type, or all girls to one type. Even the simple statement that competence is a big issue for children during the elementary period is bound to have a different meaning to the parents of different children. As I did in the previous chapter on preschool children, I shall begin this chapter by pointing out just a few of the many differences among children. My main purpose is to stimulate you to think about each of your own children as someone for whom the ideas in this book must be adapted, not someone to whom my suggestions can be applied without modification.

Boys versus girls. In the early elementary years (age six to nine or so), differences between boys and girls are less important than at any other time in life. By the end of elementary school, the differences are glaring, and their importance to the boys and girls themselves will never be greater.

The change begins in the fourth or fifth grade, when girls shoot up in height and boys do not. Soon, puberty begins for the girls, increasing the differences still more. Your child's self-esteem will depend not only on his or her own bodily changes (or lack of change) but also on what is happening to the classmates' bodies. A fifth-grader whose menstrual periods have started may feel isolated and abnormal. Four years later, some of her classmates will still not have menstruated, and they will be the ones who will feel abnormal. The same holds true for the boy who grows to six feet at age twelve, and the one who is still barely five feet at sixteen.

Even before puberty begins, the elementary-school child anticipates those changes, sees them beginning in other children, and starts to evaluate himself or herself in terms of the questions "What is a boy? What is a girl? What kind of a boy/girl am I?"

In general, throughout this period, girls are more verbal and perform better in school, and boys are more physically active, more interested in construction and moving objects than in social relationships and such role-playing games as "House." Thus our traditional stereotypes are based on truth. But there are so many exceptions and so much overlap between the personalities of girls and boys that the stereotypes are of little use.

Even if many common generalizations about boys and girls are true, what should parents do about them? Try to enhance the differences so that your sons are more "boyish" and your daughters more "ladylike"? Try to minimize them, so your sons don't get short-changed on verbal and interpersonal skills and your daughters don't get short-changed on athletics and assertiveness? Or ignore the stereotypes, letting each child have his or her own strengths in whatever areas they may be? This author declines to answer those questions for you.

In fact, you don't have much choice. Some children seem to be "all boy" or "all girl" from an early age, firmly resisting parents' more liberated suggestions. Other children are less concerned about conforming to the stereotypes and may even deliberately reject them—for instance, the girl who refuses to wear dresses. I think it is unwise to oppose these expressions of individuality. In the case of a girl who *seldom* likes to wear dresses, parental pressure to do so would tend to make her *never* like dresses, whereas respecting her right to choose, and finding a reason to compliment her no matter what she wears, enables her to feel that she can look more or less feminine, depending on the occasion.

Impulsives vs. reflectives. The variation in activity levels which I noted in preschool children continues into this period, and to ome extent the same children who were the quieter ones then are till the quieter ones. In addition, another variable observed by hild psychologists has to do specifically with mental activity.

Like adults, some children respond quickly when given a roblem to solve, and some reflect more carefully before respond- ng. Both types may get the answer right or wrong. These mpulsive-versus-reflective styles have been found to be fairly eliable characteristics of individual children across a variety of ituations. In moderation, they are simply personality differences, bout which there is nothing parents can or should do. At the ex- remes, however, an impulsive child and a reflective child have ery different needs. The former needs to be encouraged to scan ll the available information, to consider alternative responses efore choosing one. By contrast, the extremely reflective child annot commit himself to make a choice, perhaps due to anxiety ver the possibility of being wrong. This child may need reassur- nce about the fact that all of us have to make guesses in situa- ions where we cannot be certain of being correct.

How do you know when these personality styles are problems hat the child needs help with, rather than simply individual dif- erences to be accepted? I would say that they are only problems if he child's teacher or school psychologist diagnoses them as inter- ering with schoolwork; that is, the child is making mistakes ecause of impulsiveness or failing to complete work because of eflectiveness. Neither an impulsive nor a reflective style is a prob- em unless it seriously hampers a child's scholastic achievement.

Specialists vs. generalists. Another way children differ is in the readth of their interests and competencies. For some, the drive or competence in the elementary years is focused on two or three reas: a particular sport; a particular game; reading; grades in chool; perhaps a musical instrument. These children have little nterest in things they cannot do fairly well.

Other children are more scattered in their interests, ac- umulating a moderate degree of competence at a large number of activities without getting involved in any of them deeply or for long. They are more intrigued by the diversity of challenges the world offers than by the single-minded pursuit of excellence.

Parents cannot choose which strategy their children will em- ploy. Some parents who pursue a great many interests encourage their children to do likewise, but their children may be of the single-minded persuasion. These parents need to be careful not to push for breadth to such an extent that they discourage excellence. On the other hand, parents who are more single-minded and dedicated to excellence run the danger of stifling a "generalist's" other interests.

In order to avoid that kind of conflict, it helps to spend some time thinking about what kind of approach each of your children seems to be taking toward this period of life. Both types of children are normal. Either strategy can be disadvantageous to a child who carries it to extremes—the musical prodigy who never exercises her body, the star athlete who misses out on the joys of literature, or the dilettante who drops every activity before getting any satisfaction from mastering it. But in the less extreme cases, both strategies are healthy ways of developing.

Adult-oriented versus child-oriented. A difference among children in the ability to relate to adults appears quite strikingly by the time they reach age seven or eight. Although school-age children generally spend much more time playing with each other than with adults, some are more at ease with adults and better tuned in to adult conversation than other children are.

This is not an area in which much research has been done, so I can only share my impressions. When children come into my office, or when I meet my friends' children and my children's friends, I notice right away that some relate to me almost as adults—less knowledgeable, perhaps, sometimes less articulate, but *interested* in me and wanting me to be interested in them. Other children, just as healthy in terms of their psychological development, do not do that. They seem to find adults' conversation boring. Their replies to questions are courteous but peremptory, even evasive.

I assume that the children who feel at ease with adults during this period are those whose parents have treated them as interesting conversational partners, who have spoken to them in a fairly grown-up way, have included them in dinner table discussions even when there were guests for dinner, and have listened respectfully when the children had something to say. (I have to add that when this is carried too far, and children sense that there is somehing wrong with being "childish," they can develop serious neuroses.)

The more child-oriented children have not necessarily been ignored, babied, or condescended to, but their parents have probably not realized that there were many subjects on which they could engage their children on a mature level. They may have rarely stepped out of the order-giving role except when they played children's games at the children's level.

Although both groups of children are normal, the child who feels at ease in the world of grown-ups as well as among other children has a strong advantage. Teachers are adults; so are coaches, librarians, ministers, and everyone else from whom children acquire their most important competencies. The acquisition of knowledge is cumulative and self-perpetuating; skills acquired early in life lay the foundation for all later learning. The child who is less able to relate to adults, at any period in development, is deprived of valuable input. This awkwardness will make it harder to acquire all kinds of other skills. It will cheat the child of positive, confidence-building feedback from parents, teachers, and others.

The ability to relate to other children, whose interests and whose social conventions are entirely different from those of adults, is also important. In fact, if a child had to choose one orientation, it would be better to be child-oriented during this period and to let the orientation to adults wait. Fortunately, they do not have to choose one style. They can be bilingual, so to speak —fluent in the dialect of adults as well as in that of their agemates.

Parents of adult-oriented children need to remember that despite the ease of communication on an adult level, the children are still children and the parents are still parents. Don't be misled into letting your rules slip away just because your child is so articulate.

With the child-oriented child, I think the danger is that the parents may become less sensitive to the child's growth. You may need to make an extra effort to narrow the communication gap, to praise the child, to set aside time for one-to-one activities, and to include the child in some of your conversations with adults.

≡Motivation and direction in school

Your number-one tactic for inspiring your children to do their best in school is to praise their every achievement. No doubt you have been doing that from their infancy onward; but don't stop. When the first-grader brings home that first worksheet with the teacher's "Good" or ☺ at the top, show your pleasure. Praising is motivating, and it is not the teacher's job alone.

Continue taking an interest in every day's schoolwork right through to the end of high school. Don't take it for granted. Be enthusiastic about good work.

When the grades are not impressive, the first question to ask is, Who says he is doing poorly? For some children, a B in math or a C in spelling may be good grades; they should be praised as highly as another child's A. Poor performance in school is a relative matter. Before worrying about what to do about a child's "underachievement," be guided by the teacher's judgment as to what level of achievement ought to be expected of this child in this subject.

The teacher's job includes observing each child in school, interpreting test reports, analyzing the individual child's problems in understanding the material in each subject, grouping children at various ability levels, and making recommendations to parents about extra help their children might need. One question you should ask at every conference is, "Should we expect our child to be doing better work in this subject?" If the answer is yes, then ask the teacher's opinion as to what type of underachievement you have to deal with. There are at least five kinds of underachievement. The parents' job is different in each case. Depending on the type of underachievement you are dealing with, you may need to provide:

- Remedial help with basic learning skills.
- Tutoring or extra help with homework and with concepts not understood in class.
- Stricter rules about school-related behavior.
- Special incentives for improving grades.
- Psychotherapy for the child or whole family.

Different combinations of these approaches are used for each of the following kinds of underachievement.

Underachievement type 1: Significant decline. Here, achievement slips significantly below what it used to be in a particular subject, though the child still seems to be making an effort. You and the teacher should ask each other whether anything significant happened at around the same time the decline in performance began. Did the subject matter change in a way that required different skills? If so, perhaps the child needs remedial help in those skills. Was he placed in a different group? Perhaps the change was inappropriate; the teacher and/or principal might be ready to reevaluate it. Or was it something at home—a birth or death in the family, a divorce, a parent losing a job? All of those events are known to affect school performance, but not irreversibly. The child needs more opportunity to talk about his sadness and worries—with you, first, and perhaps also with a counselor.

Underachievement type 2: Discrepancy between aptitude and achievement. If the child's achievement has never been up to the level of his tested aptitude in a subject, it suggests one of two things. Either the child simply doesn't care about performing well in that subject, or certain skills necessary for achievement are not tested by the aptitude test. I would start with the first hypothesis, increasing the child's motivation by a combination of rewards and costs, as explained below. If the child is unable to bring his grades up, then you can explore the second hypothesis. When you know he is making a serious effort, the kinds of errors he makes will make it clearer to you and to the teacher just which skills he needs help with.

Underachievement type 3: Special learning disability. When certain aptitude scores are significantly lower than others, a school psychologist may identify the child as having a remediable learning disability. The test scores indicate that particular kinds of remedial work should be given to overcome or circumvent a learning disability. Thus the child need not be resigned to continuing underachievement.

The phrase "learning disability" is often loosely applied to any child with consistently low achievement in a subject. That is incorrect. A more meaningful definition of a learning disabled child is *one who can be helped by teaching the subject in a different way or by giving extra attention to fundamental learning skills before attempting to teach the subject in the traditional way.* (See the bibliography at the end of this chapter.)

Underachievement type 4: Low aptitude. Here, there is no indication of any particular learning disability. Some educators would not call this "underachievement" but would simply say the child is not bright enough to work at grade level in that subject. Nothing will enable him to master the material as rapidly as other children his age. That still does not mean he and his parents have to resign themselves to low achievement. It may mean spending twice as much time on a subject as a brighter child requires to master the same material.

Unfortunately, the way most schools are organized makes that impossible. When the majority of children have mastered a unit, the group moves on. Children who need a little more time to grasp the concepts are then at a double loss, for they also lack the foundations on which the next unit is built. For example, they have to struggle with dividing by two-digit numbers before they have mastered one-digit division. Naturally they fall further and further behind.

Educational methods designed to eliminate this kind of handicap are called *mastery learning.* If your child's school does not use a mastery-learning approach, you can provide it to your child through tutoring. Discuss this with the child's teacher or principal. (If you have some background in education, I recommend Professor Benjamin Bloom's book on this topic, *Human Characteristics and School Learning.*)

Underachievement type 5: "Goofing off." In this case, poor grades are directly due to uncooperative classroom behavior, failure to turn in homework, or absence from class. The aptitude is there, but the teacher reports that the child is simply not doing the work. This could be due to some of the same troubles in school or at home that I listed in connection with unexplained drops in achievement. However, the first step should be to make rules about homework, attendance, and cooperation with the teacher. If this is all that the child needs, then you will see an improvement in achievement, which will improve the child's attitude, which will further improve achievement, and so on. If not, *then* you can explore such other possibilities as depression, anxiety, or difficulties with other children.

Motivation by rewards and costs. Regardless of which type of underachievement you are dealing with, in addition to remedial work, tutoring, or stricter rules about school work, it is a good idea to offer extra incentives for improving.

> EXAMPLE: Twelve-year-old Karen's grades have taken a nose dive since last year, and her teacher says she simply is not doing her work. Her parents make stricter rules about homework: Television and telephone are both off limits from dinnertime until one of the parents has checked Karen's homework. This is presented as a Probation, to continue until her grades improve.
>
> At the same time, Karen is offered a reward for returning to her former level of achievement. Her parents offer to take her and her best friend somewhere special; she chooses an all-day trip to an amusement park. Her mother writes out a contract specifying exactly what grades Karen has to achieve by what deadline and exactly what reward is promised if she does.

The idea of this sort of incentive is to make the child want the intervention to succeed. Usually the child would like to do better in school as much as his parents want him to, but the remedial measures are seen as onerous. That creates resistance. The extra incentive can remove the onus, allowing the child to say to himself, "I'm not working just to please my parents; I'm working to get the tickets to the amusement park."

With or without the positive incentive, you can also increase the *cost* to the child of continuing to do poorly. Often the threat of extra tutoring, remedial classes, or stricter homework rules is sufficient motivation for the child to take grades more seriously.

> EXAMPLE: Luis has a record of nothing but A's and B's on his report cards until sixth grade, when he begins to hang out with friends every day after school. In the evenings, he watches television. Two C's appear on his first report card. After discussion with Luis and his teacher, his parents decide to tell Luis he has one marking period in which to bring his grades back up. For the next two months, Luis is still in charge of budgeting his own time. If there are any C's on his next report card, Luis will have to go to an after-

school tutor in those subjects, and his parents will put into effect a homework priority rule as in the previous example.

This example shows that you don't necessarily have to intervene immediately to produce a change in children's work habits. Why put a restriction into effect if you can get the same result with the threat alone? "Show us that you *can* improve your grades under our existing rules, or we will have to tighten the rule." Of course, you have to be prepared to follow through.

Switching teachers or schools. Although some parents are too quick to blame their child's teachers when his school achievement is disappointing, there are just as many who are too passive and who accept teachers, principals, and school psychologists as the ultimate authority.

Parents should begin with the attitude that those professionals *probably* know their business. At the same time, we have to be aware that not all teachers are wonderful; in fact, few teachers are wonderful for every type of child. Not all principals supervise their staffs adequately, and *no* psychologists or psychological tests are infallible.

You are the consumer. If you are not getting what you are paying for with your tuition or your tax dollars, be assertive. After exhausting other remedies, ultimately you might have to insist that the child be transferred to another class or even to another school.

Many parents are reluctant to be assertive for fear that teachers' resentment may have negative repercussions for the child. But being assertive does not mean being hostile; you won't generate resentment when you present yourself as a concerned parent. You respect the teacher's job, but you are also trying to do your own part to help your child. Almost without exception, teachers appreciate parents who consult with them several times each year and who respond vigorously when their children are underachieving. The parents about whom teachers complain are the ones who don't show any interest in how their children's schoolwork is going. Of course, parents who assume that problems can only be the teacher's fault are not going to be received positively.

In the early grades, if a child is reported to be having trouble in the classroom—misbehavior, inattentiveness, conflicts with the teacher—it is perfectly reasonable for the parent to ask to observe the child in class. If you are called in for a conference, ask to sit in the classroom for a couple of hours, either that day or a few days later. Even if the teacher is not receptive to this request, be persistent. Explain to the principal that you want to understand better why your child seems to be giving this teacher more trouble than most of the other children do, and why your child is having trouble this year as compared with previous years.

Undeniably, your presence in the classroom may have a moderating effect on your child, and on the teacher's behavior toward him. You won't see their interaction at its worst. But more important is the opportunity to assess how the teacher relates to all the other children. If she is authoritarian—curt, irritable, or insensitive to *any* of the children that day—you can bet that she will be that way toward your child another day. And, at the opposite extreme, if she seems incapable of managing her class, allowing not just a relaxed atmosphere but a chaotic one, then you can conclude that she is not the teacher your child needs. (A teacher who creates a structured, well-ordered environment can provide extra structure and limits for those children who seem to need them; but one whose whole class is out of control may single out the one who is most visibly suffering from her incompetence and label that child as the biggest source of her problems.)

On the other hand, if the teacher appears to be competent on the day you observe her, you have to assume she is generally so. Someone who is in control of the class, intelligent, and perceptive about the children's needs when you are observing, is not likely to be any less competent on other days.

If you don't like what you see in the classroom and your attempts to work cooperatively with the teacher have failed, discuss the problem frankly with the principal. Don't be afraid to become a nuisance, if necessary. Even if it is too late in the school year to make a change, your complaints (assuming they are not the only ones received) will help reduce the teacher's chances of being rehired and will make it much more likely that your child is placed with the most competent teacher available next year. "The squeaky wheel gets oiled."

If "nothing works." One of the most frustrating situations for parents is to have a child who just doesn't care about grades. He shows as little interest in the tutor as he shows in school. He rejects all special incentive offers—new bicycle, video cartridge, sports equipment.

In this situation, it may be best to stop pushing. The concern you have been showing is making the child more resistant. The incentive method usually works as a supplement to a child's intrinsic motivation. It does not work if motivation is completely absent, and certainly not if the child is trying to *prove* how little he cares for a subject.

Instead of pushing, concentrate on supporting the child's pursuit of whatever school subjects or extracurricular activities he does show interest in. You can actually have more effect on academic achievement in the long run by praising a nonacademic achievement, like mastery of a video game, than by criticism of the child's academic shortcomings.

Extracurricular motivation versus academic motivation. In chapter 11, I stressed the importance of praising children for the activities in which they show an interest, rather than criticizing them for all the activities they pick up and drop. Since that is particularly important in the elementary-school years, when competence is such an issue for the child, I want to say more here about the rationale for that strategy.

Competence works like a chain reaction. Every bit of increased competence leads to more competence. This happens both directly (one skill is used to acquire another) and indirectly; self-confidence makes it easier to learn, and self-esteem motivates the child to want to increase his competence still further.

Out of all the new bits of skill, confidence, and self-esteem that result, some are bound to be useful in school. So the distinction between academic motivation and extracurricular motivation is really an artificial one. Excellence in school will have later benefits for extracurricular activities. Excellence in sports, music, or model building will have later benefits in school or in the pursuit of a vocation.

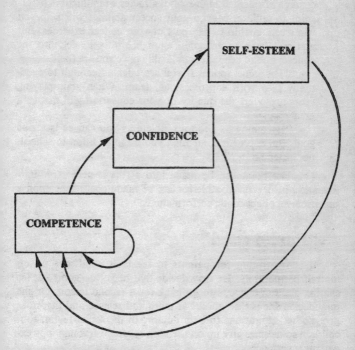

COMPETENCE AS A "CHAIN REACTION"

On the other hand, children sometimes delude themselves with the idea that they are going to be so successful as athletes, singing stars, or space warriors that schoolwork simply won't matter. Without deflating their preadolescent fantasies too much, you need to put them in touch with reality. (This is easier to do now than it will be when they reach adolescence.)

EXAMPLE: "You have to realize that only a small percentage of talented high-school athletes win athletic scholarships to college. Maybe your soccer abilities will help you win a scholarship to pay part of your college expenses. But you still have to get good enough grades to get into the college, and to keep the scholarship once you are there.

"The same applies if you are talented enough to eventually play with a professional team. When your playing years are over, the quality of your education will matter a great deal.

"Becoming as good an athlete as you can be is a fine goal. But soccer is something you do in addition to school, not instead of it."

This last point can be made into a rule if necessary. Participation in organized athletics can be made contingent upon a specific level of academic performance.

≡"I'm no good"

It is frustrating for parents to see their child give up on himself prematurely. He may decide that he is "no good" at ice skating and never wants to go back for a second lesson. Or she may decide she is "no good" at math and science and therefore give up her aspirations to be a doctor. In the social realm, too, children sometimes give up on themselves after a few unhappy experiences with peers.

First of all, you have to assess whether the child's self-evaluation is realistic. It may be a realistic decision not to invest any more effort in an activity where one is hopelessly inept. A child who can't carry a tune, for example, is acting realistically in giving up piano lessons in favor of sports; and a musically talented child with two left feet is equally realistic in making the opposite decision.

What do you do, however, if the child has not given himself a chance, if he just accepts the idea that he is a social outcast, a D student, a failure at sports, or a poor musician, rather than taking any initiative to solve the problem? You suggest inviting a friend over; the response is "I don't have any friends; nobody likes me." You suggest a summer program with a focus on sports; the child does not want to be signed up, because "I'm no good at sports." You suggest extra work in math; the child insists, "More time won't help; I'm just no good at it."

Some people become quite skilled at proclaiming their incompetence while rejecting all efforts to help them. Clinical psychology has a term for such people: "Help-rejecting complainers." The more proficient one is at the help-rejecting–complaining game, the more one loses the game of life. So parents need to stop it before it gets to be a habit.

The way to stop it is to refuse to go on performing your half of the routine. Stop making all those suggestions for the child to reject. After you have made three suggestions in response to his complaints or moping, and all three have been rejected, simply stop.

At the same time, remember that the child's negative feelings need to be accepted. You might be tempted to say, "Sure you can do it, you are good, don't resign yourself to failure"—but that reinforces the idea that the child who doesn't succeed in this area is a failure.

> EXAMPLE: Tom, in fourth grade, hates recess. "I'm the slowest runner in the class," he moans. "I can't catch, and I can't throw." His mother invites him to come jogging with her. His father offers to play catch with him. Both parents suggest that when his friend comes over after school, the two of them could play ball instead of building with Tom's construction set.
>
> Finally the parents catch on that Tom is going to reject all suggestions. "Well, Tom," one of them says, "we don't have anything else to suggest. Those are some things you could do if you wanted to be a better runner, catcher, or thrower. That's how the other boys got to be good at those things. But not everybody has to be an athlete. The jocks miss out on some of the things you do, like your construction set. If you want to put your energy into that instead of ballplaying, it's up to you."
>
> Then they stop. No more nagging, and no more going along with Tom's self-deprecations.

One warning about this advice: "Help-rejecting complainer" children are not always playing games. They may be clinically depressed, and this may be their only way of signaling it to their parents. Nonetheless, the way to respond is still to stop making suggestions. If the child is actually suffering from depression, there will be other symptoms, such as too much or too little appetite, sleeping problems, declining grades. And those things will probably get worse when you stop playing along with the help-rejecting complaints. Then you know that the child needs to be seen by a child psychologist.

≡Television and movies

By age twelve, the average American child has spent about seven thousand hours in school (including recess and lunch), compared to ten thousand hours watching television. He or she has been exposed to somewhere between five thousand and ten thousand classroom lessons, and more than two hundred thousand television commercials. It seems to me, therefore, that parents ought to give at least as much thought to what comes out of the TV as to what goes on at school. Television may not have become an issue in your family. If it does become an issue, make a rule. I have already discussed rules such as "No TV until homework is done" or "If dishes are not done by bedtime, you lose TV privileges the next night." Now I want to stimulate your thinking about the *content* of TV, and also of movies—the problem of censoring what school children watch.

As usual, I am not going to try to impose my values on you (though I can't conceal them). What I have to offer are methods for putting your own values into practice.

Trying to control what your children watch can backfire, like trying to control what they eat. When people feel deprived, they overindulge. The best way to help children become selective about what they watch is to give them choices among several acceptable alternatives.

I also doubt whether you can achieve much control over content by limiting a child's viewing to certain hours. That is fine as a matter of priorities—deferring to homework, chores, and so on—but not effective as a means of controlling content. Your children have access to garbage on TV at any time of day. They also have access to truly informative programs and creative entertainment. Your guidelines will have to deal with content, not with time slots.

Not all the violence and sexual titillation is confined to cop shows and TV movies. The evening news can be even more disturbing. A few years ago, kindergarteners in the Chicago area (and perhaps nationwide) had nightmares about the "Tapsule Man"—the killer who laced Tylenol capsules with cyanide. Tapsule Man is fun to joke about on the playground but not fun to think about alone in the bedroom when the lights are out.

Talk shows, too, like to "probe" topics of sex, violence, violent sex, and sexy violence. Nor are those the only program topics parents should be concerned about. A documentary on terminal cancer, drug addiction, or accidents at nuclear plants might be inappropriate for young children to watch without parental supervision.

Parental guidance. Since all those topics belong to the reality of our world, not just to TV, you cannot hope to keep them from your children's view for very long. But you can greatly influence how your children are affected by them. Crime, sex, violence, cancer, drug addiction, nuclear disasters, and political corruption are all occasions for answering children's questions at a level appropriate to their age.

> EXAMPLE: My six-year-old looked up from his toys as I was watching the evening news one night and asked, "What's oral sex?" It was important for me to answer him, so I said, "The man was arrested because he made the boys kiss him when they didn't want to." To an eight-year-old, I might have added, "Oral means mouth, and oral sex just means kissing in a very sexy way." To a ten-year-old: "He forced them to kiss his penis, after pretending to be their friend." To a twelve-year-old, I would say: "It would have been the man's own business if he did it with a homosexual friend, but forcing teenagers to have sex with him—whether they were boys or girls—was a terrible crime."

A married mother on a soap opera leaves her children with a baby-sitter, picks up a strange man in a bar, and goes to bed with him in a motel. Is that a damaging thing for your children to see?

It depends what you say about it. The networks stop short of showing "explicit sex," and they stop short of nudity. But your children know what nude men and women look like. What they may not know, until they see it on TV, is that some mommies and daddies go to bed with strangers.

On a police show, when a son stabs his father as the father is attempting to prevent him from taking drugs, the network censors will spare the gory details of the stabbing. But your children can imagine the father's guts spilling out on the carpet; that is not the problem. In fact, when they see blood and guts in movies, they are horrified in a thrilling sort of way, but not damaged emotionally or developmentally. What is potentially damaging is not the "explicit violence" itself but the presentation of violence as a solution to interpersonal problems.

I agree with psychologists who have suggested that TV shows should depict violence *more* realistically. In real life, victims don't always get shot in the stomach, heart, or arm, like TV victims. Real people sometimes get their heads blown off. If children saw that more vividly, it might make gunplay seem less like fun.

Research shows that watching violence and aggression on TV does not, in and of itself, make children more violent or aggressive. Nor does it necessarily disturb them. If parents comment on the violence, labeling it as part of a lifestyle they specifically reject, and *if they practice what they preach*, their children are unaffected by the televised violence.

Since you never really know what television subjects will capture your child's attention over the course of the day, being prepared to *discuss* the subject matter is more effective than trying to prohibit it. (Get in the habit of asking them about programs they watched when you were not there.) The mass media are not a school, teaching a curriculum that the community has agreed children should learn. They are a reflection of life as it is experienced in our society. They supplement children's education constructively only when parents use the broadcast material as occasions to highlight their own perspectives on life.

Parental censorship. For TV series that are principally aimed at adults, you can establish guidelines to decide whether they are appropriate for your children. If you decide to prohibit a certain show, be honest about your reasons. "That's an adult show, and we don't approve of children watching it until they're at least _____ years old. We don't care what your friends tell you their parents allow. We don't allow it." Don't make a phony excuse, such as saying a series like "Dallas" is violent if what you dislike is its portrayal of extramarital affairs. Always preserve your credibility.

With movies, your guidelines can be even more specific, because you can find out exactly what is in a movie before you allow your children to see it.

If you decide not to allow them to see a particular film, tell them why not. It may be the language used, the vividness of violence, or the explicit sex. Or you can explain that the film commends principles you abhor. For example, you consider it prowar propaganda, or disarmament propaganda. Children need to learn what their parents' values are and how they may differ from others'.

Don't depend on the PG (Parental Guidance) and R (Restricted) ratings; they mean next to nothing. Many excellent films for children as young as ten or eleven are rated R only because of strong language, which they have heard before. Many films rated PG, despite being targeted for families, are obscene in their negative attitudes toward marriage, parent-child relations, the law, women, and minorities.

The other two ratings, G (General Audiences) and X, are more reliable. In these days of pay TV and adult video cassettes, some children have access to X-rated films due to their parents' carelessness. Other parents intentionally expose their children to such material in the misguided hope of educating them. I disagree; pornography is bad for children. We adults, with realistic knowledge of sexuality, can make whatever use we want of explicit fantasy material. We can evaluate it as erotic, trashy, fun, or immoral; and we need not agree with each other. But children have no way to evaluate it, and no one with whom they can comfortably share the impressions it makes on them. It is not the way to learn about sex.

I am not suggesting that movies themselves should be more censored. It is our job as parents to make those decisions on an individual basis. Unless a picture is rated G, see it yourself first, or read a detailed review, or talk with another parent who has seen it.

Nor am I suggesting that you can put blinders on your

children. Before they reach adolescence, they are going to see and hear virtually everything. But being exposed to adult reality need not mean having their noses rubbed in it. You have considerable control over how much your children are confronted by sex, violence, and other disturbing themes in the media, and at what ages. When censorship fails, you can use the occasion to discuss the provocative or disturbing subject matter with your children, instead of merely complaining about it.

≡Live in a good neighborhood

In *How to Make Your Child a Winner*, Dr. Victor Cline includes "Live in a good neighborhood" as one of his ten crucial keys for parents. It seemed to me an obvious point, until I reflected on how few other authors mention it and how many parents let loyalty to relatives, financial pressures, or just plain inertia keep them from moving when they should. Moving might mean being further from the grandparents or selling one's house when its market value is less than one had hoped. It might mean moving into a more modest house or apartment. Yet it can be a valuable investment in your children's future.

The immediate neighborhood your children live in is more important during the elementary years than at any other time. What goes on within a few blocks of your house will influence their values, aspirations, competence, and self-esteem more than the wider cross section of society that they learn about through the media. Cruelty, stupidity, or despair on TV can be understood as belonging to another part of the world, clearly apart from their own lives. Cruelty, stupidity, or despair in a child's own neighborhood cannot be ignored. They can be overcome, to be sure, but it is a struggle.

By "neighborhood" I do not mean the school district. Attending good schools is only part of the issue. Where will they play after school, on weekends, and in the summer? Will you have to shepherd them everywhere, or will they be able to go places on their bikes and on foot? What kinds of children will they be bringing home, and what kinds of homes will they be visiting? Will their playmates be responsible children, from homes with rules? Or neglected children coping with irresponsible parents?

Of course, you can't expect to move into an ideal neighborhood and have it remain ideal for you. A community is what you make it. Your job as a parent includes active involvement in one or more of the organizations that make your community a good place for children to grow up: Scouts, PTA, park districts, sports leagues, and so forth. It is not enough to be a precinct captain or a hospital volunteer. As worthwhile as those activities are, they don't directly affect your child's daily life. By participating as an active *parent* in the community, you show your children how much you care about them, and you give them a more visible model of active citizenship.

≡Friends

Through your children's neighborhood, school, activities, and through your own choices of family friends, you indirectly determine who your children's friends are going to be. You may also have a considerable direct effect by placing certain activities or places "off limits" or by banning a particular child from your home. These measures, however, are only for *discouraging* children from forming friendships with kids whose behavior you disapprove of. That is not usually a problem during the elementary years. The more common problems are how to *encourage* relationships with other children and how to help children who have trouble finding friends.

How many friends "should" a child have? There are several different patterns of friendship, and any of them can change with age. Every child needs at least one good friend. There is nothing wrong with having only one, unless the child himself wishes for more friends. And there is nothing wrong with having many different friends without one bosom buddy—unless, again, the child is dissatisfied with that situation. There *is* cause for concern if a child is a loner: no after-school friends; no one to invite over on a Saturday, or to call on the phone about a homework assignment, or to sleep over with. Cousins can fill the bill to some extent, but brothers and sisters are not enough. Learning to make friends, to be a friend, to behave appropriately with peers is one of the major areas of competence to be achieved during these years.

The child who has no friends may be suffering from extreme

shyness. Shyness can be very painful for a child. In most cases it is just a genetic trait, to be accepted like one's eye or hair color, but often children think "They won't like me, because I'm too shy." That is obviously self-defeating; sufficient reason to consider therapy for your child. I would not expect the problem to go away of its own accord.

In other cases, the lack of friends is due to rejection by other children. This is not always an indication that therapy is needed. A child who is socially isolated for being different from his classmates in some way—because of religion or race, for instance—probably needs an out-of-school group of more similar playmates, rather than therapy. On the other hand, some children are isolated because of behavioral problems. The other children may find them too babyish, too aggressive, or sexually disturbing in some way. When you find out *why* your child is unpopular, you are a long way toward helping him or her.

> MISTAKE: "Of course they don't like you. What do you expect, the way you keep grabbing them and pulling them down off the jungle gym?"
>
> BETTER: "I was watching you play with those kids, and I noticed that they really didn't like being grabbed and pulled. I think they might be friendlier next time if you just climbed with them, without grabbing them."

"What's wrong with you that you don't have any friends?" is only likely to heighten the very feelings of inadequacy that may be contributing to the problem in the first place. Instead, try to do just the opposite: Make the child feel more self-assured. If you talk about the problem in Tom's presence, describe it this way: "Tom unfortunately hasn't found any kids in his class to be friends with outside of school."

Usually a child's biggest problem is taking the initiative. There are plenty of other children waiting for your child to make the first move. Perhaps he or she is afraid to, does not know that it is all right to, or is inept at approaching other children. You can explore these possibilities frankly with your child and help him in one of the following ways.

Get the child out of the house. You can't ensure that relationships with peers will be the result, but it is obviously much more likely than if the child hides himself indoors.

If your home video games help your child attract friends to come over and play, fine; but if all they do is entertain him while he stays home alone, you need a rule restricting their use. The same goes for model trains or any other hobby. There is nothing wrong with forcing your child out into the harsh world, provided you don't do it in a harsh way.

This might mean as little as an hour a day for a first-grader, up to several hours for a seventh-grader. Don't insist on any particular activity ("You must be on a hockey team"). Instead, suggest several alternative activities and let the child choose one. You can insist that the child find *something* to do out of the house.

Help him or her invite children over. Your firstborn may not realize, until you suggest it, that children can telephone other children or talk to them in school about coming over to play. (Your other children have an advantage in observing their older brothers' or sisters' friendships.) A specific activity helps to give the invitation structure—just as it does between adults. It takes a fairly self-assured child to call up and say, "Would you like to come over and play?" Most children feel more comfortable saying, "Would you like to play Dungeons and Dragons?" or "How about bringing your coin collection over and trading some of your duplicates with me?"

The more reticent your child is, the more you might need to create special attractions. You might rent a video-cassette movie —either a favorite classic or a new release. (Even if you don't have your own equipment, the rental fees are reasonable.) Or you can take your whole family to a museum, beach, or amusement park, and encourage the child to bring along a friend. Include some time before or after the excursion to let the children play at your house.

A birthday party seems to me a poor way to accomplish this goal. It is too much work for you and no help for the child in making friends. It puts him in the awkward situation, if he is trying to make new friends, of obligating them to bring a gift. And it only comes once a year.

Get together with your own friends who live nearby and have kids the same age. This approach requires no initiative at all on your child's part, except to be friendly when the other family comes over—for example, for a Sunday brunch. If the children enjoy one another's company, it will be obvious to you as well as to the other parents, and subsequently the kids alone can get together.

If "nothing works." Finally, if your child rejects all your suggestions, ask yourself whether you might have been trying too hard to solve his problem for him. If he still complains about not having anything to do or anyone to play with, follow the suggestions under "I'm no good," above.

In the case of a child who does not complain but merely resigns himself to a lonely existence, a family-oriented therapist is needed (see chapter 21). Remember to label the problem as "Susan is unhappy," rather than "Susan is unpopular." It is bad enough being lonely, without having to bear in addition the social stigma attached to loneliness.

≡Moral development

For nearly a century, psychologists have been investigating the growth of moral judgment—children's ideas about right and wrong. In prior centuries, there were three philosophies about children and morality. There were those who believed that children were born in "native depravity" and had to be rectified, as the Reverend Billy Graham still recommends, by fathers holding a Bible in one hand and a belt in the other. The opposing group believed, with Jean-Jacques Rousseau, that children came directly from God, to be inevitably corrupted by civilization. (Rousseau gave all his children to foundling homes rather than taking part in "corrupting" them.) Finally, there were those who saw children as blank slates, morally as well as intellectually, to be written upon by their parents.

The research has not supported any of those views. It indicates instead that normal children's moral judgment advances along with their intelligence, through similar stages from concrete to abstract. It develops as a result of all their experiences—in school, in play, with other children, and with their parents. It is certainly not a result merely of the discipline they have received. In fact, there is only an indirect connection between parental discipline and the development of morality. Let me explain what I mean by that.

If a system of rules and consequences were responsible for moral training, children would develop only the most primitive attitudes toward morality: judgments based on rewards and punishments. ("What is right is what others reward; what is wrong is what others punish.") With that attitude, anything one gets away with is all right. It is an attitude that pervades our society; but if we want a better world for our children and their children, we had better give them a higher morality than that. Higher principles are based on cooperation for the mutual benefit of all, and on ideas of right and wrong irrespective of reward or punishment.

Fortunately, most children develop those higher levels, at least in their thinking about moral questions, and sometimes in their actions as well. For example, whereas young children are more likely to cheat in games or tests if they believe they can get away with it, older children and teenagers cheat *less often* under an honor system than when they think a higher authority is monitoring them. Such research evidence supports the main principle of this book: Rules and consequences are most important in early childhood so that self-esteem, competence, and social responsibility can take over to motivate and protect the older child.

The rule system described in Part I has little direct bearing on moral education. It provides a structure for the family with respect to a relatively small number of areas in which children are not free. The moral questions arise in all the other areas of life, where children *are* free to decide how to act. A system of rules makes it clear to children what those areas are. It allows you to explain your preferences without generating too much internal resistance to your views. It allows you to convey your values without depriving your child of the opportunity to choose those values voluntarily. It frees you to be an educator rather than a dictator. And it frees your children to make responsible decisions and experience the effects of their actions upon themselves and upon others.

In other words, the extremely concrete, consequence-oriented approach you are adopting for basic rules will not represent your moral attitude. Making beds, washing dishes, and doing homework are not moral issues. Some of the rules may reflect your values (don't borrow things without asking; don't lie), but the way you enforce those rules is not a model for dealing with all situations in life. Your children will not be confused about this, for they have plenty of opportunities to learn from you, both by word and action, how decent people conduct their lives.

The greatest of all child psychologists, Jean Piaget, made this point more than fifty years ago when he said, "Given sufficient liberty of action, the child will spontaneously emerge from his egocentrism and tend with his whole being towards cooperation." Piaget also wrote:

> Thus adult authority, although perhaps it constitutes a necessary moment in the moral evolution of the child, is not in itself sufficient to create a sense of justice. This can develop only through the progress made by cooperation and mutual respect—cooperation between children to begin with, and then between child and adult as the child approaches adolescence and comes, secretly at least, to consider himself as the adult's equal.*

≡Responsibility for things

Which of the following things do you hold your children responsible for? "Responsible" means financially accountable for loss or damages due to negligence. In some cases, it might also mean routine care: washing, cleaning, mending, storing properly.

- His or her own clothes (if she loses a sweater, she buys herself a new one or does without).
- School supplies (you buy the first set of colored pencils, for example, but when the child can't find them, the second set comes out of his or her allowance).
- Sports equipment (you would refuse to replace a pair of skates if they were left somewhere).
- Bicycle.
- Pets.
- Your stereo, television, and household appliances.
- Windows, doors, furniture, etc. (beyond normal wear and tear).

Obviously, the list changes as each child grows. A five-year-old would probably not be responsible for any of the items listed

---

* Jean Piaget, *The Moral Judgment of the Child*. New York: The Free Press, 1965, pp. 190 and 319. Although it is a scholarly book, this is one of the few of Piaget's works that is readable and enjoyable by the general reader.

above. You are the one who tries to remember, when you pick him up from kindergarten, whether he had his mittens with him that morning. A fifteen-year-old would probably be held responsible for all these things.

So the elementary years are a period of gradually handing over responsibilities, making them clear, and following through with the consequences. You need to tell each child exactly what he or she will be held accountable for—write it in your rules if it is becoming a problem—and then you need to be consistent in enforcing those consequences.

Teaching children to be responsible is a matter of supporting competence and attaching a price to negligence. You would be doing neither if you took the easy way out and bought your child a new set of colored pencils, admonishing him, "Now don't lose these!" He is just as likely to lose the new ones, because it costs him nothing to do so, whereas *not* losing things costs him some effort.

If, when the child loses his pencils, you send him to the store to buy a replacement set with his allowance, you are letting him experience the cost of his negligence and enabling him to rectify the loss himself. This is for the child's benefit, not only for yours.

When the cost of repairing or replacing something is more than the child can possibly afford, yet the item cannot be done without—a winter coat, for example—decide how much of the cost the child can bear and give him a "matching grant" for the rest. You can do this even if the loss was entirely the child's fault; if he pays a reasonable share of the cost, he will get the message. (If he is guilty of vandalism or other willful damages, as opposed to mere carelessness, it may be wiser to make the child bear the full cost.)

Matching grants. When charitable foundations want to support a cause while ensuring that it has broad support from others as well, they give a "matching grant." They promise to donate a million dollars to a museum, for example, if the museum's own fund drive can raise another million. The same principle works beautifully with children.

> EXAMPLE: Harry wants a pair of skis. His parents offer to contribute two-thirds of the purchase price if Harry earns the other third doing chores for neighbors.

The advantage of this type of incentive is that children can work toward earning money for things they really want but would have no hope of being able to afford within a reasonable space of time. A ten-year-old is not going to be able to earn three hundred dollars by raking leaves in the autumn, but with industry he might earn a hundred dollars. So Harry's parents decide on a 2:1 matching grant. In another case, the grant might be 1:1, 1:2 (the parents adding a dollar to every two their child earned), or 10:1. It depends on how important the goal is to the child, what his or her earning capacity is, and how much you are willing to contribute.

≡Lying and stealing

When your three-year-old tells you there is a whale in the living room, that is pretending, not lying. When the nine-year-old tells you she did not eat any prohibited cookies, but the crumb trail leads across the floor up the front of her shirt to her face and hands, that is lying.

Don't punish your child for her first deliberate lie if you had no prior rule about lying. But make sure she knows that it is a major crisis in your relationship. Show the same amount of distress as you would to the news that your best friend was in critical condition at the hospital. In fact, the mutual trust between you and your children is your best ally as a parent; it is in critical condition when the child lies to you.

I do not think it is worthwhile to give children the third degree about *why* they lied. Two other things are more important:

1. Make a tough consequence for lying in the future.
2. Sit down face to face with the child and explain why you are so disappointed.

EXAMPLE: "Son, there are two ways people deal with each other: by trusting or by not trusting.* Up to now, you and I have always had a relationship based on honesty and trust. When you told me something, I could count on it being

---

* If you have adopted the terms used in this book, you can point out that these two kinds of relationship correspond to Liberty and Probation, respectively.

true. If you told me about some trouble at school, I knew that I could call the teacher and not hear something completely different.

"I think you've been able to trust me, too, because I've been truthful with you.

"The reason I'm feeling so concerned is that I know what life is like when we *don't* trust people. When people can't trust each other, they have to demand proof of everything. If we can't believe you when you say you're up to date on your homework, we'll have to make you bring home signed sheets from your teachers. If we can't trust you to bring back all the change when you go to the store, we'll have to check the cash-register receipt every time. That's a lousy way to live. It's the way we have to deal with strangers. Out in the world, people who don't know us don't trust us. When we come home to our family, it's nice not having to be that way.

"I have *cherished* the kind of relationship we've had up to now, and I hope it can continue. But I see plenty of other parents and children who can't trust each other. Once someone goes down that path, it takes a long time before he is trusted again, even by his parents. The choice is up to you."

If a child violates a rule and then lies in order to avoid the consequence, the consequence should be significantly greater. A simple method is to double any consequence that a child has lied to avoid. I would not escalate it for the future, just make it double for that one occasion.

The first instance of petty theft should be dealt with similarly —with a heartfelt talk and a tough consequence for the future. Don't get bogged down in semantics. Taking something that doesn't belong to you, without permission, is *stealing*. Saying something that you know isn't true, or concealing the truth, is *lying*.

Your goal is to nip lying or stealing in the bud, immediately. It is normal for children to try them once, just to find out whether anyone cares. So I would not get upset over the moral aspect, nor would I agonize over the likelihood of it leading to a criminal career. Treat it as a test, and be sure to pass the test with honors.

Of course, this will not work unless you yourself have established a model of honesty and trustworthiness in the relationship. If not, you have no chance of convincing the child to be honest with you.

Chronic lying or stealing. Normally, if you respond as I have suggested to the child's first experiments in lying and stealing, your child will sensibly choose the relationship you offer, based on honesty and trust. If he does not, and if the lying or stealing continues, *don't try to deal with it by escalating the consequences.* The second incident of lying or stealing is sufficient reason to put the child on Probation (see chapter 9).

Once you have made clear what an enormous difference there is between a relationship based on trust and one based on distrust, the latter is so obviously undesirable that no child would choose it without strong emotional reasons. He himself probably doesn't understand those reasons. If you respond severely, you are likely to exacerbate the problem. This is one of the behavior problems that definitely call for family therapy (see chapter 21).

≡Summary

Both children and parents are concerned, during the years from about age six to twelve, with *competence.* Rules are of secondary importance in helping to channel the child's energies into productive activities. Their main function is to free the child from parents' nagging and criticism, and to free the parents to provide encouragement and praise.

As your children come under the influence of a broader segment of the world, you can convey your own attitudes about the reality they are discovering; and you can convey positive feelings about their ability to cope with that reality.

One of the many things children learn during the elementary years is that the world beyond the family can be a treacherous place. By practicing honesty and trust in your own relationships, you can make your family a secure haven and a solid launching pad for adolescence.

SUGGESTED BOOKS: The Elementary Years.

Bloom, Benjamin. *Human Characteristics and School Learning.* New York: McGraw-Hill, 1976. (Requires some background in education.)

Brazelton, T. Berry. *Working and Caring.* Reading, MA: Addison-Wesley, 1987.

Cline, Victor. *How to Make Your Child a Winner.* New York: Walker, 1980.

Greene, Lawrence J. *Learning Disabilities and Your Child.* New York: Fawcett Columbine, 1987.

Holt, John. *How Children Fail* (revised edition). New York: Dell, 1988.

Kohl, Herbert. *Growing With Your Children.* New York: Bantam, 1981.

Rosner, Jerome. *Helping Children Overcome Learning Difficulties,* Second Edition. New York: Walker, 1979.

Scharlatt, Elisabeth, ed. *Kids: Day In and Day Out.* New York: Simon and Schuster, 1979.

Silver, Larry B. *The Misunderstood Child: A Guide for Parents of Learning Disabled Children.* New York: McGraw-Hill, 1988.

Smith, Lendon. *Foods for Healthy Kids.* New York: Berkley, 1982.

Ungerleider, Dorothy. *Reading, Writing, and Rage.* Rolling Hills, CA: Jalmar Press, 1987.

CHAPTER FOURTEEN

Surviving Your Adolescent's Adolescence

"**W**hat is happening to my child?"

It happened to every one of us. Between age eleven or twelve and age eighteen or nineteen, we all went through adolescence. Since then, we have watched each new wave of adolescents break upon our shores. Yet it does come as a shock when we see it happening to our own children. The abrupt changes in personality, the moodiness, the secrecy, the volatile tempers, and the slavelike adherence to peer fashions frustrate and confuse us. Most confusing of all is the way the child alternates between disdainful alienation from us at one moment and childish dependency the next.

The way to be most helpful to the adolescent child and still retain one's own sanity is to be as clear as possible about your rules and consequences. It is true at all ages, but especially during adolescence, that *it is less important for you to understand the child than for the child to understand you*. However, it is also true that parents who have a basic understanding of what adolescence is all about can not only survive this period but actually enjoy it.

From the onset of puberty, at around age twelve, to the time when high-school graduates are launched out into the world (either the "real" world or the relative freedom of college) is only about six years. During that short span there are more changes in the child's body than will occur in the rest of his or her entire life. At the same time, equally striking mental changes are taking place

—in knowledge about the world, as well as in the process of thinking. And on top of those physical and mental transformations, there are radical changes in social relationships. From a complete dependent, the child becomes relatively independent of the parents and acquires responsibilities to others outside the family.

We shall take up those three kinds of radical change one at a time. Keep in mind, though, that the child does not have the luxury of dealing with them separately. All of those assaults occur simultaneously, as if some alien force had barged into the secure, familiar environment of the child's home, shot him full of hormones, stuffed him into an adult body, set off an explosion inside his brain, and kicked him out into the street. Into a blizzard. Without a coat.

The conflict between excitement and apprehension about being thrust out into the world lies beneath most of the adolescent's thoughts and actions. Therefore the child continues to need help in building competence and confidence. Family rules are necessary but not sufficient, because your ability to supervise the child is coming to an end. How can you ensure that your teenagers acquire the skills and information to handle life in the outside world? How can you ensure that they acquire sufficient feelings of self-worth and self-confidence so that they will take care of themselves?

≡Bodily changes in adolescence

Any offspring residing in their parents' home at their parents' expense are *children.* No matter how old they are, the word *child* applies until they move out on their own. The trouble is, the adolescent child quickly acquires an adult body. He may be bigger than you are. She may have a shapelier figure than yours.

Do not be fooled. This is only a disguise. Teenagers are still children, despite all the anatomical and physiological changes.

However, it is not a disguise they can put on and take off at will. It descends upon them whether they like it or not, and even though it is exciting to be taking on all the physical characteristics of adults, it is also disturbing and frightening. Parents need to be aware of the fact that these major bodily changes have major emotional effects.

Self-image. Even before puberty, children begin to be self-conscious about their bodies. This is accentuated when puberty begins. The appearance of every new feature has significance for the child: height, weight, muscles, bra size, body hair, voice change, and, of course, pimples. What are the implications for parents?

In the first place, try to recognize every sign of maturation. Compliment the child on his or her appearance whenever you can do so sincerely. Don't call attention to the awkward symptoms of transition—the squeaky voice, the clumsiness, the acne. If the child seems upset by those aspects of puberty, you can listen sympathetically and assure him that they happen to everyone.

Second, since the child wants so desperately to present a good appearance, especially to peers, you might be tempted to exploit his or her self-consciousness as a convenient consequence for disobeying rules. For example, you might prohibit your daughter from using your face cream or devise some punishment that would publicly embarrass your son. *Don't do it.* The child's self-esteem is your most valuable ally. Do everything you can to build it up, unconditionally.

Another thing that should be unconditional is your availability to the child as a counselor about the physical changes he or she is experiencing, as well as about matters of beauty, physical appearance, and grooming. For the most intimate matters, it should be the parent of the same sex. On the other hand, for things having to do with their appearance, teenagers are often especially interested in the advice of the other parent, who is a representative of the opposite sex.

Menstrual tension and cramps. This can be a problem for about forty years, not just in adolescence. But self-consciousness, the novelty of the experience, and the fact that periods might be quite irregular at first, make it a special problem for girls in their early teens. Fathers as well as mothers need to be sympathetic at those times, as you would with any physical ailment.

When trying to discover why your daughter seems particularly cranky today, you might consider the hypothesis that she is about to have a period and needs a hug or needs to be left alone more than she needs a sharp response from you. However, to accept menstruation as an excuse for disobeying your rules would be to reinforce the idea of "the curse," which women of our generation have worked hard to overcome.

> EXAMPLE: Paula's weekly responsibility is cutting the grass. If it is not done by noon on Saturday, her allowance is cut by five dollars. One week she comes to her mother on Saturday evening, just as she is about to go out, and explains that she did not feel well that morning because her period started. She promises to do her job the next day.

> MISTAKE: Paula's mother gives her the full allowance and tells her husband to mow the lawn himself this week.

> BETTER: "If you had come to me early in the day and asked for an extension, I would have explained to Dad and it would have been fine. This way it looks as though you forgot and are just using your period as an excuse. I am going to give you a forty-eight-hour extension, because this is the first time the situation has come up. But from now on, if you are sick or have any good reason why you can't meet the deadline, you have to get the extension *before* the deadline or take the consequences."

If menstrual cramps or other symptoms are frequently so severe that she has to stay home from school, the girl's doctor should be consulted.

Sexual awakening. The whole of chapter 16 is devoted to adolescent sexual activity, but two things need to be said here about changes in the child's body. The first is about family members respecting one another's privacy. Nudity has a definite sexual significance to adolescents that it did not have when they were younger. Some children bathe and dress themselves privately from an early age and never see their parents in the nude. Other parents are less inhibited. This is fine, but it can be a mistake to continue that after puberty. Do not hesitate to make rules about closing the bathroom door, not coming downstairs in one's underwear, and so forth. And you should follow the same rules yourselves.

The second word of advice is that you need to start from the beginning—before puberty if possible—encouraging the children to come to you with any questions at all about the changes their bodies are about to undergo. A girl should feel comfortable about talking to her mother, stepmother, aunt, or an *adult* female friend; a boy should feel the same about his father, stepfather, or another adult. If you are a single parent with a child of the opposite sex, instead of insisting that you must become the child's confidant, you can say, "I'm willing to try to answer your questions, but if it's something you think I might not understand because I'm a man [or woman], don't hesitate to call Dr. Jones or ask the school nurse. You're old enough to learn the facts, and you can't always rely on the information you get from other kids."

≡The adolescent mind

Less obvious, but every bit as consequential as the physical changes of adolescence, are the changes in the way the mind works. How do adolescents react to the logic of parents' rules? How can parents provide a firm structure without provoking revolution?

In the elementary-school years, children can think logically about concrete objects that they see or visualize, but they still fall short of abstract thinking or "formal" logic. An example that I gave in an earlier chapter was:

> Jenny is bigger than Kenny.
> Kenny is bigger than Lenny.
> *Is Jenny bigger than Lenny?*

Elementary children usually answer this correctly with no trouble. But they cannot necessarily think through the same syllogism with abstract symbols and nonsense words:

> J is more "dreft" than K.
> K is more "dreft" than L.
> *Is J more "dreft" than L?*

Most high-school students can answer this correctly. One of the reasons that we have junior high schools for twelve- and thirteen-year-olds is that this is the age when children go through the *transition* to formal logical thinking. The child begins to be capable of logical deductions and, for the first time, capable of thinking about hypothetical propositions such as this one: "If they changed the rules of baseball so that players could be taken out of the game and put back in, as in football, then we would see fewer fielding errors and higher batting averages."

What is the effect on adolescents' behavior once their thinking becomes capable of this higher level? They find themselves able to think about all sorts of hypothetical propositions, including ideal worlds to which the human imagination can aspire. They suddenly realize that much of what they had taken for granted as inevitable is only one of many possible permutations and combinations that nature could have contrived. The result is that they are ready to challenge the necessity of every characteristic of the world.

This continually renewed challenge to established ways of viewing the world and established ways of doing things is one of mankind's greatest strengths. When adolescents appear contemptuous of our values, traditions, institutions, and lifestyles, they are manifesting the essential free-spirited questioning without which mankind would still be living in caves. They are expressing Martin Luther King's "I have a dream" and George Bernard Shaw's "I see things that never were, and ask, why not?" At the same time, they can be a pain in the neck.

It is the adolescent's job to question everything. It is your job to keep him in touch with reality, but *you only have to confront him with reality in the few areas that you have rules about.* You do not need to get into arguments about politics, music, clothes, hairstyles, sports, or anything else, unless you and the child enjoy such discussion. If the matter is so important that you want to insist upon your view, then make a rule and enforce it with consequences. Otherwise, you can discuss it on a purely intellectual plane if you want to, but it does not have to become an emotional issue.

> EXAMPLE: Randy, seventeen, has started to smoke, and his parents are shocked. Neither of them smokes, and they consider it an abuse of Randy's health, as well as a socially offensive, filthy habit. They should say, "We consider it an abuse of your health, as well as a socially offensive, filthy habit. You have to decide the question for yourself at this point in your life. However, you are not allowed to

smoke in our house." This makes it very clear which part is the preference and which part is the rule. Then, when Randy replies that it is not socially offensive, his parents should not argue the point. They can simply say, "Well, it's a matter of opinion. We could be wrong about what other people think, but we find it offensive and we do not allow it in our house."

Some parents feel they have to come down very strongly in defense of the values and institutions that their adolescents are questioning. The result is constant confrontation, provocation, and bitterness between the generations. Adolescents are likely to feel their parents are attacking not only those ideas but their right to have *any* ideas of their own. (You will have to get used to the fact that they think their ideas are novel even when they are slavishly copying their friends and idols.)

Adolescent idealism can be a great strength. It motivates them to care about themselves, their own safety, their own future. Don't pop their bubble by disputing all their unrealistic goals. Let them be "into" something—anything from sports to computers to chess to car repairing. You achieve more of your own goals as a parent by encouraging your kids to put their utmost into doing their own thing than you could ever achieve by making rules and restrictions.

When parents criticize the teenage culture, it feels to teenagers like an attack on themselves as persons. It sounds to them like "Don't grow up." And sometimes they are right; parents are sometimes upset by the very fact that their children are growing up. Often this is what leads children to overreact, to rebel to a greater extreme than they had ever intended.

Other parents take the opposite approach. Not wanting a confrontation, they try to accommodate their teenagers as much as possible, going along with everything, even adopting some of the adolescent styles of dress and speech. They do not understand why their children fail to accept them as peers. They are astonished that their children keep testing their limits even though their rules are the most liberal in town.

That is not what teenagers want or need. They want us to remain ourselves, consistent with the values and realities of our community and our generation, even while they are questioning those realities. If their job is to "see things that never were and ask why not," our job is to show them what is and will remain. However, we only have to do this in relation to the rules we insist upon; we can acknowledge that they might be right in theory.

EXAMPLE: Terri inherited some money from her grandfather, which her parents are saving for her college tuition. She wants to use some of the money now, to pay for a demo tape that will launch her singing group on the road to stardom. She argues that the potential return on this investment is so much greater than the 10 percent she is earning in the money market that it justifies risking the capital. "And it's my money," she says. "I should be able to decide how to spend it."

MISTAKE: Her father gets into an argument with Terri about the wisdom or stupidity of spending the money in this way. They also argue about what it means to say the money is hers.

BETTER: "You might be right. It could be a very wise investment. But you can't have the money."

"Why not?" the child is sure to protest.

"We are going to spend it on college tuition. Whatever is left after you have graduated from college, you will be able to invest in any way you want." Beyond saying this, Dad would be wasting his breath. Listen to the child, acknowledge her feelings, but do not feel obliged to get into a debate.

EXAMPLE: Barry, seventeen, wants to buy his own car. His parents do not consider him ready for that much responsibility yet. They have told him that he will have to wait until he is eighteen. "But it isn't going to cost you anything. I'm going to pay for it from my lifeguard earnings. You act like I'm a reckless driver or something. You think I'm a baby."

"No, we don't," his parents should reply. "You would probably take excellent care of your car. You seem to be a safe driver." They do not need to defend all their fears; they do not need to go into their reasons more than once. "We might be wrong, but we have set eighteen as the minimum age for anyone in this family to own a car."

EXAMPLE: Sam is another seventeen-year-old who wants his own car, and his parents have decided to let him buy one. His uncle is willing to give him a ten-year-old station wagon in good condition, for one hundred dollars. The insurance would cost several hundred more, but Sam argues that his parents should contribute at least the amount they would have paid to add him to their existing insurance policy. They feel that if he wants a car, which they consider an extravagance, then he should pay every penny himself. They explain that they are willing to allow him to buy a car but not willing to subsidize the purchase.

"To each according to his needs," Sam cries, "from each according to his abilities." He has proclaimed himself a socialist.

"Sam, if you want your own car, you'll have to pay all the expenses yourself," his parents say. "It is your decision."

EXAMPLE: Susan, fifteen, can get a part-time job at a fast-food restaurant if her mother will write a letter saying that Susan is sixteen years old. She explains that most of the kids working there are younger than sixteen and the manager knows it; he just needs the letter as a formality. Susan's mother at first agrees to go along with the scheme but later talks to a friend about it and realizes that she does not think it right to collude in a lie.

"Well, then *you lied to me*," shouts Susan bitterly. "You said you'd do it. I told my friends I was going to be working there. You should set a good example and stick with what you told me the first time."

"I'm sorry that I changed my mind. I'm sorry that I hadn't thought it through before saying anything. I'm sorry that you had to be disappointed. But I will not lie about your age, and you may not take any job that fifteen-year-olds are not allowed to have."

"Then you'll have to pay me forty-five dollars a week, because that's what I would have earned. There's no other job I can get."

"I'm sorry, Susan, that's all there is to it."

This way of talking with adolescents requir exactly the opposite of what you feel like doing. defending yourself. You want to explain that your in was not a firm promise and to explain why your later decision is wise and reasonable. You do not feel like apologizing.

Following those inclinations would be a big mistake. Susan can always find a rationale by which, in principle, she has justice on her side. That sort of mental gymnastics is part of the wonder and excitement of adolescence. It is not your job to suppress it. All you have to do is present a consistent reality, and over the period of a few years the child's mind will gradually go through the inevitable transformations toward the more constrained rationality of our adult world.

By the same token, you do not need to be afraid to apologize. It does not necessarily mean you were wrong. It means acknowledging that the child is hurt a little by your specific ruling and also by the more general pain of being relatively powerless in a world that does not appreciate her superior reasoning.

Challenges to authority itself. The younger child challenges parents' rules but does not challenge their right to make rules. Teenagers, however, often direct their arguments not just at the fairness of the rules themselves, but also at their legitimacy: As free citizens, why should they have to be bossed around by their parents?

Instead of arguing about this or defending your responsibilities as parents, you can simply agree that it is hard to let one's freedom be limited by others. Growing up means acquiring freedom. But it is a gradual process and never culminates in total liberation. Point out that we adults are constrained by a great many rules. Point out that we, too, are frequently "bossed around"— by employers, by clients or customers, by the government.

Try saying, "We know it is frustrating. You are mature enough now so that you feel ready for more freedom than society is willing to give you. That is why we wrote out our list of rules— so you could rely on the fact that you only have those specific obligations to meet as long as you are living in this home. Other than the rules on this list, you are as free as an adult."

If the child wants to argue about that rationale, I would

refuse to get roped into the debate. You do not have to convince him that your authority is morally, politically, or philosophically legitimate. (Deep down, he knows that it is.) You only have to convince him that, legitimate or not, this is the way things are going to be.

Changing relationship with the family

It is true that teenagers normally get deeply involved with other teenagers, spend a lot of time with them, and let their tastes be ruled by whatever is currently "in" with their generation.

However, it is not true that teenagers care more about their peers than about their family relationships. Nor do they care more about their friends than about their parents.

There is a common misconception that children become less interested in their parents when they start school, and then even less interested when they reach adolescence. Probably this misconception is based on the amount of *time and attention* they devote to peers versus family. But time and attention are not good indicators of emotional significance.

As involved as teenagers are with their peers, and as passionate as many of their friendships are, those peers are often interchangeable. This week's best friend may not be next week's. Meanwhile, the relationships within the family grow more sophisticated, more sensitive to the strength and vulnerability of each family member.

It is the adolescent child, not the younger child, who suffers more when parents divorce. It is the adolescent whose self-esteem is supersensitive to parental criticism. It is the adolescent who is obsessed with the parents' every imperfection, who stews and sulks over the injustice of having been born into the wrong family. All these observations, though they involve negative rather than positive feelings, indicate how concerned and involved adolescents are with their parents' behavior, thoughts, and feelings.

What is really going on during this period is their development of a more autonomous role in the family. It is not a matter of caring less. In fact, mature relationships between young adults and their parents involve deeper caring than the younger child, who evaluates everything in terms of his own desires, is capable of. Nonetheless, those more mature relationships require more freedom, more time and space to be a separate person.

That is why the system of family rules described in Part I works so well. You reward maturity and responsibility with freedom; you respond to irresponsibility and immaturity by restricting freedom. The adolescent has the power to set his own pace of development along that path toward autonomy.

The "peer pressure" myth. Another common misconception is that teenagers cannot resist peer pressure to go along with whatever is in fashion and parents are powerless to set standards that conflict with those of the peer group.

You can impress upon your children that you hold them responsible for their own choices about how to behave. What their friends do is irrelevant; if necessary, they may have to choose different friends. If your child goes off with friends and gets involved with drugs, it is because he or she chooses those friends and chooses those drugs.

When teenagers invoke peer pressure as an excuse for their behavior, they are simply attempting to evade responsibility for their own decisions and actions. Don't let them evade that responsibility.

Parents, too, often use the "peer pressure" myth as an excuse for failing to set limits, to write clear rules, and to find effective consequences. Sure, the adolescent culture exerts powerful pressure. Sure, your children's friends will encourage them to test you in every conceivable way. You simply have to decide that you are more powerful. And you are—not only because you pay the rent and stock the refrigerator but also because your child desperately wants your approval, your respect, your confidence in his ability to make it in the outside world.

You may be interested to know that therapists who work with troubled adolescents do not consider the peer group as necessarily a negative force. On the contrary, instead of trying to isolate irresponsible youngsters from peer pressure, we often rely on group therapy as part of the treatment. Group therapy helps because the peers are a more convincing voice of reason than the authoritative adult can ever be. They pressure the adolescent to conform to the rules of the group, and ridicule his immature behavior.

This sort of positive influence happens all the time in informal, everyday peer groups as well. There are more *positive* effects of peer pressure than negative ones. You can have some influence in fostering the beneficial effects by establishing good relations with your children's friends, making yourself a good listener to them, and making them aware when you have concerns about your child (anything from skipping homework assignments to using foul language), where the friends' cooperation might be helpful.

Influencing the choice of friends. Is it a good idea to let your children know when you do not like their friends? Or does it only provoke them to keep their friends away from you and be more secretive about whom they are associating with?

Conversely, should you encourage them to associate with kids who fit your image of appropriate teenagers? Or would that only look as though you were meddling in their affairs and result in alienating them further?

I feel that we should indeed let our children know which other teenagers impress us positively, and which ones negatively. This comes under the heading of *preferences*. If you try to make a *rule* about it, it is likely to backfire. Make your rules about behavior, and leave it to the child to choose friends who will not interfere with following your rules. You thus *indirectly* encourage the child to seek a more responsible group of friends. If you try to legislate *directly* whom they can associate with, it will seem like an illegitimate invasion of their rights and they may feel compelled to thwart your choices even if they would otherwise have agreed with you.

Believe it or not, your children really want to know which of their friends you like and which ones you do not like. Your daughter may bring some of her friends' friends over to the house just to see what your reaction will be. You owe her an honest reaction. As I said above, the adolescent's job is to challenge all our values, and our job is to remain honest and clear about what those values are.

Before you go too far in evaluating your child's friends, a couple of words of warning. Be sure to express yourself in reference to the friends' *behavior.* If your judgments are merely based on race, religion, or social status, your child is likely to lose respect for you and to reject your opinions on a great many other subjects as well. He knows the other kids better than you do, on an individual basis; your stereotypes may not apply.

Nor can you tell from clothes, grooming, or manners which other teenagers are dangerous for yours to be associating with and which are harmless. Many kids who disguise themselves as hippies, bikers, or punk rockers are really responsible, self-respecting young people. Conversely, many high-school drug dealers and addicts look like "preppies." Again, you are better off commenting on your children's friends' *behavior* than trying to deduce their personal qualities from their appearance. (You may be a very good judge of character in adults and yet be all wrong in your assessments of adolescents.)

The one area where you *can* enforce rules about friends is where you have rules about specific behavior that is unacceptable in your home—smoking, swearing, teasing your pets, or whatever —with the consequence that the friend who does this will not be allowed to come again. Here, it is the *behavior* that you are being firm about, not the other child personally. It is a good idea to ban the friend as a guest for a period of time—say, one or more months—rather than permanently. If the banishment is temporary, your own child is less likely to consider it unreasonable; and at the end of that period, either the other child will come back radically improved in behavior or your child will have dropped him as a friend.

≡Your two best controls: Transportation and communication

The fact that most sixteen-year-olds can get drivers' licenses is surely their most cherished freedom. Therefore the hand that dispenses the car keys wields great power. Instead of thinking of your child's license as a tremendous nuisance, a threat to life and limb, and an insurance-rate catastrophe, think of it as *something you have the power to suspend.*

Besides the fact that the freedom to use the car is so highly valued by teenagers, it has the virtue of being divisible into convenient units of time. You can withhold the car by the day, week, month, or year.

Actually, there are four different aspects to adolescent transportation, all of which lend themselves easily to natural consequences, logical consequences, or, if necessary, arbitrary consequences:

1. The chauffeur service you have been providing all these years. When you drive your kids someplace or pick them up, you are doing them a favor. You can say, "If you want me to do favors for you, you'll have to start showing more consideration for. . . ."

2. The right to operate a motor vehicle. The sequence in most states is a learner's permit at age fifteen (requiring parents' permission), a driving course sponsored by the school (also requiring parents' permission), a written test and a driving test that can be taken after the sixteenth birthday (but only with parents' permission), and then a license that parents can rescind at any time up to the child's eighteenth birthday.

EXAMPLE: "If it comes to our attention at any time that you have been in a moving automobile of which the driver—you or anyone else—even *appeared* to be drunk, we will personally suspend your driver's license for one year." You suspend a minor's driver's license by tearing it up and writing a letter to the state department of driver's license registration, explaining that your child, a minor, does not have your permission to obtain a new license before a certain date. This will not affect his driving record for insurance purposes (since you do not have to tell the state the reason), nor will it count against him in any way in the future. (Call the general information number of the appropriate bureau in your state for specific details.)

3. The right to borrow your car. This should be a reward for responsible behavior. You can lend your car not

just by the day, but by the hour, or in so many odometer miles per week (which can be reduced, for a Probation, in the same way that curfew times can be reduced). You can make it perfectly clear how you expect your car to be treated, which expenses the child is responsible for, and what the consequences will be if these expectations are not met.

4. The right to own a car. In "our day," twenty years ago, it was not uncommon for high-school seniors to have their own cars. My best friend bought a '51 Chevy for one hundred dollars. His summer earnings enabled him to pay the insurance premiums—another hundred dollars—and he made the rest of us chip in every time he stopped to fill the tank (at twenty cents a gallon!). This is one way in which today's adolescents have *less* freedom than their parents had; rare is the teenager today who can afford a car, or even whose parents can afford to buy him one. If you happen to be that fortunate and generous, you should certainly use it as an opportunity to set forth clear conditions.

Last-minute calls. What do you do when your child is due home at midnight and calls at five minutes before midnight to say that no one is willing to leave the party to give him a ride home? Would you mind getting dressed, he asks, and coming to pick him up? Or should he wait until his friends leave (they don't have to be home until 1:00)? Or do you want him to walk home—he can make it in ten minutes if he cuts through the city dump—where those kids were murdered last year—maybe somebody can lend him a flashlight—and a raincoat.

Don't be a sap. Tell him to take a taxi, at his own expense. The kid is responsible for arranging transportation home in advance. If it falls through, he takes the consequence. It does not matter what the reason is; there is always a reason. When an adult is late for work, he has to take the consequence even if it was not his fault the bus was late. "Next time," says the boss, "you had better take an earlier bus just to be on the safe side."

So you need one rule about what time the kid is to get home, with a consequence that overrides all the usual excuses. (If he is late because he stopped to rescue an invalid from a burning building, I would make an exception—if there are witnesses!) But you need another rule about calling you. On those occasions when the child is going to be late, do you want to be called or do you just want to deal with it the next morning? This probably depends on the child's age.

In fact, sometimes when parents have been discussing this with me, they suddenly realize that they don't care when the child comes home on a weekend night so long as he does not wake them. So they discover that they don't really want a curfew time at all. You should talk with your spouse about *why* you have a curfew on the weekends. Is it just so that the child doesn't wake you when he comes in? If so, maybe you want to make a rule about waking you instead of a rule about the time.

You also may need a rule about what the consequences will be if you have to get dressed and go out on a pick-up mission. You have to define what you consider to be a sufficient emergency to warrant such a call. Then you may also need a rule about any alternatives the child is not allowed to use in order to avoid paying the price of making an "emergency" call to you. (In Chicago, for example, the elevated trains are not safe for teenagers at night. Parents need a consequence for their children calling them and asking to be picked up downtown, but a worse consequence for *not* calling them and taking the El instead.)

If you do make a last-minute pick-up, the time you get the child home should count exactly the same as if the child had come in on his own at that time, for purposes of the curfew rule. He might have called you at 11:30 and was in the car by 11:55, but if you don't get home until 12:20, the kid is twenty minutes late.

The phone. As with the car, a hierarchy of privileges can be constructed around teenagers' other absolute necessity, the telephone. You will soon discover the need for very explicit rules to govern incoming and outgoing calls on your phone. The next thing you will discover is that you can change those rules—that is, reduce the minutes of use per day—as a highly effective consequence.

Taking away telephone privileges is a logical consequence when children fail to get other things done that have a higher priority, such as homework and chores. In addition, it makes a good logical consequence for misbehavior that has to do with communication: disrespectful or obscene language, fighting with siblings. "If the two of you cannot communicate with each other without degenerating into warfare, you will both lose the privilege of communicating with anyone else, on the telephone, for the rest of the evening."

Less extravagant than giving adolescents their own car, and very convenient for parents who can afford it, is to give them their own telephone (with a different number) or to let them get one with their own money. That gives you another potent consequence: What Ma Bell installeth, Ma Bell can take away.

> EXAMPLE: The Davises have a second telephone for their three children. Monica is allowed to be on the phone only during the first quarter of any hour, Brian during the second quarter hour, Kevin during the third. Any friend who calls during the wrong time slot is called back later. Thus there is no arguing, and the schedule guarantees that no child can spend more than fifteen minutes in any one call or more than 25 percent of the evening on the phone. If the system is abused, the phone will be unplugged for an appropriate period of time.

≡Summary

The physiological changes of puberty disturb a child's self-image. This is partly because of the suddenness of the change; the massive shock to the body takes getting used to. It is also because of the transformation in the child's sexual feelings, from simple feelings of physical pleasure to complex feelings about individuals of the opposite sex.

The whole period of adolescence is a function of our culture. Every little change in the body is evaluated in relation to the culture's "ideal," which itself has changed every decade or so. One generation's Troy Donahue and Sandra Dee are the next generation's John Travolta and Brooke Shields. Of course, certain evaluations are fairly constant: How tall am I? How pretty? How perfect a figure? How clear is my skin? How deep is my voice?

During this same period, the mind goes through changes that are every bit as radical as the body's. Able to reason for the first time about hypothetical propositions, the adolescent naturally has to test those propositions against the reality that parents and teachers impose.

For that reason, you can expect adolescents to manipulate your rules to their own advantage. The attempted manipulation is usually all right; it means that they accept parental authority and are trying to assert their growth and independence within your constraints. Whenever the rules do not work in the way they were intended, parents can change them.

The final area in which adolescence involves fundamental changes is in the child's relationship to the family. There is a *double bind* in the messages we modern-day parents send to our teenagers. We tell them, "We aren't going to keep a roof over your head and feed you forever. You are going to have to go out there and make it in the world, responsible for yourself. But remember, you're still a member of this family, dependent on us and subject to our rules." That sounds like "Grow up, but don't grow up"—a double bind. Double binds can make anyone a little crazy. Any adolescent who isn't a bit crazy must not be getting the message.

However, the full message is "You're still a child as long as you continue to live in our house. We make rules for our children. As you grow up, as long as you prove to be responsible, our restrictions will be fewer and fewer, and we will treat you as more of an adult. If your behavior is immature, we may have to start treating you as more of a child again."

SUGGESTED BOOKS: Adolescence

Brusko, Marlene: *Living With Your Teenager.* New York: Ballantine, 1987.

Davitz, Lois, and Davitz, Joel. *How to Live (Almost) Happily With a Teenager.* Minneapolis: Winston Press, 1982.

Ginott, Haim. *Between Parent and Teenager.* New York: Avon, 1973.

Miller, Derek. *The Age Between: Adolescence and Therapy.* New York: Aronson, 1983. (Requires some background in psychology or psychiatry.)

Orbach, Susan. *Fat Is a Feminist Issue.* New York: Berkley, 1979.

Sussman, Alan. *The Rights of Young People.* New York: Avon, 1977.

CHAPTER FIFTEEN

Drugs

A *drug* is anything taken internally that produces an effect on the body's functioning, other than simple nourishment. *Drug abuse*, in the case of children, is taking any drug, in any dosage at all, without their parents' knowledge and instruction. *Drug addiction* is only one form of abuse; one need not be an addict to suffer injury or death from an overdose or from taking the wrong drug.

It is obviously frightening for parents to contemplate their children's experimenting with drugs. What makes parents feel so hopeless is the fact that teenagers try drugs when they are with their peers, out of their parents' surveillance. This makes it difficult to follow one of my cardinal principles, "Don't make any rules you can't enforce." You are not going to know when and if your child starts experimenting with drugs, *especially* if you try to make a rule against it.

The solution to this dilemma is to use your most important ally, your child's *self-esteem*. You build that by being a firm parent in other areas, before drugs even become an issue, and by praising children's specific actions when they sincerely impress you. You then make maximum use of that strength within your children by providing them with accurate *information* about the natural consequences of various courses of action they may choose. The third step is to think beyond your vague fears to the specific likely outcomes of drug dependence—effects on school performance, jobs, trouble with the law—and to *make rules* about those observable things rather than about the unobservable experimenting.

This three-step approach—first building self-esteem, then educating your children about the dangers and giving them ways of dealing with the dangers, and finally making rules only of the kind that are enforceable—applies to other concerns besides drugs. It applies to your concerns about adolescent sexuality (chapter 16), about respect for other people's feelings, about responsibility for property. Although drugs may be the severest problem facing today's young people, the following discussion should suggest a general model for dealing with all sorts of concerns.

This chapter begins with some general considerations about protecting adolescents by building self-esteem. Then we shall move on to steps two and three: how parents can educate themselves about the drugs teenagers commonly use and abuse, how to communicate with your children about these problems, and, finally, how to make enforceable rules about drugs.

≡The problem of protecting the adolescent

Both this chapter and the next deal with potentially destructive adolescent activities. These problems differ from problems with such things as homework, chores, and curfews. In the case of drugs, promiscuity, reckless driving, and the like, adolescents are *not* just testing the limits of their freedom. They are actually, though perhaps unconsciously, toying with self-destruction. To shy away from that unpleasant fact is to misunderstand the whole problem.

Therefore, just as we cannot enforce rules against people taking poison or shooting themselves if they really do not want to live, we cannot prevent children from becoming pregnant or drug-addicted if that is what they want to do. These are not really the same kinds of choices as the ones for which your system of rules is designed.

We shall, in these two chapters, discuss some rules that *discourage* children from experimenting with drugs or with sex earlier than you think they should do so. However, we will not pretend that these rules can ever provide the full protection you might like to provide. The best way to protect your children is to make them feel good about themselves and about their futures so that their own health and safety are precious to them, so that they become their own best guardians against self-destructive actions. Children who value themselves as human beings and who feel confident about their futures will protect themselves; children who do not will not.

But where do children get self-esteem? It comes directly from their parents. As the diagram shows, there are two immediate and long-standing influences upon children's self-esteem: how much their parents care about them and respect their feelings, and how much their parents respect themselves.

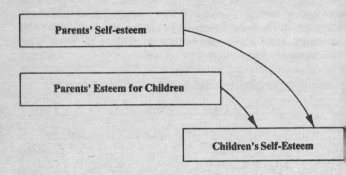

When you consistently enforce rules, you show your children *both* that you care about them and what happens to them *and* that you have plenty of self-respect. Those two facts are more important to children than anything else, believe it or not—even more important than being fed and entertained and catered to. Furthermore, your clarity and consistency allow you also to be warm, loving, actively listening parents. Because you rarely nag or yell or criticize, you have more opportunities to convey in both action and word how impressed you are with each child's growth and achievements.

With such support, your children have no intention of throwing away their lives, and you do not need an elaborate set of rules to prevent them from doing so.

On the other hand, your family rules cannot ignore your specific concerns about these dangerous activities. It is more than likely that your child will have tried marijuana before the tenth or eleventh grade (in some communities, long before). It is highly probable that by that time the child's tolerance for alcohol will have been tested, and it is also likely that your child will experiment with the effects of any or all of these activities upon driving an automobile.

How do you feel about those eventualities? Your personal preferences and worries will depend not only on your attitudes but also on the grade level of each individual child, the child's physical maturity, the child's emotional maturity, norms in your community, and your child's friends in particular.

With so many variables, this book can only deal with the problem of *how* to enforce whatever standards you choose and leave the choice of those standards to you. Some families are very restrictive about things like marijuana, alcohol, and premarital sex. Other families treat their adolescents, beyond a certain age, like adults in these matters, leaving such things to their discretion. Many families try to find a compromise in the middle ground.

"All-or-none" thinking. It is difficult to think about these issues sensibly if you fall victim to "all-or-none" thinking—for example, if you think that once the teenager loses his or her virginity, promiscuity is sure to follow, or that the kid who experiments with drugs even once is automatically on the path to destruction. That kind of unrealistic panic gets in the way of rational planning, and if you talk to your adolescents in catastrophic terms, you only insult them. The question is not how to prevent experimenting with sex or drugs but how to maximize the maturity with which your kids will approach them.

Anyway, you have no chance of succeeding with an absolute, blanket set of prohibitions: "No alcohol, drugs, or tobacco." (I wish it were that simple.) The kinds of rules that work are different for different specific substances or activities.

An illustration: Tobacco. Cigarettes are less upsetting to most parents than other drugs, but they will serve as a good first example of the problems that arise when you try to protect your child from any drug. You can state your *preference* that your child not start smoking. You can back up that preference with medical data, with the cost of a carton of cigarettes, with the smell of a used ash-tray. You may be able to make a good case, even if you yourself smoke. My father's heavy smoking and coughing were all the evidence I needed to make up my own mind on the subject. But suppose you were to try to make a rule: "If you ever smoke a cigarette, you'll be grounded."

Your son knows as well as you do that he can try a cigarette over at his friend's house without your finding out about it. He can do this on a regular basis, stock up on breath mints, and he will either become addicted to nicotine or be wise enough to stop in time. Your unenforceable rule will not have had anything to do with it, so it would have been better expressed as a preference: "I personally think smoking is a waste of one's health as well as one's money."

That does not mean there is nothing you can do. You can frame a rule in terms of the results that would eventually come to your attention. You do not really care about that one cigarette, anyway. With this particular drug, your concern is about the addiction that may follow. Are there any consequences of addiction to tobacco that you can let the child know about in advance? For instance, who will pay for all those cigarettes? You?

> EXAMPLE: Fifteen-year-old Lisa gets fifteen dollars per week in allowance. After the bus fare to school and her lunch money, she is left with about six dollars to spend as she chooses. Her parents know that one of Lisa's friends spends about five dollars per week on cigarettes. They say, "We hope you're smart enough not to become a smoker." (Caring)
>
> "Don't worry," Lisa reassures them.
>
> "We're not worried," her parents say. "But in case you do, we will interpret that to mean you can afford to waste five dollars per week." (Education) "So if we find out that you are buying cigarettes, your allowance will go down to ten dollars." (Enforceable rule)

If Lisa's parents have previously established credibility in firmly enforcing their rules, this threat will carry some weight. She can conceal occasional smoking, but occasional smoking is not what they were worried about. The main reason they preferred her not to experiment with cigarettes was the likelihood that it would lead to addiction. Lisa knows that if she were to become a nicotine addict, she would not be able to hide the fact for long. So she now has a good financial reason not to smoke. It is only an extra rationalization that she adds to her own reasons, but it could tip the balance.

Closing the credibility gap. In this chapter on drugs and in the following chapter on sexuality, we shall discuss bigger worries than cigarettes. We shall approach all these worries in basically the same way as in the foregoing example:

> • Don't try to make rules about the experimenting that your children will probably do in secret.
> • Ask yourselves what the consequences are that you really fear; what might the experimenting lead to?
> • Those consequences will almost always be things that you will find out about (drunken behavior, truancy, declining grades, pregnancy). Make rules in advance about what your reaction will be if any of those things happen.
> • Educate your children accurately about the probable natural consequences of pursuing certain actions. If they do not understand the risks, confront them with reliable published information. If you are not sure your own ideas are correct, educate yourself first.

The last point may be the most important. Many parents undermine their authority by creating a credibility gap. If you tell your children that marijuana usually leads to hard drugs, they are going to dismiss not only that falsehood but also the truth you tell them, such as the fact that they can never know exactly what is in the various pills they will be offered or the fact that cocaine is addictive.

Credibility is your most essential asset as a parent. If you throw it away, you throw away whatever degree of control you might have had over those aspects of your children's lives that worry you the most.

Honest, accurate information is vitally necessary to children. It is much better if it comes from the parents, or if the parents at least confirm the information from other sources, including school, the media, and peers.

When should children be educated about sex? In a general

way (the "facts of life") by the time they start school, more specifically before they reach puberty, and with accurate, detailed responses to their questions thereafter. Similarly, when should they be educated about drugs? Before they are offered any, as well as later, they continue to need a reliable source of specific information.

There is no justification for parents saying, "We don't plan to discuss such things with our children, because we don't want to put ideas into their heads." The ideas are going to be put into their heads by others. The question is, will they be able to evaluate those ideas? With what knowledge? It is your business how liberal or conservative you decide to be with regard to your children's behavior. But keeping silent is not a legitimate form of conservatism; you are abdicating your responsibility. Keeping silent about these important matters is almost as destructive to your credibility as telling the child untruths.

In short, tell your children the truth, the whole truth (gradually, as it becomes age-appropriate), and nothing but the truth.

≡Alcohol

Let's apply the same kind of logic that we have used with cigarettes to beer, wine, and liquor. The rule "Do not drink alcoholic beverages" is unenforceable. It draws the line at the wrong place. Once the child has crossed your line and gotten away with it, there is no effective boundary between one drink and many. "One might as well be hanged for stealing a sheep as for a lamb."

A better set of rules would deal with the behaviors that you are most concerned about, the *reasons* you worry about a teenager getting started with alcohol:

1. Between seven million and ten million Americans are alcoholics, and an even larger number are "problem drinkers," people whose lives are habitually disrupted by abuse of alcohol but who have not yet established a physiological addiction. More than one million of the addicted alcoholics and as many as five million problem drinkers are between the ages of fourteen and seventeen. Alcohol abuse is

responsible for the loss of more lives than all other drugs combined. It has been estimated that it costs the American economy ten billion dollars per year in lost productivity.

2. You are justifiably concerned about how drinking will affect your child's school performance. You cannot rely on the school to enforce rules about drinking, but you can expect the drinking to affect grades and attendance reports, and you can set consequences for that.

3. Finally, you are justifiably terrified about driving under the influence of alcohol. You cannot be sure of finding out about every incident of driving while intoxicated, but you can be specific about what you will do if it does come to your attention. Even if you are sure that you can trust your teenager, it is a good idea to have an extremely strict rule about drinking and driving, and also about being a passenger in a car whose driver is drunk. (A majority of the teenage girls killed in alcohol-related auto accidents, and more than 40 percent of the boys, are passengers rather than drivers.)

Your rules, then, can focus upon drunken behavior—when, where, and how frequently you will tolerate it. They can include an absolute prohibition against being *seen* drinking before or during school hours. Many parents would extend this to school nights, depending on their values, the age and responsibility of their children. Others, especially with children under seventeen or so, would punish drunken behavior at any time.

EXAMPLE: Ruth is fifteen. The first time she is to be driven home from a party by one of her friends, her parents say, "You are responsible for the sobriety of anyone from whom you accept a ride. If we ever find that you have been in a car with a drunk driver, the consequence will be that getting your own driver's license will be deferred for a year. And we don't need as much evidence of intoxication as a court of law requires—so be sure that anyone who gets behind the wheel is not only sober but *drives* like a sober driver."

EXAMPLE: Steve has just received his license to drive. His parents say, "If you ever give us reason to believe that you have driven our car or anyone else's car while intoxicated, your license will be suspended—by us—for one year."

Here are some examples of more liberal rules. This system allows you to set your own standards and then to be firm about wherever you draw the line:

> EXAMPLE: "You are expected home at the required time, drunk or sober. And if drunkenness becomes a pattern—more than once per month—we will consider that you are developing an alcohol problem and we will crack down harder."

> EXAMPLE: "Now that you're a senior, we're going to start offering you beer and wine when we ourselves are drinking it. But you don't have permission to help yourself at other times. Any other drinking you do will have to be paid for with your own money." This is a reasonable way to begin treating the seventeen- or eighteen-year-old as an adult. But if pilfering occurs, you'll need a rule dealing with the specific consequences of that, and you'll need to keep track of your supply.*

The two toughest questions that parents ask about how to handle teenage drinking are "How drunk is drunk?" and "If we prohibit our children from drinking in our presence, won't we just drive the problem underground?"

How drunk is drunk? I suggest you forget about objective criteria like blood alcohol levels, the ability to walk a straight line, and so forth. Never get into an argument over how much your adolescent has had to drink. Refuse to engage in debates over the meaning of "drunk," "high," "tipsy," "loaded," etc. As parents, you have the right to punish your children for *appearing* to be drunk, if your rule is stated in those terms. They have the responsibility to see to it that they never lead you, their teachers, the neighbors, or the police to believe that they are intoxicated.

Therefore, if you want to have rules about drunkenness, state them in terms of "intoxicated *behavior*." Don't argue about it. "I'm sorry, I'm not a detective. I don't know what you did or

---

* Teenagers who persistently sneak alcohol from their parents' supplies and let themselves be caught may be sending messages for help.

didn't drink. I can only go by what I saw (or by what the principal reported to me). Justice isn't perfect, but you'll have to accept the consequences and be more careful what impression you give others in the future."

On the other hand, if you feel uncomfortable about making the judgment that your child is drunk, you can bypass the issue of intoxication entirely. You can simply make rules about loudness, disorderliness, violence, and abusiveness. Many "intoxicated behaviors," such as violence and abusiveness, are things that parents normally have rules against anyway. Amazingly, they sometimes forgive these same things if the child is drunk! That is an excellent way to encourage drunkenness. *Under no circumstances should intoxication or any other artificially altered state of consciousness ever be allowed as an excuse for violating parents' rules*. The message you want the child to come away with is "I'd better be careful not to let myself get so drunk that I lose control over my behavior."

"I'd rather have them doing it at home than elsewhere." Many parents feel it is a mistake to prohibit drinking at home, because it only encourages teenagers to find other places to drink. "It seems like the wrong place to draw the line; it might convey the idea that we don't care what they do as long as we don't know about it." Another parent adds, "If my children and their friends are going to get high, our home is the safest place they could choose. At least they won't have to be in the car when the others drive home."

I understand the reasoning behind these arguments, but I still think it a mistake to condone behavior in your house that you would not consider acceptable if it happened somewhere else. There are some important general principles at stake. Adolescents are in the process of deciding what standards of behavior they want to take out into the world with them as they spend more and more time away from home. One of the important sources of information they use in those decisions is your own set of standards. You are not the only source, and not one that they accept unquestioningly, but you are a very important source. Sometimes they will incorporate your standards; sometimes they will go the opposite way; and sometimes they will make compromises to fit their own chosen lifestyles. But the best thing you can do for them as a parent is to remain consistent and clear about your own attitudes. Even when they choose to reject your preferences, let them be perfectly aware that this is what they are doing.

You will not necessarily imply that "we don't care how much they drink as long as we don't find out about it." You do care, and your children know you do. Of course you can only enforce rules about behavior that comes to your attention. But through those rules, you let your children know exactly what your standards are, and they will take those standards into consideration even in situations that you probably would not find out about.

Dr. Lawrence Kohlberg, a psychologist at Harvard who studied moral development from early childhood to adulthood, found that the highest levels of morality are based on standards of right and wrong regardless of whether other people are there to observe one's behavior and reward or punish it. Most of us would like our children to be so virtuous; but it would be a mistake to let our ideals make us unrealistic. Few adults reach that highest level, let alone adolescents. Besides, drinking is not really a question of *moral* judgment but of practical judgment: Which of my faculties am I going to require in the next few hours, and how much can I afford to dull those faculties with alcohol? Who else is going to be involved, and what are their reactions likely to be? By making your own reactions clear, you can help your adolescent make responsible judgments about drinking.

Parties. I am impressed by a set of guidelines printed and distributed by the parents' and teachers' committees in many high schools around the country. With the permission of the Committee on Drug Abuse in Deerfield, Illinois, I quote from their brochure:

GUIDELINES FOR HOSTING A PARTY

1. Do not offer alcohol to guests under the age of 21 or allow guests to use drugs in your home. You may be brought to court on criminal charges and/or have to pay monetary damages in a civil lawsuit if you furnish alcohol or drugs to minors.

   —Be alert to the signs of alcohol or drug use by teens.

   —Guests who try to bring in alcohol or drugs or who otherwise refuse to cooperate with your expectations should be asked to leave,

—Notify the parents of any teen who arrives at the party drunk or under the influence of any drug to ensure the teen's safe transportation home. DO NOT LET ANYONE DRIVE UNDER THE INFLUENCE OF ALCOHOL OR DRUGS.

2. Set the ground rules with your teen before the party.

—This will give both a good opportunity to express feelings and concerns.

—Let your teen know what you expect.

3. Notify your neighbors that there will be a party.

4. Notify the police when planning a large party.

—This will help the police protect you, your guests, and your neighbors.

—Discuss with the police an agreeable plan for guest parking.

5. Plan to have plenty of food and nonalcoholic drinks on hand.

6. Plan activities with your teen prior to the party.

[*This is the one suggestion that seems unrealistic to me. The teenagers I know don't want preplanned activities; they want to listen to music, talk, sometimes dance or play games, but all spontaneously. "To party" means specifically not to be programmed.*]

7. Limit party attendance and times.

—When possible, make a guest list and send out invitations beforehand. It is important to discourage crashers.

—Avoid open-house parties. It is difficult for parents and teens to keep control over this kind of party.

—Set time limits for the party that enable teens to be home at a reasonable time, definitely before the legal curfew.

8. A parent should be at home during the party.

—A parent can bring in snacks and nonalcoholic beverages. Not only will your presence help keep the party running smoothly, but it will also give you an opportunity to meet your teen's friends.

—Invite other parents to help if your party is large.

9. Do not allow any guest who leaves the party to return.

—This will discourage teens from leaving the party

to drink or use drugs elsewhere and then return to the party.

10. Other ideas

    —Get to know your children's friends and their parents. Keep in touch with them during your children's teen years.

    —Many parties occur spontaneously. Parents and teenagers should understand beforehand that the above guidelines are in effect at ALL parties.

    —If, despite your precautions, things get out of hand, do not hesitate to call your local police department for help.

Unfortunately, the reality of life in many communities is that teenagers will not have parties in their homes under such rules. They believe, sometimes correctly, that no one will come to the party if parents are going to be home and if no alcohol is allowed. This is a sad state of affairs, but it will change if more parents agree to adopt the guidelines.

What about parties at someone else's house? We have already discussed the general principle: Limit your rules to actions that would come to your attention, including curfew. You cannot monitor your child's behavior at someone else's house, but you can monitor what time he comes home, in what condition, and whether there are any complaints from others about his conduct. Let me also quote four of the Deerfield committee's guidelines:

GUIDELINES FOR TEENAGER ATTENDING A PARTY

1. Know where your teen will be.

    —Obtain the address and phone number of the party giver.

    —Let your teen know that you expect a phone call if the location of the party is changed.

[*The only way this can be enforced is in terms of consequences should you later discover that the child was not where he said he would be.*]

2. Be sure your teen knows when he/she is supposed to be home.

3. Know how your teen will get to and from the party.

    —Assure your teen that you or a specific friend or

neighbor can be called for a ride home (make sure your teen has the phone number).

　—Discuss with your teen the possible situations in which the teen might need to make such a call.

4. Contact the parents of the party giver to:
　—Verify the occasion.
　—Offer assistance.
　—Be sure that a parent will be present.*
　—Be sure that alcohol and other drugs will not be permitted.*

The last two suggestions, which I have starred, I consider unrealistic in most American communities today. Up to the age of thirteen or fourteen, perhaps, one can prohibit one's children from attending unsupervised parties; but after that age such a prohibition is neither practical nor fair.

The reason it is not practical is that we had better hold our teenagers accountable for their actions and the actions of their group, whether or not they are being chaperoned by other adults. Teenagers have to assess the situation at every party or get-together, and if they do not feel secure about taking responsibility for what may happen, they have a responsibility to leave the party. That is true whether parents are in the kitchen, or upstairs out of sight, or out of town.

It is not fair to prohibit teenagers from attending unchaperoned parties if, in fact, practically none of the parties *among their age group* are chaperoned. (I would not allow thirteen- or fourteen-year-olds to go to unsupervised parties with older children.) Although I myself would insist on being home during any of my children's parties—to help them stay in control of things if uninvited guests show up or if anyone brings alcohol or other drugs—I am aware that some other parents are less cautious. If they are stupid enough to allow their children to hold a party when they are away, it is not my place to call them up and tell them to stay home. It is their house. My children may go to the party so long as they are willing to share in the responsibility for whatever happens. If things begin to get out of hand, it is up to them to exercise leadership, or call for help, or leave.

The Drinking-Driver Contract. An organization called Students Against Driving Drunk (S.A.D.D.), which has spread from

Massachusetts to high schools across the country, has drawn up a sample contract for parents and teenagers to sign. Because it is worth discussing in every family, I quote it verbatim:

> TEENAGER: I agree to call you for advice and/or transportation at any hour, from any place if I am ever in a situation where I have had too much to drink or a friend or date who is driving me has had too much to drink.

*Signature*_____

> PARENT: I agree to come and get you at any hour, any place, no questions asked and no argument at that time, or I will pay for a taxi to bring you home safely. I would expect we discuss this issue at a later time.
>
> I agree to seek safe sober transportation home if I am ever in a situation where I have had too much to drink or a friend who is driving me has had too much to drink.

*Signature*_____

The students who designed this contract showed their concern about their parents' safety as well as their own. They also showed an understanding of the most basic principle of child-rearing: If parents want their children to act responsibly, the parents have to act responsibly.

If you or your spouse has a drinking problem. Just as alcohol can interfere with children's schoolwork and development, so can parents' excessive drinking interfere with their ability to be parents. In fact, that is one of the most frequent things adolescents complain about.

The parent who has a habit of drinking too much will often be *too lax* when sober and *too rough* when inebriated. Alcohol tends to suppress one's self-control, which often means releasing pent-up anger and sometimes violent rage. Some parents, when drunk, may physically abuse their children. More often, they fall back on futile arguing and verbal abuse. The next day, when sober, they feel guilty. They feel they have no right to criticize anyone else's actions. So they are inclined to be lenient, even when the children may need punishment. Powerless over alcohol, these parents feel powerless over anything and anybody, even the people who most need them to be firm and consistent.

The next thing that happens is that the two parents stop working as a team. If only one of them has a drinking problem, the other one takes over the parental responsibilities. It doesn't work.

Parents who have become dependent on alcohol already know what they need to do. They have to quit drinking. Otherwise, the illness inexorably takes its downward course; and it drags the whole family down with it. But giving up alcohol is not easy. It may require a brief stay at a rehabilitation center. It will certainly require total abstinence, not just "cutting down." In the meantime, while they are postponing that crisis and desperately trying not to let their lives fall apart, they still want to be good parents.

Frequently, when parents seek counseling to help control teenagers, the teenagers point the finger back at the parents' drinking. Some therapists refuse to work with such families until the parent goes through detoxification and joins Alcoholics Anonymous (AA). I certainly encourage the latter, but usually the drinking problem has not become bad enough yet for the parent to face up to it and go on the wagon. The children's behavior problems need help *immediately*, not months or years in the future when the parents finally get help with their problem.

What is needed, therefore, is a system of discipline that can be implemented by parents who occasionally get drunk but who do not label themselves alcoholics and are not prepared to give up drinking. The system of written rules and consequences described in Part I fills that need. Parents must agree on their family rules and state them explicitly when sober; then they can follow through with the stated consequences even when one or both of them have had a few drinks. The parents' drinking problem cannot be used by the child as an excuse for ignoring rules. At the same time, the written rules and predetermined consequences protect the child from unreasonable, violent, or abusive spur-of-the-moment reactions.

EXAMPLE: Mary Ann's parents are both problem drinkers. In addition, they are divorced, and Mary Ann and her younger brother live with their father. The father does not drink every night, but on Saturday afternoons he usually has several beers, continuing through the evening, so that by the time Mary Ann's curfew rolls around, he is in no shape to enforce it.

MISTAKE: When Mary Ann comes in late, her father yells a lot and calls her ugly names. "You're grounded," he shouts—sometimes he says she's grounded for a week, sometimes for a month, but never with any effect.

BETTER: After a number of counseling sessions, Dad is able to say, "I admit I sometimes drink too much."

"You *always* drink too much," his daughter says.

Dad does not argue about how often or how much he drinks. "You have to follow the rules; my drinking is a problem, but I don't stop being your father no matter what." However, Dad promises to put off any *decisions*, including interpreting rules and imposing consequences, if he has had anything to drink that day.

I cannot guarantee that this sort of promise will help you avoid ugly scenes when you have drunk too much, because it depends upon how alcohol affects your personality. (For many people, promises made beforehand are thrown out the window after a few drinks.) In any case, this is not the ultimate solution, as you know. Parents whose children accuse them of a drinking problem have an extra handicap. Making a system of explicit rules can help you provide clear expectations and defer your decision-making until you have a clear head. But it is only the first step, showing the child that you are still a parent, despite any problems you may have. *Then* go through a detoxification program and join AA.

≡Marijuana

At the end of the 1960s, use of marijuana (and hashish, the more concentrated form of cannabis resin) became commonplace among young people in our society. Those of us who were in college, in military service, or just entering the work force at that time are now becoming the parents of teenagers and preteens. Many of us have warm, friendly feelings toward cannabis yet do not want our children getting involved with it. Parents who themselves have smoked marijuana may be less upset about their kids trying it than most parents were in the 1970s. They may feel reluctant to make any rules about it at all.

On the other hand, marijuana is illegal. To condone it is to condone law-breaking. Furthermore, a ninth-grader smoking a joint in the morning before school is a completely different situation from the earliest experiences you may have had with marijuana (sharing a joint on a Saturday night in your college dorm or around a campfire on the beach). The difference is not only in the user's age but also in the strength of the marijuana currently on the market, and in its daily, not just occasional, use. For a frightening number of young people, marijuana is not an occasional "high" but a constant condition.

Although parents who have used marijuana may run the risk of being too tolerant, there are still many to whom it is completely unfamiliar. They are at risk of succumbing to "all-or-none" panic ("one joint and you're a drug addict").

Before trying to make any rules about marijuana, parents need to have an accurate picture of how it is used by teenagers today. You have to be clear to yourself about your concerns before you can make rules that are clear to your children. The place to start is with some facts:

Marijuana is not physically addictive. The body does not build up tolerance to tetrahydrocannabinol (THC), the active ingredient in marijuana. Tolerance would mean that larger doses were required for the same effects, as is the case with alcohol. In fact, habitual marijuana users can get high on smaller doses than novices. The high depends as much on the state of mind before lighting up a joint as it does on the marijuana itself. Nor does cannabis lead to the use of such addictive drugs as heroin. Heroin users are likely to have smoked marijuana previously, but very few marijuana users ever consider trying heroin. (In a national survey, 49 percent of high-school seniors who used marijuana said they had also tried other illegal drugs, but the vast majority of those drugs were, like marijuana, nonaddictive.) The proportion of marijuana users who do go on to become drug addicts is small enough so that I do not consider it a realistic concern for parents. Harping on the threat of addiction may do more harm than good, by lowering your credibility.

But marijuana is dangerous. There are potentially harmful effects of using marijuana that are worthy of a parent's concern:

1. Contrary to some teenage mythology, no one does better in school—or in any other environment requiring a clear mind and a high energy level—when stoned. They do worse.

2. Also contrary to myth, there is clear evidence that driving an automobile, or any other work involving reflexes and sensorimotor coordination, is significantly degraded under the influence of marijuana. Even one or two joints produce an impairment of driving skills that lasts for several hours after the high is gone.

3. Psychological dependence can be just as serious as a physical addiction. Although the body does not become addicted to the drug, some individuals come to rely more and more on the euphoric, tranquilized state of mind and on the lifestyle that encompasses it. The term "pothead" is used pejoratively by "nonheads" but cheerfully accepted by heads themselves. In other words, they pride themselves on being social dropouts and lifelong nonachievers.

Some authors argue that the drug itself produces this psychological dependence so that it *is* addictive. There is no real evidence for that. The result, however, can be the same as with a physical addiction: strong resistance to doing anything about the problem.

4. The marijuana on the market today is estimated to be up to ten times more potent than what you may have smoked ten or fifteen years ago. Research is still coming in, but studies based on today's average THC dose have shown that it can cause reduced fertility in men (lower sperm count), as well as genetic defects. In addition, much marijuana is adulterated with other chemicals (including poisons) that have unpredictable effects.

5. Most of us who are over thirty-five did not smoke grass until late adolescence or adulthood. A recent study found that in rural Maine, where social change is relatively slow, 6 percent of *fourth-graders* had tried marijuana. Nationwide, 31 percent of boys admitted to using marijuana

before the tenth grade. One in ten high-school seniors smoke pot *every day*, averaging three or four joints a day.

Use of marijuana at such an early age makes today's situation very different from the college drug scene of our generation. Besides disrupting the educational process, drug users tend to halt their emotional development at whatever point they become seriously involved. A twenty-one-year-old who is rehabilitated from a drug habit of eight years typically has the emotional maturity of a thirteen-year-old.

6. Like alcohol, marijuana is a depressant, not a stimulant. Anyone who is already depressed will only make matters worse by smoking dope. Suicide attempts by adolescents are often preceded by ordinary social consumption of alcohol or marijuana. This does not mean the drug causes the suicidal feelings. It releases feelings of emotional pain and despair that are already there.

7. Purchasing any illegal drug, especially in multiple doses, tends to involve relationships with the sort of "adult" who serves as liaison between organized crime and the high-school marijuana market. A dealer's typical routine is to wait until the child becomes dependent on him as a marijuana supplier and then pretend to be out of marijuana but offer another drug as a consolation.

How can we make rules that deal with these concerns? In the first place, let us realize that the mindless "pothead" lifestyle, the psychological dependence, the depression, and the involvement with unsavory characters are not caused by smoking marijuana. Marijuana is only the vehicle by which some already troubled adolescents, low in self-esteem and despairing of success at anything else, drop out of the competitive world while at the same time embracing, to extremes, the fashionable attitudes and behavior of their age group.

So if your child is leaning in that direction, you will not solve the problem by cracking down on pot. It is similar to the situation with teenage alcoholism. There, too, the major concern is psychological dependence, which has to come first before the physiological addiction process begins. A parent's job is to get help for the child's original problems, which the child has tried to solve by abusing marijuana or alcohol. (In chapter 21, I will have more to say on when and how to get professional help.)

Your rules should focus on your concerns about the probable *effects* of marijuana that you will be able to see: deterioration in school attendance and performance, irresponsibility with motor vehicles. As with alcohol, you can make rules about the consequences of unexcused absences and tardiness, consequences of a significant drop in grades, consequences of being reported in a car whose driver has smoked marijuana, and so forth.

You can also enforce a rule against possession of marijuana, or even paraphernalia like hashish pipes, cigarette-rolling papers, and roach holders (clips, often decorated, to hold a joint down to its last embers). Kids may be able to keep such items out of sight, but that is not the point. The point is that if they can anticipate the consequence of being caught with the stuff, you have made your standards very clear. The mere fact that you care so much will improve the adolescent's self-esteem and make him much less likely to feel like "dropping out," which is your bigger concern.

What if you yourself use marijuana? In our diverse society, some readers may be shocked by that idea, whereas just as many will appreciate its pragmatism. I know parents who have shared a joint with their teenagers as casually as they might offer a sip of wine or beer. I know others who keep their marijuana usage secret, and still others who stopped when they became parents, so as not to set a bad example. In general, whether you continue to smoke marijuana or have stopped, I advocate telling your children honestly about your experiences. It would be worse for them to learn that you had been dishonest than it would be for you simply to acknowledge a double standard: *What is all right for you is not necessarily all right for your children.*

With alcohol, my concern was that excessive drinking would interfere with your ability to be firm but fair. With marijuana, I have two different concerns. One is that you may hesitate to prohibit marijuana if you smoke it yourself. You probably don't feel guilty about drinking alcohol, but you may feel guilty about marijuana. Don't let that interfere with your rules. My other concern arises from the fact that alcohol is not against the law, whereas marijuana is—for adults as well as minors. If the child knows that you occasionally smoke grass, you are setting an example of disrespect for the narcotics laws—and laws in general.

Although setting such an example is regrettable, you can still show that your actions are consistent with the idea of rules and consequences. You can simply explain that our society is ambivalent about marijuana and has some laws on the books that are rarely enforced. However, you need to stress that if arrested for possessing marijuana, you would take the consequences. Thoreau did not merely refuse to pay the poll tax that he considered unjust; he willingly took the consequence: a night in jail. You are going to make some rules because your children are not old enough to make the decisions you have made for yourselves about marijuana. Unlike the state and federal marijuana laws, the family rules *are* going to be enforced consistently.

What you do from that point on will be the same as parents who have much more negative attitudes toward marijuana. You have to sit down and decide what you consider acceptable at your children's age, what limits you want to enforce. And you have to phrase the rules in terms of visible events.

≡Uppers, downers, acid, coke, and other "trips"

The first thing you need to do is educate yourself. Several excellent books are suggested at the end of this chapter. I shall provide only a brief introduction to the different types of drugs children are playing with today; then I shall make some suggestions about rules.

Hallucinogens. LSD ("acid"), PCP ("angel dust"), quaaludes, mescaline, DMT, and DOM ("STP") are a few of the more popular synthetic drugs that produce hallucinations. In the days of Ken Kesey and Timothy Leary, a lot was written about "mind-expanding" and "altered states of consciousness" in relation to creativity. The adolescents who use these drugs today don't describe themselves as searching for any higher truth. They simply say they want to get "high." When they speak frankly about their goals, these kids do not seem to have much confidence in the future. To those of us who, at twenty, condemned those over thirty for having "sold out" to materialism, now that we are pushing forty, the ones under twenty seem to have sold out. What could be more materialistic than the instant unearned pleasure of a "trip"?

So that is one danger of hallucinogens—that the "high" becomes the most important thing in life. You combat that danger by building up self-esteem and confidence about the future, by generating an interest in sports and other healthy activities, rather than by merely enforcing rules.

But there are other dangers:

1. The question of *addiction* to a drug has two parts: *dependence* and *tolerance*. Dependence may be only psychological ("needing" the drug) or both psychological and physical. Tolerance means requiring an increasing dose to get the same effect.

Whereas marijuana does not produce tolerance, but can lead to psychological dependence, hallucinogens do just the reverse: They usually do not create dependence, but they do create tolerance. In fact, chemical similarities between different hallucinogens can cause a user of one drug to develop tolerance to others. The frequent user of mescaline will require a bigger dose of LSD to get high, and vice versa.

The consequence of tolerance to hallucinogenic drugs can be similar to what happens in alcoholism. Problem drinkers may be proud of their "capacity," but what is really happening is that they have to drink more before they feel drunk. Ultimately, the effective dose approaches the level of a lethal dose, producing brain, liver, and other organ damage. "Acid freaks" (heavy hallucinogen users) may similarly flaunt their capacity to take more and more drugs in dazzling combinations, but this does not mean their bodies or brains are impervious to those doses.

2. The long-term effects of these drugs are unknown. It is fairly clear that they can damage the developing nervous systems of fetuses whose mothers take them while pregnant. Findings that indicate genetic damage or other effects on future pregnancies are still inconclusive.

3. Users never actually know what they are taking. The so-called "controlled substances" (the illegal drugs) are not controlled at all. They could contain anything. The people

who manufacture these drugs use whatever alternative ingredients are cheaply available at the time. Those who sell them on the street call them whatever is most popular at the time.

In 1970, The Haight-Ashbury Free Clinic in San Francisco found that 90 percent of the "hallucinogen" samples they analyzed were different substances than they were alleged to be. In a study on the East Coast, of thirteen samples purported to be mescaline, seven were found to be LSD, four were STP, one was aspirin, and one could not be identified. None was mescaline.

This unreliability can be extremely dangerous, because the ability to control one's reaction to the psychedelic distortions of a "trip" depends greatly on getting the trip one expects. A youngster may have tried mescaline previously and had a certain kind of experience. The next time someone sells or gives him some "mescaline," it may be something quite different. Not knowing when or how the experience will end, he panics. Most accidents due to "freaking out" (jumping through a window, for example) are caused by panic.

The symptoms of an LSD trip may include tingling, numbness, nausea, loss of appetite, chilly sensations, extreme emotionality (exaggerated laughing or crying), and, most noticeably, dilation (widening) of the pupils. Many of the same symptoms are produced by marijuana, mescaline, DMT, and STP; they differ mainly in their quickness, intensity, and duration of effects. Do not hesitate to get medical attention for a child with any of these symptoms. Hospital emergency rooms deal with them every day.

The foregoing drugs usually come in the form of pills. PCP (phencyclidine, or "angel dust") can be in pills or powder, or be impregnated into cigarettes of tobacco, marijuana, or spearmint. Because it is relatively inexpensive, PCP is one of those drugs frequently sold as something else. It is an extremely dangerous drug, producing an astonishing variety of effects: depressant, stimulant, analgesic, hallucinogenic, anesthetic, and/or convulsant. In low doses it can produce euphoria and distorted perceptions similar to LSD. But daily use of PCP develops tolerance: Larger doses are required. High doses have bizarre, psychotic, unpredictable effects: violent aggression, unusual accidents, suicides, impulsive homicides. Along with complete loss of control, there seems to be an amnesia, so unlike LSD users, PCP users who have a "bad trip" have no bad memories to dissuade them from trying it again.

Any teenager who is believed to be on a PCP trip should be contained as calmly as possible. Because even a gentle person can suddenly become incredibly strong and destructive with an overdose of PCP, the police should be called to provide immediate transportation to a hospital.

Uppers. Amphetamines, or "uppers"—such as Benzedrine, Dexedrine, and methylamphetamine ("speed")—are a big drug problem in adults of all social classes, as well as in adolescents. They are stimulants, which means that they activate the sympathetic nervous system, constricting blood vessels, increasing heart rate and blood pressure, dilating the pupils and the windpipe, relaxing intestinal muscles and tensing other muscles, increasing blood sugar, and stimulating the adrenal glands. The results are alertness, wakefulness, attentiveness, and the kind of emotional stress reaction that comes when one feels as if one is about to be attacked.

These drugs are highly addictive, producing both dependence and tolerance. If you were to get your physician to prescribe an amphetamine as diet pills, they would help to suppress your appetite but only if taken every day. Soon one would need more pills just to keep from slowing down and feeling depressed. The same dependency arises in an athlete who takes speed as a pep pill or to increase endurance, and in a college student who uses it frequently to stay awake to finish a paper.

Ironically, these pills will not solve anyone's weight problem in the long run; they damage an athlete's physical conditioning; and they actually impair mental performance. A student who has not done three months' worth of reading assignments and lectures might improve his chances of passing the final if he stays up all night cramming (and stays awake during the test), but he is not going to learn anywhere near as much as the student who did the reading over a longer period with an unfatigued mind.

Speed is also used as a social drug, like marijuana or alcohol, to produce a "buzz," euphoria, and sensuality. After its use becomes chronic and a larger dose is needed, users may switch to intravenous injections, with the added risk of developing hepatitis or other diseases from contaminated needles. Few teenagers do this, but it is worth pointing out that those "helpful" pills you may have been depending upon, with your doctor's cooperation, can mushroom as a major threat to your children's lives.

Downers. Sedatives, or "downers," include *barbiturates*—drugs ending in *-al*, such as Amytal ("blues"), Nembutal ("yellows"), Seconal ("reds"), and Tuinal ("tooeys" or "rainbows")—and *tranquilizers*, such as Librium and Valium. They all have the opposite effect of that of stimulants, with equally disastrous possibilities.

These drugs do not create dependence as long as they are used in prescribed doses. Unfortunately, one's system gradually develops tolerance, so that larger doses are required to get the same amount of sedation. The larger doses then produce dependence in many users. It is said that more Americans are addicted to Valium than to any other drug, including alcohol. Most of these Valium addicts are women over thirty. With teenagers, barbiturates are more popular than tranquilizers.

Barbiturates serve different purposes for different users. One type of barbiturate abuser seeks more and more escape from stress, eventually retreating into oblivion. Another type seeks the opposite reaction, since, paradoxically, after one can tolerate large doses, barbiturates begin to have a stimulating effect similar to that of amphetamines. The third type is someone who takes sedatives in combination with other drugs—either in alternation with stimulants or LSD, to produce a cycle of ups and downs, or together with alcohol, which gives a quicker "high" but also a deeper depression soon afterward.

All three types are courting addiction. Again, we have to recognize the precedent we parents establish by our own overdependence on over-the-counter, as well as prescription, drugs. If you yourself have a problem with any of these drugs, the best thing you can do for your kids is to let them know how it came about, how it affects you, and what you are doing about it. Children can learn from negative role models as well as from positive ones, if their parents are honest and open with them.

Cocaine. If your children can afford this drug even occasionally, they have too much spending money. You should be as concerned about where they are getting the money as about the cocaine itself.

Whether sniffed or injected, cocaine produces a tremendous euphoria, similar to the effects of marijuana but more powerful, including sporadic paranoia and tactile hallucinations. Unlike marijuana, cocaine is energizing: continued use can produce insomnia and loss of appetite. "Crack" is cocaine in a form that is smokable, relatively inexpensive and uncontrollably addictive. It can damage lungs and promote the spread of AIDS through burned and bleeding lips. Worse, the violence that follows it from community to community make crack a terribly destructive element in our society. It is not enough to educate one's own children about this. We must all get involved to keep crack out of our towns.

Heroin and other "hard stuff." I consider all of the drugs discussed above very serious indeed; children who use any of them are drug abusers. Unfortunately, adolescents often reserve the phrase "hard stuff" for drugs that are "mainlined" (injected into the veins). If your kids are doing anything with needles, your problem is already beyond the scope of this chapter. Take the kid directly to a drug rehabilitation hospital.

An overdose is a medical emergency. Too many young people die of drug overdoses when their friends could have saved them by dialing 911 (or the equivalent emergency number in their area). Often the friends panic and run away, or they stay and try to restore consciousness while waiting for the effects of the overdose to wear off. They hope to save their friend (and themselves) from getting in trouble. For the person who has "OD'd" this can be a fatal or brain-damaging error; it is then also devastating for the friends who have let it happen. An injection or other proper medical treatment could have saved their friend's life.

Be sure, therefore, that your children know that they *must* call the police or paramedics if anyone they are with appears to have lost consciousness or to be physically out of control in any way. They must also recognize it as a medical emergency if anyone, who may be only moderately drunk or stoned, swallows a number of pills out of the medicine cabinet, perhaps in a suicide attempt. Regardless of how harmless the pills are believed to be, his or her friends must not wait to look for symptoms of an overdose.

The best rule of thumb for all situations is "If you're scared by what you see happening to your friend, call for help." They should be prepared to tell the paramedics as much as they can find out about what drug was taken, when and in what amounts, and what else the person had to eat and drink.

Possession. You don't need a rule in your family about possession of drugs unless you have reason to believe that your children are toying with them. However, if you do find drugs in your children's possession, or if one of your children is reported to be using any drug, then you need an immediate firm rule that will apply to every child in the family.

Although you have the legal right to search your children's rooms at any time, it is not a good idea unless other evidence first comes to your attention (a friend or teacher tells you your child is using drugs, or the child leaves clues where you can't help finding them). The principle to follow is: *Trust each child to the full extent that he or she has been trustworthy in the past.* Even learning that your child's best friend has been arrested for dealing quaaludes is not necessarily sufficient cause for invading your child's privacy. But if you find an unidentified tablet on the floor of the child's bathroom and your pharmacist tells you it looks like a quaalude, then that knowledge combined with the fact that the child's friend was selling quaaludes would be sufficient reason to do a complete search.

The first time you find any drugs at all, other than something you have authorized your children to take on their own (vitamins, perhaps a headache tablet), you should flush them down the toilet. If you want to know what the drugs are, and you do not believe your child's explanation, you can have them tested. But it is not really necessary to identify them before taking action.

Make sure all the children in the family know that you have found and destroyed a drug that should not have been in the house. Since no one is being punished the first time this happens (assuming you don't already have a specific rule about drugs), it is not important whose pills, powders, or joints they were. Announce a new rule for the future. A logical consequence might involve restricting relationships with other kids, since that is where the drugs come from. Let us say you choose grounding as the consequence. In this case it can't be a brief grounding. A month might be about right, for the first offense after you have given warning. "If we ever again find any unauthorized drugs, the one responsible for bringing them home will be grounded seven days a week, for a month. And we won't play detective: If we don't know which of you to punish, you will all be grounded." This speech contains two important phrases. "Unauthorized drugs" means anything you have not told your children to take; it avoids quibbling over what the pills or powders are that you have found, whether they are illegal, and so forth. "Person responsible" enables you to ignore the child's claims that the drug was left behind by a friend, or a friend of a friend.

This consequence will not prevent your children from experimenting with drugs in the future. It may make doing so less convenient. The most important result, however, is that it gives your children a very clear answer to their question "What do you think of this?" That is what they are asking, unconsciously, when they leave stuff where you are likely to find it.

If your rule is subsequently tested, make sure you follow through with it, *no questions asked*. There really is no need to hear all the excuses, all the extenuating circumstances.

> EXAMPLE: David, Laura, and Jim Robinson—ages sixteen, thirteen, and eleven, respectively—all swear they have no idea where the little heart-shaped pills their mother found in the TV room came from. Since neither parent brought the pills into the house, all three kids are punished. "How can you punish us, when we don't even know how they got there?!"
>
> "Maybe it seems unfair," Dad says calmly. "I'm willing to believe that those pills were not yours. But you are all responsible for making sure that no unauthorized drugs appear in this house. I guess you didn't do an adequate job of policing some of the kids that you brought home. It may just be bad luck, but you'll still have to take the consequence."

Should you be a tattletale? Yes. If your children name another kid as the possessor or purveyor, you may want to bar that kid from your house for a period of time (one or more months), in addition to punishing your own kids. *You should also call the friend's parent.* Many people are reluctant to do this. They use excuses like not having definite evidence, not wanting to be accused of libel, protecting their children from retaliation—but the truth is they are just too timid. Their reluctance prolongs and exacerbates the problem. If other kids were telling their parents that *your* kid were a pusher, wouldn't you want to know about it?

> EXAMPLE: You pick up the phone and a stranger nervously introduces himself: "Mrs. Jones, this is Frank Smith calling. My daughter Sandra is friends with Robert."
>
> *You:* Oh yes, I know Sandra.
>
> *Caller:* I feel a little awkward calling you like this, but my wife and I are very concerned about drugs, and we seem to have a problem.
>
> *You:* Oh my. Well, I hope Robert isn't involved.
>
> *Caller:* I don't know if he is or not, frankly. What I do know is that the kids say he is very involved. We found some pills and confronted Sandra, and she said that Robert brought them over here.
>
> *You:* So you really don't have any evidence. She could be blaming him just to get out of trouble.
>
> *Caller:* Yes, that's correct. However, Sandra is not out of trouble. She has been grounded for a month. We're not concerned with prosecuting Robert, though he won't be allowed over here for another month after Sandra's grounding is over. The only reason I called was to share with you what Sandra told us. Maybe it isn't even true, but you know Robert better than I do.
>
> *You:* Well, this is very upsetting. I have seen a package of pink pills, but he said they were just candy.
>
> *Caller:* They're not candy. I took them to a pharmacist, and he identified them as Secobarbital, a barbiturate.
>
> *You:* Oh. Well, thank you for calling.
>
> *Caller:* I'm sorry it wasn't pleasant news.
>
> *You:* No, it wasn't. But I'm glad you told me.

I made "You" the receiver of this call so that you could see that you would appreciate the other parent surmounting his embarrassment and telling you the facts, in a nonjudgmental, constructive way. Now you can feel confident about being the caller, if that occasion arises. You may not meet with the same friendly response this caller got. The other parent might hang up on you. Don't worry about it. You have done the responsible thing. It is the only way we parents can make inroads against teenagers' infatuation with drugs, and against the criminals who exploit it.

≡Know and use the laws

Whatever rules you make for your own children should be consistent with the rules of their school and your state and local laws. Parents put themselves on shaky ground if they try to be *less* strict than the law itself. For example, if the law prohibits possession of marijuana but you decide to allow possession of marijuana while prohibiting quaaludes, you are sending a confusing message.

Regardless of your attitude about the marijuana law—even if you strongly believe, as many do, that marijuana should be classed with tobacco—your best strategy as a parent is still to accept majority rule and support the law. That way the law supports you, and your position is clear, not only on the issues you have discussed explicitly with your children, but also on law-breaking in general.

Most schools publish a booklet that clearly enunciates their policy on drug possession, sales, or gifts on school grounds, buses, and at school functions. Usually there is a suspension for the first offense and expulsion after the second or third offense. Counselors may meet with the student, parents, and principal to arrange participation in an appropriate treatment program before the student is readmitted.

When you know the school rules in advance, you can frankly discuss with your children what the further consequences of suspension or expulsion should be. In addition, both you and the child should know exactly what your local and state laws say. You should know how the laws are normally enforced in your community.

- Do you and your teenagers know the legal age in your state for purchasing or consuming alcohol in a public place? Is the age requirement younger for wine and beer? Are minors arrested in your community under this law? What is the usual fine or jail sentence? In practice, the first offense usually results in only a warning, but if your child were fined, who would pay the fine? Make it clear.

- Possession of a small amount of marijuana, at any age, in any place, is illegal throughout the United States. However, enforcement of this law varies widely. For what amounts of marijuana, and for what other drugs, have there been arrests and convictions in your area? Are only the dealers arrested, or are the purchasers arrested, too? Who would post bail? Who would pay the fines?

• For how long are driver's licenses suspended after the first arrest for driving while intoxicated in your state? What about the second arrest? What happens to the insurance rates of a parent whose teenager is arrested for drunken driving? Who will pay the difference? (It is worth noting that judges are under increasing pressure to enforce drunk-driving laws more consistently than they have done in the past.)

• Any adult who furnishes alcohol to a minor (even in his own home) may be liable in a civil suit for monetary damages brought by anyone who suffers injury or property loss through the actions of any person intoxicated by that alcohol.

• Recently, many local communities have passed ordinances that allow adults to be fined (up to one thousand dollars in some towns) for serving alcohol to minors even if no damages result. These ordinances are serving as models for new state laws, which promise to have significant benefits if police departments and courts will enforce them. Does such a law exist in your town or state?

To get the answers to these questions, try calling your local police department. Ask to speak to the commander of the juvenile division. Or call the office of the chief judge of the juvenile court in your county or municipality.

≡"My friends do it, but I don't"

Mr. and Mrs. Roth were in my office with their ten-, thirteen-, and fourteen-year-old children, discussing their feelings about teenage drug use. They had made considerable progress in learning to communicate as a family, but drugs remained a topic on which, as one of the boys put it, "Mom gets hysterical."

Mrs. Roth was saying that if any of the kids' friends started using drugs, she would want them to drop that friend and have nothing to do with him. Her fourteen-year-old interrupted, "You don't drop your friends just because they've got problems. What about Mrs. Collins? She drinks too much. You're worried about her, and you tried to tell her she should go to the hospital. You didn't just tell her, 'Don't call anymore, I'm not your friend anymore.' "

The Roths had to admit that Roger had a good point. I think he was right. It is a natural impulse for parents to want their kids to separate themselves completely from any friends or acquaintances with serious problems, but that is neither realistic nor an action that we would consider moral in our adult relationships.

We will have to accept the fact that within any group of adolescents, some are more involved in drugs, some are less. If your child claims to be a nonuser among users, he may be telling the truth—or nearly the truth.

You should make it clear to your kids, however, that you will hold them responsible for any trouble their group as a whole gets into. If your daughter's friends are drunk, and one of them throws a bottle through a store window while she is with them, it is reasonable to say that the group as a whole was responsible. There should be a consequence for your daughter as well as for whoever actually threw the bottle. If she was together with peers who were engaged in anything you prohibit—drunkenness, vandalism, shoplifting, reckless driving, or whatever—and did not remove herself from the situation, she should be punished.

There are two principles involved. First, you simply cannot be a detective and evaluate the truth of your child's claim not to have been doing what the others were doing. You don't want to have to take a position as to whether you believe your children or not. If you challenge their claim, you undermine your relationship of mutual respect. But if you accept their statement on the basis of inadequate evidence (whether or not they are telling the truth), they may be tempted to lie in the future.

When the rule prohibits being in a group in which any members are doing the acts in question, you do not have to worry about degrees of guilt. You can say to your fourteen-year-old, "I'm glad to hear that you personally didn't have any beer. But because you were in the group that went out behind the school and passed some bottles around, you have to take the consequences. Our rule says that you will be grounded if you are in a group of kids in which *anybody* gets in trouble for consuming alcohol. The rule doesn't get into issues of how much you did or didn't join in with the others. Next time something like that happens, make sure nobody can even get the slightest impression that you might have been one of the ones involved."

The usual excuse is that "I didn't want to leave him because I was trying to get him home and keep him out of trouble." But this is such a universal cop-out that you should never yield to it unless you have independent evidence that your teenager really did everything possible to prevent trouble.

Parents may actually harm children when they accept their unsubstantiated protestations of being the innocent member of the group—the claim "My friends do it, but I don't." Although it is *possible* for your children to refuse drugs and still be accepted, you should be realistic. If the only friends he has are users, and if a majority of his social activities are of the "other people were doing it but I wasn't" variety, then he is probably lying to you.

≡How can kids refuse drugs and still be accepted?

The truth is that the child who declines offers of alcohol, pot, and pills does *not* automatically become unpopular with peers. The other kids will only exclude him or her from one kind of activity: parties whose sole purpose is to get high. Whenever there is any other purpose—playing music, going to the beach, making a homecoming float—the group is almost always tolerant of an idiosyncratic member who is not a part of the drug scene.

Keep in mind that even in communities where drugs are quite prevalent, not all teenagers follow that Pied Piper. If a high percentage do, that still leaves some who have the courage to refuse. Your children can choose friends from that group.

Furthermore, if their friends do get involved with drugs, your children do not necessarily have to lose them as friends. At a party, when they are offered something they do not want, they can say, "No, thanks." At that point, they may very well get an argument from the kid who is offering the drug. It is important to realize that this kid is not really as concerned about getting his friend high as he is about protecting and enhancing his own self-image: If other kids imitate him, he must be great. So it is a mistake to argue the merits or dangers of drug use if one doesn't want to be rejected as a friend. The most effective thing the child can do is simply to ask, "Can we still be friends even if I don't do drugs?"

If the answer is no, at least the nonuser has clearly established that he is being rejected because the other kid doesn't want straight friends, rather than because of anything else he did or said.

More often, however, the answer will be yes, and the group will find ways of including the nonuser in most of their activities. If he has a driver's license, his value to the group may be greater when everyone else has been drinking or smoking grass, and they can count on him to drive them home.

In any group, there is a range of differences. Some kids will be looked down on for going off the deep end, whereas your kids may be teased for being too straight. Yet if they do not argue the point but merely make a personal decision and stick to it, they will be respected for their courage and appreciated for the way they balance the excessive members of the group. Their individual decision reassures others that they, too, have a choice. Instead of having four beers, for example, the others can choose to stop at one or two; instead of using LSD, they can stop at marijuana.

An exercise to prepare children to say, "No, thanks." I suggest holding a family meeting when your oldest child is still only in sixth or seventh grade. You can discuss the kinds of peer pressure that the children anticipate, and you can rehearse different responses that they can try. Have the kids play the parts of the drug offerers, and you be the refuser; then switch roles. They will probably be more creative than you in thinking of ways to handle the situation.

Do not accept assurances from your kids that this sort of thing does not go on among their friends or at their school. It does go on at their school, and if none of their friends are involved in it yet, some of them soon will be. Point out that the rehearsal is only an exercise to reassure you that they would be able to handle a difficult situation if it should ever arise. It is just like a fire drill at school.

Going along with this role-playing exercise is not necessarily a promise from your kids that they will never experiment with drugs. It is a demonstration that they *can* choose to refuse. Thus it makes clear that they must be held accountable for whatever decisions they do make when the situation arises.

≡ Summary

The major part of what parents can do to prevent drug abuse involves making adolescents feel good enough about their bodies, their minds, and their futures so that they do not want to throw them away. A second part of the parents' task is seeing that children have accurate information about the effects of drugs. Direct rules about the observable results of using those substances are the smallest part of the parents' task.

It is not possible to draw up a ranked list of dangerous drugs, from least to most harmful. Their relative danger depends as much upon how they are used as upon the substances themselves. For example, everyone would agree that alcohol addiction is much worse than tobacco addiction. But occasional cigarette smoking is more dangerous than occasional consumption of alcohol, because continued cigarette smoking will almost surely lead to nicotine addiction, whereas most social drinkers will not become alcoholics.

Therefore parents are better off avoiding second-guessing (for example, "We'd better crack down on marijuana because it might lead to heroin"). Instead, make rules about the very things you are concerned about. When you and your partner sit down and ask yourselves *why* you want to insist that your children stay away from drugs, you will usually list things like school, jobs, family responsibilities, and other behavior that you really do have the power to enforce rules about.

SUGGESTED BOOKS: Drugs

Alibrandi, Tom. *Young Alcoholics.* Minneapolis: CompCare Publications, 1978.

Dusek, Dorothy, and Girdano, Daniel. *Drugs: A Factual Account* (4th ed.). New York: McGraw-Hill, 1986.

Milam, James, and Ketcham, Katherine. *Under the Influence: A Guide to the Myths and Realities of Alcoholism.* Seattle: Madrona, 1981.

Talbott, Douglas, and Cooney, Margaret. *Today's Disease: Alcohol and Drug Dependency.* Springfield, IL: Thomas, 1982.

Vaillant, George. *The Natural History of Alcoholism.* Cambridge, MA: Harvard University Press, 1983.

Wegscheider, Sharon. *Another Chance: Hope and Health for the Alcoholic Family.* Palo Alto, CA: Science and Behavior Books, 1981.

Books for Children

Hemming, Judith. *Why Do People Take Drugs?* (32 pp., grades 1-3). New York: Watts, 1988.

Hyde, Margaret. *Mind Drugs* (grades 7-11). New York: Putnam, 1986.

Hyde, Margaret and Bruce. *Know About Drugs* (64 pp., grades 4-6). New York: McGraw, 1979.

Martin, Jo, and Clendenon, Kelly. *Drugs and the Family.* New York: Chelsea House, 1990. *(Note: This is one of 50 separate volumes in the Encyclopedia of Psychoactive Drugs, which you will probably find in your school library or the children's section of your public library. Each title is on a specific drug or on a drug-related problem. They are equally good for parents and children to read together, or for 9-12-year-olds to read on their own.)*

CHAPTER SIXTEEN

Sex

Martha and Alan were in their twenties and engaged to one another before they "went all the way" for the first time. Now their children are in high school, and Martha and Alan want them to remain virgins at least until adulthood.

In the house next-door, Jim and Kate have a different attitude. They know that adolescents are becoming sexually involved much earlier (on the average) than was the case a generation or two ago, and they feel their children will be better prepared for marriage as a result. Kate took their daughter to a birth-control clinic when she started dating, although she was still a virgin; and they are seeing to it that their son is also completely informed about sex, contraception, and venereal disease.

Down the street live Jeff and Carolyn, who disagree with one another on the whole subject of teenagers and sex. Jeff is extremely worried, but only about his two daughters; he assumes that his son "can take care of himself." Carolyn is open to the idea that all three of their children are likely to have intercourse while still in high school. Carolyn wants her son to be as cautious and responsible about sexuality as she expects her daughters to be.

Parents in our society differ from one another in their attitudes about adolescent sexuality even more than they differ in their thinking about drugs. Yet I think we can make some assumptions about all the parents just mentioned, and about all readers of this book. I assume that you do not want your children plunging into sex irresponsibly; you do not want them procreating before they are ready to assume the responsibilities of parenthood; you do not want them to have to face the trauma of an abortion decision; you want them protected from venereal diseases, and you would want them to get proper treatment if they ever did contract a venereal disease; you do not want them hurt in ways that might spoil their enjoyment of mature sexuality throughout their lives; and you do not want them to hurt others.

There are differences between those kinds of concerns and the concerns we have about our children experimenting with unprescribed drugs. Drugs are something they can live without entirely; whereas sex is a source of joy and beauty, an expression of love, and our means of reproduction. Becoming a sexual adult is a central part of growing up. A child who learns to fear sex is as unfortunate as one who becomes involved with it too early or incautiously.

Nonetheless, my advice for parents is exactly the same as in dealing with concerns about drugs. The most important task is to build self-esteem, beginning practically from birth. The second task is education, which begins with "the birds and the bees" and adds honest explanations as soon as children are interested and capable of understanding them. Rules come in as a distant third. In fact, it is absolutely impossible to impose your standards about adolescent sexuality by trying to enforce rules about it. You can state your preferences, and you can provide information. Short of a twenty-four-hour-a-day chaperone, you cannot prevent your children from going as far as they decide they are ready to go.

There are many implicit rules, however, in the facts your children must learn about sex. Sex is replete with natural consequences. For example, "If you have intercourse without contraception, you are more than likely to become pregnant." Your discussions of sex will inevitably focus upon the various natural consequences of irresponsible sexual behavior.

But your children need more help from you than that. They also need to learn that sex is a fine thing, in the context of a warm, trusting relationship between willing and secure partners. They need to know where they can turn for answers to questions they may not feel comfortable asking you, or to which you may not have answers. And they need to know how to say "No" until they feel emotionally ready to have sex, or whenever they do not feel it is what they want with a particular partner.

No one can impart that knowledge better than a child's parents, if they can get past their possible discomfort in bringing up the subject. It does not matter if your own sexual experience is limited, or disappointing, or not the sort of model you hope your child will follow. You are not going to talk about your own experiences specifically. But the most effective way to show your children that questions about sex can be answered straightforwardly is by taking the lead in opening up the topic.

As with drug questions, you probably need to educate yourself first, about such questions as how teenagers can best prevent conception, how to recognize the symptoms of various diseases, and what to do about them. Again I shall only provide a brief outline of the kinds of information teenagers need. (The books listed at the end of the chapter provide detailed information.) First, however, we need to deal with the more general problem of how to talk about these issues with your children.

≡Don't wait for the child to ask

Despite the barrage of sexual stimulation all around us, and despite the revolution that has brought once-taboo topics into everyday social conversation, it is still not easy for most parents and children to talk with one another about sex. Although we may be more comfortable than our parents were about explaining the basic facts of reproduction, we are no more inclined than they were to go into detail. Nor do our children want to know anything specific about our sex lives, or to tell us anything specific about theirs. Yet they do have many questions, and there are many things they absolutely need to know. If the only way they can piece together answers to those questions is from what they hear on the street, they will be sadly misinformed.

Although your children probably have good books they can refer to, and although they may have a good sex-education program at school, they still need to hear a few words about essential topics from you. If they get the impression that their mother or father regards these as shameful or distasteful matters, it is difficult for them to feel positive about what is happening to their bodies or about the natural desires they are feeling.

Certain basic topics ought to be introduced during the elementary-school years, mostly to help children make sense out of the frequent allusions they hear and see, but also to prepare them for puberty and to establish certain attitudes. I think it is important for preadolescents to acquire the attitude that sex is a normal, happy part of adult life. I also think they should be made to feel that sex and all its natural consequences are topics about which they can get accurate information from reliable adults. (Sex is enough of a mystery for us adults; we needn't present it as even more of a mystery than it is.)

Most experts on sex education would agree that during the elementary-school years, children should be taught about procreation, gestation, and birth; about menstruation and other changes that will come with puberty; and they should be given correct explanations and reassurances to counteract misinformation that they are likely to get on the playground about masturbation, homosexuality, sexual deviance, and sexual abuse.

Procreation. The "facts of life" should be explained in a simple way, with pictures of the reproductive system, by the time a child is six or so. (There is no harm in telling them at four or five, if they are interested.) The emphasis should be on the miracle of how a baby grows from a fertilized egg. At this age, all the child needs to know about the sex act is that conception occurs when the father's penis deposits sperm from his testes into the mother's vagina, and that the sperm swim up the Fallopian tubes to meet an ovum from the mother's ovaries.

Over the next five or six years, the explanation will need to be repeated as occasions arise. Each time, the parents should be sensitive to new questions the child may have, as well as to old questions repeated.

You should explain—if not at the first telling of the story, then at one of your later retellings—that a baby is created only if the sperm get into the Fallopian tubes at just the right time to meet the ovum of the month. The implications of this point may not be fully understood at first, but it opens the way later to explain that mothers and fathers have intercourse as a part of making love to each other, not just one time for each child they want to have.

Menstruation. Girls need to learn about this part of growing up, from their mothers, *before* their first period, which often comes at age ten or eleven. It is astonishing and distressing how many girls, even today, have no idea why they are suddenly bleeding from their vaginas. They may then hear a speech from their mothers about how natural and wonderful it is, a manifestation of their capacity to bear children, but the rhetoric is belied by the fact that it has been kept a taboo topic until that moment, and by the mother's evident discomfort in having to talk about it.

Boys also need to learn about menstruation by the time it begins to happen to the girls they know. It is not unusual for a fifth-grade girl's period to start when she is in school, and for her not to discover it until it is obvious to all. Your son might be taken aback by this, or he might be one of those who intensify the girl's embarrassment. On the other hand, if you have prepared him, he might be the one who leads his classmates in reacting tactfully and maturely.

Masturbation. It is estimated that about two-thirds of all women masturbate on occasion, and nearly all have tried it at some time in their lives. As for men, the saying is that 95 percent of us admit to masturbating and the other 5 percent are lying. Among teenage boys, the ratio is probably more like ninety-nine to one. By the time they reach puberty, both boys and girls need to be told simply that masturbation is normal and harmless. Once you are sure your children know that much, it will probably require no further discussion.

Nearly all children play with their genitals as toddlers, but they usually stop at around age five, and when they resume doing so around the time they reach puberty, they do it privately. If your elementary-school child has a habit of rubbing himself or herself in public, it is best to say, "That doesn't look nice, and I wouldn't want kids teasing you about it. Let's get out of the habit of rubbing your crotch so much." If the habit doesn't begin to disappear, you can set up a reward system contingent upon stretches of time without public crotch-rubbing, similar to what you might do with gold stars for not wetting the bed (see chapter 5). The next step would be a rule with a negative consequence, such as being sent out of the room. If the problem persists, then it is a symptom of anxiety, and the child should get professional help.

Homosexuality. During the elementary-school years, children hear the word *gay*, call each other gay and use coarser epithets such as *queer* (which they pretty much mean literally), and they gradually learn that these words have something to do with effeminacy in men. By the time they are in fifth or sixth grade, they know that the words somehow imply deviant sexual relations, and they are sufficiently confused so as to need a reliable explanation. I suggest telling them that homosexuals are a minority (one man in about ten and one woman in about thirty) who prefer making love with members of their own sex. You can point out that homosexuals obviously can't make babies, but they can and do kiss and hug each other just like men and women do when they make love. I would also discuss the fact that some people make fun of homosexuals just because they are different, as others make fun of those whose race or religion is different. Don't be afraid to say anything positive about homosexuals, or to defend their rights, or to mention homosexuals of whom the child has heard, such as Tchaikovsky. Doing so will certainly not foster homosexuality in your child. Nor will any insulting remarks about homosexuals ensure your child's heterosexuality.

After puberty begins, both boys and girls frequently engage in a kind of sex play with members of their own sex, which would be called homosexuality if adults did it. For example, girls kiss and pet each other, or boys masturbate together. If you see that happening, you and your child may both need to be reassured that this is *not* an indication of incipient homosexuality. In most cases, the sex play includes fantasies about doing such things with the opposite sex.

Child molesters. The greatest sexual dangers to children do not come from their peers and are not a matter of voluntary choices. They come from adults: in the form of sexual abuse by relatives, rape by strangers (far less common), and exploitation in exchange for money, drugs, or simply shelter. This is a tragedy of severe proportions in our society.

It is important to make children aware of the fact that to a very small number of disturbed individuals, children are sex objects. You don't want them to get the idea that every stranger who says hi to them on the street is a potential child molester. Chances are that they will never have occasion to say no to a stranger offering them a ride, or run away from someone who exposes himself in the park or talks to them in a dirty way. But that is what they must be prepared to do, in case it does happen.

The real danger, it seems to me, isn't so much the existence of disturbed adults as the likelihood that the child will feel obligated to go along—either in fear of being hurt, or just not wanting to be rude. They should be taught, in advance, that any stranger who would put a child in that position is not a nice person and does not need to be treated with deference. Unfortunately, though, not all child molesters are strangers. The vast majority of people who succeed in sexually abusing children are relatives, probably because the child feels more obligated to go along and more frightened of being hurt—perhaps even blamed—if the acts become known. I would not suggest warning children about specific relatives or neighbors who have a history of acting "strange," but neither would I leave them alone with those persons.

Because there are safe ways to handle intimate advances from strangers, your child does not need to go around in fear. A child molester is not like a bogeyman who pounces on you from behind a tree. He (and he is never a she) is quite likely to be a timid person who will run away if the child runs away. The most intimidating thing he might say could be, "If you tell anybody, I'm going to come back and get you." When you are talking to your child about these hypothetical situations, tell him not to worry about a threat like that; the police will see that the person doesn't come back.

If you have informed your children, if you see that they are always accompanied or supervised by reliable adults until they are old enough to take care of themselves, and if you have provided them with a secure environment including rules of behavior, then you do not really need to be concerned about sexual abuse by adults. Then all you have to worry about is precocious sexuality between your children and their friends!

Talking with adolescents about sex. If you have taken the initiative during the elementary-school years to make sure your children have the accurate information they need at that age, then it won't be difficult to continue to take the initiative during their adolescent years. Do not say to yourself, "My child would feel comfortable coming to me with any questions or problems."

Your child probably would not, no matter how good a relationship you have. Your daughter might not spontaneously say to you, "I have had intercourse with Doug and I plan to do so again; how can I prevent pregnancy?" Your son might not initiate the question "Marilyn says she won't get pregnant if I withdraw before ejaculating; is that true?" *You* need to bring up these subjects, or at least the general subject.

In the following section, I shall list briefly the most important facts you should be sure your teenager knows. What I said in chapter 11 about active listening applies to this educational process just as it does to conflicts between parents and children: Take turns speaking and listening. When you are expressing your concerns as a parent, talk about your own feelings, including your fears, and avoid criticizing the child's character. When you are listening to the child, ask questions to be sure (and to show the child) that you understand what he is saying, but don't interrupt, and don't respond with your own point of view until the child is ready for you to become the speaker.

EXAMPLE: Marianne overhears one of her fourteen-year-old son's closest friends ask another friend, "Did you fuck her?" She thinks about the implications of this for a couple of days and then decides to have a talk with her son about it.

Marianne: Is this a good time to talk with you about something?

George: About what?

Marianne: I overheard something the other night that kind of upset me, and I wanted to be straight with you, ask you to explain what was going on, and tell you how it made me feel.

George says nothing.

Marianne: Can we talk now?

George: I guess so.

Marianne: Barry was telling you and Peter something about a girl, and I think I heard Peter ask him, using a crude word, whether he had had intercourse with her.

George: So you listen in on our conversations.

Marianne: Well, I was in the living room, and you three were here in the kitchen. I wasn't making an effort to eavesdrop, but since that's not the kind of word I usually hear in this house, it did catch my attention.

George: I can't control what my friends say.

Marianne: That's not why I mentioned it. I was more concerned about Peter's question, and I didn't hear Barry's answer.

George: His answer was yes, but he was lying. We always say stuff like that. Guys brag about their exploits. Don't worry, nothing like that really happens.

Marianne: Well, I've got a couple of things I want to say. I just want to express my feelings. I'm not giving you the third degree; I just need to feel that you're listening. Okay?

George: Sure.

Marianne: It would help if you'd turn around and look at me. (George turns halfway toward his mother.) Thanks. The first thing I want to say is that it's not true that things like that don't happen at your age. They do happen. If you and your friends aren't getting involved with sex yet, some of your classmates undoubtedly are, and it's likely you and Peter and Barry will have girlfriends in the next few years, with whom you may decide to have sex.

George: Come on, Mom, I don't need a lecture. Don't worry—I'm not going to get in trouble.

Marianne: Please don't answer me until you find out what I'm concerned about. I guess it might sound like a lecture, but it's not. It's exploring whether you have thought about certain things.

George: I have.

Marianne: You have thought about sex, or you have thought about what I'm talking about?

George: Both.

Marianne: Well, you haven't heard what I want to say yet. It's about the word *F-U-C-K*. It's a word that is demeaning, especially the way Peter used it. It implied doing something *to* the girl, like she was an object, not a human being. And it also implied a one-time thrill, rather than part of a relationship between Barry and whoever he was referring to. You know what I mean?

George: Yeah.

Marianne: You do?

George: Yeah, but it didn't really mean that. They were full of bull anyway.

Marianne: Well, I figured that was probably the case. But I wanted you to know that as a woman, and also as someone who cares about you, it hurts my feelings to hear sex talked about that way even in jest.

George: I didn't say it.

Marianne: Do you understand how I feel?

George: Yes, I do. And I've heard all this before. Sex is a relationship between two people.

Marianne: Well, I'm glad you've heard it, and I hope you believe it.

George: I do.

There is no denying that this mother was lecturing her son, but she did so in a way that focused upon her own feelings, avoided accusations, and was frank and unembarrassed without violating the appropriate gap between generations.

A big mistake parents sometimes make when trying to convey their preferences about sex (as also about drugs and other issues) is to try to support their arguments with ominous consequences. This invariably backfires.

MISTAKE 1 (mythology): "If you don't remain a virgin, men will think you're a tramp and you'll never get a husband." This is not true today (probably not yesterday either), and she knows it. You'll lose your credibility.

MISTAKE 2 (theology): "If you get involved in sex before marriage, God will punish you." Not true. God does not have a good record for following through with consequences in this world, and the expectation of divine retribution in the next world has rarely been an effective deterrent against human temptations.

BETTER: Talk about the moral aspect of sex in terms of love and respect—for God, if you will, but also for other human beings. Morality is a matter of social responsibility and of treating others as you would want them to treat you.

MISTAKE 3 (empty hyperbole): "If you get a girl pregnant, I'll kill you." You won't, and he knows it. So you're sending the message that you feel strongly about birth control, but you are failing to state the explicit consequences besides the fact that you will be upset.

BETTER: "Getting involved in sex just for the physical or emotional thrill of it, without regard to the consequences, is irresponsible. Within marriage, or within a long-term, loving relationship between adults, sex is very positive and important. But in your situation, there are hazards. We want to be sure you're aware of them so you can make responsible decisions."

In all three of these cases, the attempted "consequences" are empty threats. Yet sexual relations do have consequences—natural ones—and the purpose of talking with teenagers about sex is to be sure they are aware and have thought about those risks. Your purpose is not to scare your children but to focus them realistically upon the considerations that a responsible person would keep in mind.

≡What adolescents need to know about "getting involved"

I think most Americans realize that their children will get involved with sex long before marriage. We are in less of a hurry than our parents were for our children to marry. In the light of unprecedented numbers of divorces, more parents are encouraging their young people not to marry until they are mature enough to make responsible choices and a permanent commitment to each other. At some point in that process of maturing, they are very likely to have sex with somebody. There is an increase in teenage sexuality as compared with previous generations, but even more significant is the decrease in guilt and secrecy among teenagers who are nonvirgins, compared to the way their counterparts felt in the 1950s and early 1960s. Although many parents still imply that there is something illicit about sex between adolescents, television, the movies, and popular magazines glorify sexuality. Adolescents cannot help but identify themselves with the images that surround them, especially when the sexy models and movie stars are adolescents like themselves.

Nationwide, by 1973 (when the most recent large-scale surveys were done) it was estimated that 30 percent of girls and 44 percent of boys had had intercourse by age fifteen, 72 percent of boys and 57 percent of girls by age nineteen. In the last ten years, those figures may have risen somewhat (probably not a great deal).

You can adjust the age upward or downward based on what you know about your own children and their peer groups, but on the average, it is a reasonable guess that half the sixteen-year-olds you know have already had intercourse with someone. This means that the vast majority of adolescents will have had to make *decisions* about sex prior to that age. It is certainly not something that parents can close their eyes and wish away.

The phrase *sexually active* is often used for nonvirgins, but it is a misnomer. In the first place, most sexual activity among teenagers does not include intercourse; many actively sexy teenagers are still virgins. In the second place, most teenagers who have had intercourse do not have it very often. So in that sense, not being a virgin does not make them sexually active. Many have had intercourse only once or twice—perhaps to find out whether they were ready, perhaps to prove something to themselves or their friends —and then decided to go more slowly in subsequent relationships. So it is a mistake to assume that if one's child has had some sexual experiences, subsequent relationships necessarily involve intercourse. And it is an enormous mistake to confuse "sexually experienced" with "promiscuous," which might be implied by "sexually active." (Indiscriminate coupling with many partners will be discussed later.)

Teenagers should be educated about three different kinds of hazard they face when they decide to begin having sexual relationships: pregnancy, venereal infection, and emotional damage. For each area, I shall briefly outline the facts that you should be sure your teenagers understand. A short chapter on this subject is no substitute for the thorough treatments in the books suggested in the bibliography, but it will serve to get you thinking and talking about subjects you might have been tempted to avoid.

Pregnancy. The chances are that while your child is still a virgin, he or she will hear of someone getting pregnant "accidentally." This is a wonderful opportunity for you to say, "Anyone who has intercourse without any birth control is trying to make a baby. It is ridiculous to call it an 'accident.' What do people do when they are trying to make a baby? If a couple want to get pregnant, they have intercourse without taking any contraceptive precautions. So if you do that, you have as good a chance as anyone of making a baby. If that happens to you, we won't call it an accident.''

You should also be sure that your children realize:

- that a girl can get pregnant the very first time she has intercourse.
- that a boy can get a girl pregnant the first time he has intercourse.
- that there is a chance of conceiving at just about any time during the menstrual cycle (the rhythm method works only if a woman has kept daily temperature records to ascertain precisely when and how regularly she ovulates).
- that the number of one's different partners has nothing to do with the likelihood of conception.
- that the female orgasm has nothing to do with conception.

Teenagers circulate many erroneous myths about conception and contraception. The biological explanation of reproduction is not enough. They understand about the sperm and the ovum, but many crucial details have been left out of the accounts they were given when younger. Unfortunately, these additional "facts" are often supplied by misinformed peers. You don't have to weed out those myths one by one; you can simply state the truth and say, "Anything you may have heard to the contrary is not true; don't believe it, and don't let your friends believe it."

Talking about birth control does not mean you are encouraging your teenagers to have intercourse.

EXAMPLE: A sensible approach, which does not suggest or endorse early sexuality, is to say, "At some time in the next ten years it is pretty likely that you will be in love with someone and want to get involved in sex with them. That doesn't mean you'll have to gamble with having a baby nine months later. Frankly, young adults are ready for sex before they are ready to be parents. I suggest you wait until you are sure you are ready for sex and the relationship is the kind in which you can feel very comfortable about having sex. But when the time comes, birth control is something you must plan for in advance and be responsible about."

"Birth control" may mean the pill or diaphragm (both of which require a doctor's consultation), condoms, or refraining from intercourse before and after ovulation each month (the "rhythm" method). Withdrawal before ejaculation is a method of birth control only in principle; among teenagers, it does not work in practice. Obviously, no method works unless it is used without error and without exception.

The most reliable method of contraception for teenagers may be condoms used with vaginal spermicidal foam. The reason is that this combination of two moderately effective methods has the best chance of being used as directed; other methods are more effective under ideal conditions, but also more likely to be improperly inserted (diaphragm), forgotten (pill), or miscalculated (rhythm). Also, because birth control pills can have side effects for some women when used for many years, it may be unwise to start a girl on this method when she is still in her teens, especially if she is not going to have intercourse on a regular basis.

However, I think this decision should be made by the young people themselves, and they should not be asked to report to you. Let your son and daughter know why you are concerned; make sure they have all the facts and know how to get a doctor's advice; and then leave the decision up to them. It is important to make it easy for them to visit a doctor or clinic without discussing the visit with you. If this discussion takes place when you know your teenager is already involved in a sexual relationship, then you can insist that he or she (with partner, preferably) consult a particular doctor immediately. But I think it would be an invasion of their privacy to insist on knowing the results of that consultation.

If the discussion takes place earlier, merely as preparation, it is a good idea to present the medical consultation as something you expect the child to do when the time comes, without necessarily telling you about it. (You can even reimburse them in advance for the cost of the visit, telling them you will hold them accountable for the money, with interest, if they get pregnant.) Recently, rumors circulated among teenagers in the Northeast that clinics dispensing birth control were required to notify a girl's parents. That rule had been proposed in Congress but was not actually in effect. The rumor alone was sufficient to reduce by 34 percent the use of the pill, IUD, and diaphragm by girls under fifteen and the pregnancy for that same age group increased by 93 percent.

Birth control is not merely something for parents of girls to be concerned about. It is just as important to be sure your son is aware of his responsibility for precautions against pregnancy. Perhaps it is even more important, because girls know that they will bear the consequences of any "accidental" conception, whereas a boy can delude himself into thinking that it is only the girl's problem. He may be tempted to believe that "she can always get an abortion," or "no one can prove I'm the father," or he can use such excuses as "I assumed she was on the pill." You need to make him realize that you would consider him as responsible as the girl. If she were to elect to keep the child, he would be its father; if you would expect him to take on that role and contribute to the child's support, let him know that now. If she were to have an abortion, would you expect him to pay part of the cost? Go with her to the clinic? Let him know that now. If she were to put the child up for adoption, he would have no legal right to stop her. That, too, he should think about in advance.

All such considerations involve decisions by parents. Before they ever become an issue, you need to think through what your response would be if your daughter were to become pregnant, or if your son were to make a girl pregnant. Of course you do not know exactly what your reactions would be, because they depend on the ages of the two young people, who the partner is, what their options are in terms of education and jobs. But you can discuss all the possible outcomes that might occur as a result of extramarital pregnancy. You don't know which of these consequences your family would wind up choosing, but you and your teenager do know that none of them would be desirable.

Venereal disease. Venereal diseases—literally, "diseases of Venus" goddess of love—include dozens of different infections communicated through sexual contact. Some are easily treated; others have as yet no cure. The most important thing for teenagers (and adults) to know is that none of these diseases goes away by itself. Without exception, every venereal disease gets worse the longer the treatment is delayed. Not only does it spread to every new sexual partner, but in the case of some diseases—gonorrhea and syphilis, in particular—the infection spreads through the nervous system, causing brain damage and eventually death if it is not treated. Therefore, any genital itching, pain, inflammation, or unusual discharge should be reported immediately to a physician.

Teenagers are usually even worse informed about venereal diseases than they are about conception. Many think gonorrhea is like a cold: "You just cut out sex until you get over it." Be sure that your kids and their friends know that they will not "get over it" without prompt medical treatment. Sometimes, unfortunately, the symptoms do disappear for a while, so one thinks the infection is gone. But it is certain to return, and in the meantime one can still infect others.

The second thing every teenager who has sexual relations should know is that it is possible to be carrying a venereal disease without being aware of it. A boy can catch gonorrhea or chlamydia, to name only two examples, from a girl who never knew she had it. It is not enough for him to be treated with penicillin. Unless she, too, is treated, he will be reinfected the next time they make love. Conversely, the vaginal infection called trichomoniasis produces symptoms only in the female, but her partner will carry it back to her after she has been cured, unless he too has taken the pills.*

Venereal diseases are not only spread through intercourse. They are also spread by external genital-genital contact, and some can be spread by oral contact as well. Teenagers must understand that contraceptive precautions, such as condoms, are not sufficient protection against venereal disease.** The infection occurs without penetration, without ejaculation, without an orgasm; it is simply a matter of contact between the infecting agent and any warm, moist environment.

At least three venereal diseases—gonorrhea, chlamydia, and

* Often teenagers will share their VD pills with friends, hoping to save them the embarrassment and expense of visiting their own doctors. However, this leaves them with an inadequate dose of medication, and no one is cured.

* * Furthermore, birth-control pills actually increase the chances of a girl becoming infected. The normal acidity of the vaginal secretions kills many germs, so that a single act of intercourse with a male who has gonorrhea will infect the female only about 45 percent of the time. But the pill changes those secretions from acid to alkaline, and makes the likelihood of her infection nearly 100 percent.

herpes simplex 2—are epidemic among American youth. The reason we hear so much about herpes is that no cure for it has yet been found. Someday a cure or preventive vaccine (since herpes is a virus) may be found, but in the meantime its victims suffer occasional bouts of intense pain. The outbreaks recur periodically, affect all the subsequent sexual relationships, and endanger their children during pregnancy. Herpes is no joke.

AIDS has done a lot to heighten our awareness, and our children's, about venereal infection. Somehow its deadliness and the acceptability of speaking frankly about it have made more people realize what was equally true of syphilis, gonorrhea, and herpes: When you have sex with anyone, you are having sexual contact with everyone that person had sex with, and everyone *they* had sex with (or shared a needle with), for years in the past. Teenagers and young adults who regard the AIDS risk seriously enough to use condoms will protect themselves from all other sexually transmitted diseases as well. Unfortunately, if AIDS gets so much attention that it becomes the only risk they consider, and if they consider their partners very unlikely to have been infected with the AIDS virus, they may risk contracting the routine diseases like gonorrhea, which have been with us much longer and which are just as common among teenagers who have sex as among adults.

Therefore, in addition to the point about the network of sexual contact, I think it is important to be sure young people understand the following facts. Heterosexual men and women are just as capable of transmitting and of contracting the AIDS virus as homosexuals are. Worldwide, as many women as men have died of AIDS; this will be true in the United States, too, before a cure is found. In fact, the U.S. Army now finds as much AIDS virus among its adolescent female recruits as among males. Any prostitute or promiscuous person (or anyone who has had even one sexual contact with a prostitute or with another person who has had contact with a prostitute, etc.) should be regarded by your daughter or son as a dangerous sexual partner.

Besides the bacterial and viral infections, one should mention crabs and scabies, itching conditions caused by insects that burrow into the skin. Unlike the diseases mentioned above, these can be spread from one person to another even without sexual contact— for example, by sleeping in a bed or a sleeping bag previously occupied by someone with crabs. Teenagers, being less scrupulous about where they sleep than their parents might be, are more prone to crab lice and scabies mites.

The purpose of giving young people all this information is not to scare them into vows of celibacy—that would not work anyway—but to make them think about their sexual partnerships in advance. Every effort should be made to select partners who they can be reasonably sure are uninfected, or to refrain from sex until they have been treated. Contracting a venereal disease is not an inevitable result of adolescent sexuality. But it is an inevitable result of promiscuity.

It is important not to impose any additional consequences on an adolescent who contracts a venereal disease. The symptoms themselves, the embarrassment of divulging them, and the diagnosis and treatment are more than enough punishment. In fact, a teenager who behaves responsibly in these circumstances, seeking appropriate medical care for self and partner, is to be praised. If they expect to be punished, they may fail to get medical attention until the disease has advanced to a more dangerous stage.

Feelings. There is a third set of considerations that adolescents should be made to think about, besides the risks of pregnancy and infection. In some ways, these issues may be more difficult for parents to talk about with their children, because they involve some candor about our own sexual relationships. It has to do with the fact that sex is a bond between two people. It is never just a physical act.

I consider this an essential area in which parents should educate their children. You will find occasions like the one that Marianne found (earlier in this chapter) when she overheard her son's friend refer to sex crudely, as a demeaning exploitation of a girl.

In fact, more than feelings are at stake. Both pregnancy and venereal disease result, in most cases, from too much concern with the sex act and too little concern with one's responsibility to the partner and others. When boys begin to talk in terms of "scoring," suggesting that sex is a game with winners and losers, or when girls think of sex as the price with which they purchase a boy's attention, the risk of pregnancy and of venereal disease is high. On the other hand, when neither partner is out to exploit the other, when both are interested in intimacy and mutual caring, and when their sexuality is not an act of defiance against their parents, they are likely to take appropriate precautions.

Sociologists have discovered a disturbing change in adolescent norms over the past decade or so. In the fifties and sixties, there was much more passion in the high school set than there was sex. "Going steady" was the ultimate bliss; it rarely meant "going all the way." "Love me tender" had to do with interpersonal feelings, perhaps with kissing and petting. Teenagers who were known to be promiscuous were looked down upon, while those who were in love were admired. I had been in love several times before I went to college in the early 1960s, but I was a virgin and so were most of my classmates.

More recently, the opposite values have prevailed among teenagers. Sex is acceptable at an earlier age, but only if it is casual. An intimate relationship between two adolescents is likely to be laughed at by their peers, or simply discouraged by the norm of socializing in groups of three or more. The sex taboo has been replaced by a love taboo.

The principal danger for our children might not be sex itself, but the attitude that sexual liaisons are merely a two-person variation of masturbation. They are not supposed to be romantic: As the Beatles suggested, "Why don't we do it in the road?"* Parents who see this attitude in their kids might want to express their feelings about it. How can this be done?

One way to make your attitude clear is by approaching your child privately, as Marianne did in the earlier example, and using the active-listening techniques to have an open dialogue. "I just want to express my feelings," she said. "I'm not giving you the third degree; I just need to feel that you're listening." Another thing Marianne might have done would have been to confront George and his friends on the spot.

Confrontation requires sensitivity, because there is a thin line between confrontation and harassment, or between embarrassing the adolescent a little and cruelly humiliating him. If you succeed in pulling it off forthrightly, it can be very effective.

* There is a direct parallel between the deromanticizing of the drug experience, reducing it from "consciousness-raising" to "getting high," and the deromanticizing of sex, reducing it to "getting off."

EXAMPLE: You overhear George boasting to two friends about a sexual exploit, real or imagined. You enter the room and say, "It doesn't sound like Sharon is a human being to you. I don't know whether you're telling the truth about your encounter with her, but if you are, I wonder if she cared as little for you as you seem to care for her." That's all, then you walk out of the room. You have taken the opportunity to confront George with the discrepancy between his behavior and a set of values that you would respect. You have pulled off this confrontation without hostility, but with just enough public embarrassment to make it a negative experience for George. It works because you focused on how his description sounded to you rather than on him as a person.

Rules about privacy and modesty. There is one area in which you can and should enfore rules about sexuality: with respect to privacy. Exactly as with drugs, you cannot control what your children do in private, but by controlling what they do in public, you can convey a set of standards. Therefore, I see nothing wrong with rules that force your teenagers to keep their trysts private, even if it is no secret that they occur.

EXAMPLE: Debbie's parents know that she and Carl have a sexual relationship, because she asked her mother for birth-control information. Nonetheless, Carl is not allowed to sleep over, nor may Debbie invite him up to her bedroom and close the door. "The only reason I can give you," her father explains, "is that it makes us uncomfortable. In our house, we have the right to be comfortable."

On the other hand, Carl's parents have taken a different attitude. "We expect you and Debbie to be as discreet as we have been all these years in our own bedroom. You can have privacy behind your closed door, so long as we don't hear or see any X-rated scenes."

The same principle extends beyond sexual activity, to modesty and decorum in general. You may feel that your daughter's bikini top is too sexy to be worn downtown, or that your son's jeans with the hole worn through on the buttock are unseemly. If your feeling is only a preference, don't go on expressing it again and again; that is nagging. But parents have the right to make rules about clothing, makeup, and decorum—provided that the rules are stated in a form you can enforce.

Promiscuity. I don't want to list promiscuity as one of the "hazards" of teenage sexuality, because it is not a hazard for the vast majority of young people. Adolescents do not become promiscuous (have intercourse with many partners, and without regard to relationships) as a result of having started at an early age. Those who do become promiscuous are using a faulty solution to try to deal with deeper problems, just like those who turn to drug abuse. If you have reason to believe that your son or daughter is using sex in that way, don't try to deal with the problem by strict rules. This child needs professional help, probably through family therapy.

≡Summary

Raising adolescents who will be responsible about their developing sexuality is not accomplished by rules about sex itself. It is accomplished by making young people feel so good about themselves that they want to protect their own futures, and good enough about other people that they will automatically want to protect their girl- or boyfriends from being hurt, too. You do this by being clear about many other rules, before sex even becomes an issue.

Equally important, at puberty, parents have to educate their children about the biological and interpersonal aspects of mature sexuality, and especially about the natural consequences that follow irresponsibility in sexual activity. Those consequences include pregnancy, venereal infections, and damaged relationships.

Only as a third step can we add some explicit rules and consequences about the superficial details of sexuality—for example, what things are to be kept private, what standards of modesty you expect.

SUGGESTED BOOKS: Sex

AIDS: Answers for Everyone (96 pp., grades 6-12). Treehaus Communications, 1989.

Calderone, Mary, and Johnson, Eric. *The Family Book About Sexuality.* New York: Harper and Row, 1981.

Cartland, Cliff. *You Can Protect Yourself and Your Family From AIDS.* Old Tappan, NJ: Revell, 1987.

Lewis, Howard R., and Lewis, Martha E. *The Parent's Guide to Teenage Sex and Pregnancy.* New York: St. Martin's Press, 1980.

There are many excellent books for children on reproduction, puberty, and sexual relations. Because it is so important that your choice be appropriate to your own communication style as well as to your children's maturity, I recommend reading as many books as you can in your library or bookstore before selecting them for your children.

PART III.

Special Topics

Parts I and II were for all parents. The remaining chapters are for those who face special problems. Chapters 17, 18, and 19 deal with the difficulties of being a single parent, a stepparent, or a divorced parent without custody. Chapters 20 and 21 discuss extreme behavior problems—how to recognize them and what to do about them—and what to do if you cannot make the author's system work in your family.

Many other special problems are not discussed—for example, the special child, the adopted child, the only child, and families belonging to racial or religious minorities. Whatever makes a family's experiences different—for example, the questions that arise for the adopted child, and the awkward or ignorant remarks about adoption that he may hear from others—should be acknowledged within the family, *not* denied. However, such special difficulties only increase the importance of everything that has been said in Parts I and II.

CHAPTER SEVENTEEN

Single Parents

Thus far, I have emphasized the importance of both parents' agreeing upon their rules and collaborating in enforcing them. But what if there is only one parent? If you are one of the 6.3 million parents in the United States who must do the job without a partner, you can still use the system described in this book. You won't need to worry about getting another person to agree with your rules, unless there is someone else in your home (a grandparent, for example) whose help you rely on in enforcing them. But you will need a consultant or two, friends with whom you can share your thinking and planning.

For purposes of this book, a single parent is anyone with legal custody of a child and with no live-in partner helping to maintain that child's home.* If a new partner moves in with you and your child, I no longer call you a single parent (see chapter 18). If you are a parent without custody, whether single or remarried, your situation raises different issues (see chapter 19).

In the first part of this chapter, I address all single parents without partners, who have custody of their children. Then I shall

---

* Some married mothers feel like single parents because their husbands are away a lot or take no active part in the child-rearing. If you are one of those, this chapter is *not* for you. What you need to do is insist that your husband start acting like a father. If that leads you into marriage counseling, fine. If it leads to divorce, *then* you will need this chapter.

discuss some issues that depend upon whether the children also have a relationship with their other parent.

≡Cautions for all single parents

Are single parents more likely to need written rules than married parents? Not necessarily. Many children of single parents are extremely cooperative, so they and their parents never fall into the vicious circle of behavior problems . . . nagging instead of clear rules . . . more behavior problems. It is *parents under stress* who need written rules; and being single is one factor that might make you a parent under stress.

Whether you are divorced or widowed, with daily responsibility for one or more children, some of your biggest difficulties are likely to relate to time and money. Two people can handle their children's needs as long as one of them can earn enough money alone, or as long as they can earn enough by both working and sharing the child care. A single parent, on the other hand, not only has to support the family but also must pay for child care.

In addition, there is the problem of spending time with other adults. No child can or should meet the parent's need for companionship. But your social life decreases your time with your child and adds to your expenses as you pay for extra child care. If, instead, you cut back on adult relationships (romantic and otherwise) you probably increase the stress in your two full-time jobs as worker and parent.

Along with the problems caused by being a single parent, you may have emotional sources of stress—for example, grief over the loss of your spouse, or anger and depression following a bitter separation. Clear rules and expectations for your children will help you to be a better parent under stress, but they will not make the sadness, grief, anger, loneliness, or depression go away. Those internal stresses require time, friends, and sometimes professional counseling.

Stress tests. When children sense that their parents are under stress and fear that the parents may not be able to cope with that stress, they don't always react in the way we might wish them to react, in order to reduce the stress. Instead, they sometimes become depressed and withdrawn, which gives the parent something else to worry about, or else they test the parent's breaking point.

That sounds crazy. Why would children who are afraid their parents may reach the breaking point go ahead and push them toward it? The answer is expressed in the Irish saying "Better the devil ye know than the devil ye know not." Your child knows what you are like when you are furious with him: You are not happy, you are not nice, but you are alive and attentive and engaged with him, even if what you are engaged in may feel like mortal combat. That is far less terrifying than the possibility, which he unconsciously fears, that you might just cave in. The child does not want to believe that you could run out of energy, literally "break down." So he keeps testing you.

The only solution is to pass that test so decisively and consistently that the child gradually gets over that fear. Be a clear parent; use the system described in Part I. Children of all ages feel reassured when they find that their parents can be relied upon. There is no better way to demonstrate your reliability than by making rules (which are really just predictions about your own behavior in particular circumstances) and following through on them.

You don't have to do it without help. When you are ready to draw up your list of rules, or to add to the list, or revise it, or experiment with different consequences, talk it over with a friend first. If you know other single parents, you can be sounding boards for one another.

In the two-parent situation, the fact that they have to agree with one another and help each other enforce the rules guarantees that the two parents will do some discussing and debating. Thus they serve as checks and balances on one another. If one parent is inclined to overreact about an issue, the other can suggest moderation.

> EXAMPLE: I was upset at my five-year-old's persistent habit of lying on the floor two feet from the TV, looking up at it. Convinced that he was straining his neck and searing his eyeballs (that was what they told me when *I* was five), I had told him many times to move back. Finally, I indicated a line on the carpet and threatened that if I saw him closer to the

TV than that line, it was going to be turned off for the rest of the day. His mother came to our rescue by asking whether turning it off for five minutes might not be just as effective. We made it a written rule. He still tended to forget the rule, so we raised the penalty to ten minutes and the problem soon disappeared. The "rest of the day" threat had been an over-reaction to my own frustration.

During most of the child's waking hours, he is with one parent or the other, not both, even in a two-parent household. In applying a system of rules, the two parents' main benefit to one another is in the planning phase, having somebody to talk over the problems, crises, and decisions with at the end of the day. There is no reason that single parents cannot arrange to have that opportunity, too; two single parents can perform that service for each other. That is also what neighbors and sisters-in-law are for, not to mention hotlines, pediatricians, and counseling services.

Boundary confusion. Testing the parent's ability to cope is not the only explanation for problem behavior in single-parent families. Another problem is the child's possible confusion about the normal boundary between the generations. Throughout this book, I have referred to the importance of that boundary. It is even more important in single-parent families. The child may misunderstand his role, thinking he is supposed to replace the lost spouse as your best friend, emotional support, and equal partner in decision-making.

Children do not really want that kind of responsibility for their parents' welfare. Yet if they sense that their parent needs to have them in that role, they will try to take it on. They may even see some short-term advantages (later bedtimes, more choices) in being treated so democratically. Yet we know they don't feel comfortable about it, as shown, for instance, by the fact that arguments and tantrums increase. As one mother told me about her thirteen-year-old son, "I told him if he would act more mature, I'd treat him like a friend instead of a child. But the more I let him get away with, the more childishly and irresponsibly he acts."

Children of single parents. It is difficult to generalize about children in single-parent families, because many other factors have greater influences upon their personalities, needs, and problems than the mere fact that they live with only one parent. The child who has never known a father; the child whose father or mother has died; the child whose parents have been through a relatively amicable divorce (as compared to a bitter divorce or a desertion) —all these experiences are so fundamentally different that there is no reason to expect the children to resemble one another at all in terms of self-esteem, competence, or behavior problems. Other factors that make a difference are the age at which the loss occurred, the number and ages of siblings who suffered it together, and the personalities of the parents both before and after it occurred.

For those reasons, I have listed some valuable books that focus separately on coping with divorce, death, or never having known the father, and which offer detailed discussion of the issues related to the number of children, their ages, and other family circumstances. (See also the books listed at the end of chapter 21.)

One generalization can safely be made about all such children: The events that create a single-parent family are powerful forces in shaping a child's development. A parent's death, desertion, or divorce leaves emotional wounds in the child just as it does in the remaining parent. Discipline may be necessary, but it will not be sufficient to heal the wounds. Don't be afraid to acknowledge, "My child is in pain and needs professional help."

≡When the other parent is in the picture

Up to this point, I have been referring to all single parents. Your own particular experience will depend on many different factors, including your economic situation and your social-support network. Perhaps the biggest factor is whether the children's other parent is still involved through weekend visits, telephone calls, or letters. This section assumes that the other parent has maintained contact with you and sees the children on a regular basis. Of course, this is a positive thing, for you as well as for the children. It gives you some time off.

Furthermore, when the bitterness between you and the ex-spouse has slacked off a bit, it feels good to exchange a remark or even just a knowing smile with the one other person in the world to whom your children are as special, their development as marvelous, their needs as urgent as they are to you.

But there are dangers on that road. All forces converge to pull the two of you into overinvolvement with one another. The reality is that your family *has* broken up. You are divorced, or you are getting divorced, and if the children are living with you, then *you* have to make the decisions. (If you have joint custody, it may be even harder to remember that you are a single parent.) Keep the coparenting consultations to *the minimum necessary to sustain the other parent's cooperation in your decisions.* For instance, the other parent should not be the main person you rely on as your sounding board or counselor.

Since you cannot afford to be undermined, you will need to respect the other parent's feelings, values, and opinions. But divorced families too often use joint decision-making as a way of denying the reality of the divorce, or of maintaining the same habitual patterns of conflict that characterized their marriage. When you catch yourself falling into that trap, you will know that you have carried the idealistic notion of coparenting too far.

Whether you have a traditional custody agreement or some sort of joint custody, remember the difference between at-home rules and elsewhere rules. As I said in chapter 4, the fewer elsewhere rules you have, the better off you and the child will both be. The principle is that when the children are not with you, other people are in a better position to enforce rules than you are; but they can only be expected to enforce their own rules, not yours.

MISTAKE: Doris's ex-husband is a pediatrician, so she respects his judgment about the children's biological needs. She asks him how much sleep they need, and he suggests a bedtime of 8:30 on school nights and no particular restriction on weekends. Doris encounters no problems over this until the first time the children stay with their father on a school night. Although she has reminded the children to be sure to go to bed by 8:30, their father and stepmother do not even serve dinner until nearly 8:00, and it is 9:30 before the children are in bed. Guess what the children say to Doris the next time she tells them it is bedtime? These adults would deny it, but I think they are playing games with each other.

BETTER: Doris can reply by explaining that she makes the rules for her house and that Daddy and his wife can make whatever rules they want for their house. She might like to have more control over her ex-husband, for a variety of reasons, but the reality is that she cannot. What she can and must do is keep his independent decisions from having any impact on her own ability to be an effective parent.

Often, fortunately, the noncustodial parent—the one whom the child merely visits—sincerely wants to be helpful. That parent should *also* have a set of at-home rules, and some of them are bound to be different from those of the custodial parent. You don't have to resolve those differences. *Such differences in rules for different situations cause no problems for children.* They are used to it, from infancy onward: Grandmother has her own rules, the day-care center has its own rules, school and playmates' homes all have different rules. Children can learn two or three languages (for example, Spanish with grandparents, English with parents) as masterfully as one. So they are never traumatized by the fact that rules are situation-specific. They are traumatized when adults are inconsistent within the same situation.

═When the other parent has no contact with the children

The truth is that the other parent is never really "out of the picture." He or she may have died, or been institutionalized, or disappeared before the child's birth, or moved to the other end of the country and left no forwarding address. Nonetheless, a child will normally wonder about that parent, entertain fantasies about what they were like or about the possibility that they might return. There is typically some anger toward the deserting parent—even if the desertion was unintentional, through death. Because the child feels guilty about that anger, it may be denied or repressed or transferred onto the remaining parent (you).

So the departed parent turns out to be very much "in the picture." However, he or she is no material help to you. Quite the contrary, for the fantasy may be a superparent, warm and affectionate, always understanding and tolerant of all the child's desires. The banal reality that you offer cannot hold a candle to that fantasy. You may find yourself in considerable conflict between the desire to maintain your children's positive feelings about their origins and the equally understandable desire to destroy that fantasy once and for all by saying, "Your mother was a tramp" or "Your father took one look at you and packed his bag."

That can be extremely destructive (though factual questions should be answered honestly). You can afford to ignore the child's fantasy and concentrate on the reality, which is that you are the only parent the child has. Don't let yourself be put in competition with a remote fantasy. Your rules, like your love, deal with today and tomorrow and next week. A system of concrete written rules will actually help you stay on a different level from that missing parent.

Another mistake to avoid is feeling guilty about the child's missing the other parent. Don't try to compensate for that loss by overlooking problem behavior.

> MISTAKE: In chapter 12, when discussing tantrums, I used the example of Matthew, a five-year-old whose father had died. His mother, grieving as much as he was, had a hard time coping with Matthew's tantrums. Since she understood that they were probably related to his grief and anger over the loss of his father, she was tempted to use each tantrum as an occasion for talking about their sadness.
>
> That would not be helpful. Matthew was unaware of the connection between his tantrums and his sadness. When he was crying over a toy that didn't work, he sincerely believed that was the only thing upsetting him. If Mother rewarded him with extra attention and closeness, she was likely to see more tantrums in the future.
>
> BETTER: Matthew's mother should deal with the tantrums just as any parent would (see chapter 12): by grabbing him firmly and making it clear that tantrums will not get him anywhere, and then by teaching him appropriate ways of expressing frustration. Then she should find other occasions and other ways for the two of them to talk about the husband and father they have lost.

If some parents try to compensate for the child's loss by overlooking problem behavior, others do the opposite. In my experience, single mothers sometimes overdo it where rules are concerned. Perhaps it is a symptom of what a stressful job they have, or of a fear that if they do not keep a tight grasp on the reins, their whole family might just gallop out of control. As a family therapist, I have worked with a number of mothers who seemed to be trying to compensate for the missing father by being unnecessarily strict. I know of no research showing how widespread this is, but here is an example.

MISTAKE: Sally is a single mother of three children, ages nine, eleven, and fourteen. Her rules are reasonable, but she has more of them than the U.S. Navy. The children feel compelled to test each rule. They find novel ways by which complying with one rule can be an excuse for challenging another. Instead of producing a sense of relief in the children after the former chaos of their home, Sally's list only makes them feel as if they were under martial law. Revolution is the only honorable way out.

Furthermore, indications that the system is going to meet with heavy resistance throw Sally into a panic, and she reacts by escalating the punishments rapidly. Swearing was to have been punished by a half hour's ostracism in the child's own room, but now the punishment doubles with each offense, and before Sally knows it she is sending the eleven-year-old to his room for two hours. As he trudges off, she has to pretend not to hear the stream of profanity he mutters.

BETTER: Sally should start with as few rules as possible —perhaps with just one rule. She should add rules only as needed, to change the behavior that she feels is really important. (I happen to agree with Sally that she needs a rule about swearing.) Remember that the rule only applies *next time*. (Do not be upset when there is a next time; expect it. The child needs to find out whether you can be trusted to follow through.)

As for the punishment, why not start with five minutes of ostracism? And instead of doubling it if it does not work, Sally can increase it by one minute. With one-minute increments, even if it takes the child ten trials before realizing that he is making life harder for himself, he is still only up to a fifteen-minute punishment. It is the *direction in which things are going* that must be impressed upon the child, not how powerful and punitive his mother can be.

≡Summary

Single parents need clear rules for the same reasons married parents do. But single parents have a greater need for a support network, especially for at least one close friend with whom to discuss decisions as a spouse would do. Two heads *are* better than one, for this purpose at least.

As in any family, children of single parents need to know that the parent is firmly at the helm. Resist the temptation to be more egalitarian than you would be if there were two of you.

On the other hand, don't panic and take an overly strict approach just because you are *alone* at the helm. As long as you are clear and consistent, you can create a system that reflects your own values and concerns, and that gradually gives your children all the freedom they can handle responsibly.

SUGGESTED BOOKS: Single Parents

Bustanoby, Andre. *Being a Single Parent.* New York: Ballantine, 1987.

Dodson, Fitzhugh. *How to Single Parent.* New York: Harper & Row, 1986.

Gardner, Richard. *The Boys' and Girls' Book About Divorce.* New York: Bantam, 1970.

Gardner, Richard. *The Parents' Book About Divorce.* New York: Bantam, 1970.

Salk, Lee. *What Every Child Would Like Parents to Know About Divorce.* New York: Warner Books, 1979.

Scarr, Sandra. *Mother Care, Other Care.* New York: Warner, 1984.

Turow, Rita. *Daddy Doesn't Live Here Anymore.* New York: Anchor/Doubleday, 1978.

CHAPTER EIGHTEEN

Stepfamilies

A stepfamily is created when a single parent acquires a new partner who moves into the home and helps to maintain it. The classic type consists of mother, children, and a stepfather who either has no previous children or whose children live with their mother. But this chapter applies also to father/stepmother families, blended families with "his" or "her" children, and families like Al and Betty's (see chapter 1), where one child is from a former marriage and the rest are "theirs."

Exactly when the new partner begins to take on the role of stepparent is bound to depend on the situation and on the personalities involved. In general, I believe that being a partner in making and enforcing rules has to go along with being a partner in maintaining the household. If the person you live with has children, it is nearly impossible for you to be a good partner financially and emotionally without being a partner in parenting.

The time when a new stepparent joins in the enforcement of rules marks a significant and probably stressful transition for the whole family. How should such a change be handled? Should you ease into it by degrees, calling as little attention to it as possible, hoping that no one will be too upset and everyone will get used to it eventually? Absolutely not. That makes it much *more* stressful in the long run.

It is easier for children to get used to changes that are clear, substantial, and openly acknowledged than ones that are subtle and confused or even denied. So there should be a marked change from "father alone," for example, to "father and stepmother" as the parental team. Coinciding with a stepmother's move into the home, a wedding-type party helps mark that change. Whether or not the legal arrangement is important to you, a celebration of some kind may serve to symbolize an event that is affecting the structure of the family.

Mankind has always dealt with major changes in families through *rituals*: weddings, funerals, baptisms, Bar Mitzvahs, graduation ceremonies. Whenever someone moves in or out of a family home, or moves to a new status within it, the traditional ritual helps everyone prepare for the change, acknowledge it, and refer back to it later by sharing memories and photographs of the occasion.

Because our society is going through a period of change in attitudes toward marriage, we have not yet established a customary way of marking the occasion when unmarried people begin living together. But we need some such ritual, especially if one of them has children.

As a stepparent, your authority comes from your status in the home as coprovider of the children's needs. Do not allow yourself to be sidetracked because of the lack of a biological relationship to the child. Nor does it matter that the love between you and your stepchildren cannot be the same as between them and their biological mother or father.*

EXAMPLE: The child says, "You can't tell me what to do. You're not my father."

MISTAKES: Stepfather backs down or appeals to mother to handle the situation, or lashes out angrily at the child because of hurt feelings.

BETTER: "No, I'm not your father. But this is not your father's home. In school you follow the rules that the teacher and principal make, and here you have to follow the rules that your mother and I make." (Optional comment, if the timing is right: "I would like to be a good stepfather,

---

* This chapter does not necessarily apply to stepparents who go on to adopt the children. By the time that happens, you should no longer be thinking of yourself as a stepparent. You are then the child's father or mother.

though, and when you say things like that, it makes me feel I'm not doing very well. Do you want to talk about it?'')

In such a confrontation, the implications of "You're not my father" would be quite different if the child has a father elsewhere (implying, "Don't you try to take my father's place") as opposed to his being fatherless (implying, "I wish I had a father, but I don't"). As with single-parent families, it is useful to discuss stepfamilies in two categories, depending on whether there is a noncustodial parent in the picture.

Stepfamilies when the other parent is also actively involved

If the children have a "real" father who takes them every other weekend, or a mother who lives out of state but telephones regularly and takes them on vacations, their attachment to that other parent is likely to be strong. In fact, it can remain very strong even if the noncustodial parent is less than wonderful— even in the face of disappointments, broken promises, and the most irresponsible behavior on that parent's part. As the responsible parent or stepparent, this is likely to infuriate you.

The secret is for stepparents to establish their own distinct relationships with the children. (The same applies to a "weekend" stepparent, typically the wife of a man whose children live with his former wife.) You are not replacing the other parent, not usurping the love and respect due that parent, not pretending to have the same feelings toward the children that you would have toward your own natural children. What you really want and deserve is to become a respected and loved person in your own right. The love between adults and children is nonexclusive. Just as a parent can have equally caring but different relationships with several children, so can children have close relationships with several different adults. Father means one sort of relationship, mother a different sort, grandparent another, and stepparent yet another.

Make no mistake about it—you mean more to your stepchildren than friends, teachers, even uncles and aunts. You are so important, in fact, that you can expect your share of the anger, tears, resentment, and abuse that are an occasional part of all intimate relationships. But most of the serious trouble—the prolonged antagonism that some stepparents experience from their stepchildren (often *mutual* antagonism)—can be avoided if you make it very clear that you are not interested in taking anyone else's place.

Small gestures can carry great weight. A stepfather who wants to be called "Dad," for example, is blurring that crucial distinction between father and stepfather. (I think stepparents should be called by their first names.) If you buy the child a new watch when she already has a watch her father gave her, you are asking for trouble. Birthdays and Christmas call for some advance communication between the two sets of parents to protect the child from conflict. You should also refrain from negative remarks about the other parent. Religious or ethnic slurs, comments in the child's presence about that parent's values, occupation, appearance, or behavior are all like waving a red cape in front of a bull. Peaceful coexistence is your goal, because if it comes to a war—even a cold war—the stepparent will certainly lose, and no one will win.

EXAMPLE: Nancy and Jerry normally have his six-year-old daughter every Friday night and Saturday. This week, Jerry is out of town and won't be home until 11:00 Friday night. Nancy picks up Jennifer at the usual time, gives her dinner, and wants to put her to bed as Jerry usually does, with a story. Jennifer wants to wait up for her father. Nancy wisely allows her to stay up, which allows the two of them to have a special evening together and does no harm whatsoever to the enforcement of bedtime on normal occasions.

EXAMPLE: Morris lives with Judy and her two children. It is a school night, Judy is at a meeting, and the children want to watch TV. Morris asks to see their homework, since he and Judy have a standing rule that there is to be no TV until both children have finished their homework. The children explain that they want to watch one show before they do their work.

In this case, Morris says, "Sorry," and turns off the TV. It is more important to show solidarity with Judy than to promote himself as a "nice guy."

Unfortunately, the children know how to get under

Morris's skin. Robert, the eleven-year-old, says, "When we're at our father's, we can watch our favorite programs and do our homework later."

MISTAKE: "Your father is probably half-tanked, so he doesn't care."

BETTER: "At home, you can't." (Terse and firm, but not unfriendly; Morris does not need to defend the clear family rule.)

It is good to remember that you *have* taken the other parent's place, in two important ways. As Dad's or Mom's new spouse, you are the model for what kind of person they would now choose for a partner. And together you provide the model for what a successful marriage and family can be. However, there is no reason to point this out explicitly to the children.

Mourning the dead marriage. One of the hard things for a stepparent to deal with is a situation in which the children are still feeling sad about the break-up of their original family. And the stepparent's spouse is sad, too—even if the first marriage was awful.

A study has shown that people typically take two to four years to complete the period of mourning that follows the end of a marriage. Even a bad marriage is a powerful emotional bond, which, when torn apart, creates a wound that will heal slowly. Healthy mourning for any loss requires talking about the thing that was lost, remembering the good parts, thinking about what life might have been like if it had continued.

The average divorced person remarries in less than three years, still in the midst of that process of recovery. The children, especially, have barely begun to give up the fantasy that their parents' marriage will be restored. A stepparent who demanded that those slow processes of adjustment to reality must be curtailed or pushed underground would only endanger the new marriage and inflame the children's resentment of the situation.

MISTAKE: Sandra became involved with Peter shortly after his divorce, and during the first year of their relationship, she listened patiently as he rehashed his disastrous marriage, his anger at his wife's leaving, and his sadness and anxiety about the children's welfare. After they married, however, Sandra resented having to listen to the continuing emotional travail over Peter's first marriage. She especially resented it when Peter and his children would recount some event from those years in which she had not taken part. She tried changing the subject gently, but when the problem did not go away, she confronted Peter about it and got him to promise to avoid talking about the first marriage when she was within earshot.

BETTER: A friend points out to Sandra that when Peter and the children talk about the past, it has nothing to do with their feelings about her. Getting to know and love someone includes hearing about their past and understanding their present feelings about that past—happy as well as sad. Getting to know and love children includes letting them talk about their life in another family, even if you are not part of that family and dislike the other parent.

Sandra decides to regard the children's and Peter's conversations about his ex-wife as though they were accounts of a movie she had not seen. With the proper distance, she finds she can be an interested outside observer yet still be warm and empathic when sad feelings arise. The secret is not taking their nostalgia as a reflection upon her.

However, when one of the children tells Peter, "I wish you and Mommy would get married again," Sandra responds openly and honestly.

"That hurts my feelings," she says. "I love your dad. We have a happy marriage. I hope your mommy will find someone else."

Although the stepparent is not trying to take the other parent's place with the child, he or she certainly has taken that person's place with the spouse. Both facts have to be acknowledged. But the purpose of doing so is not to induce guilt and make the child act lovingly toward you, the stepparent. The purpose is to be entirely yourself—a whole new person, not Mother, not Father. Those biological parents really are not your rivals.

≡Stepparents when the original parent is gone

The foregoing advice—to avoid entering into a contest with the mother if you are a stepmother, or with the father if you are a stepfather—applies to stepparents when both of the original parents are still involved in the children's lives. The situation is more complicated when the parent has died or, worse, deserted. Then, often, children show a real need to have a stepparent fill the gap, but they may also feel ambivalent. The intensity of the conflicting feelings depends on their age, how long it has been since they lost the parent, how well they knew the parent, the personalities of all those involved, and how the surviving parent seems to feel about the relationship between the stepparent and the children.

At one extreme, a two-year-old who never knew her original father can easily be adopted if her stepfather wants to be in the role of a "real" father. On the other hand, a ten-year-old who has been told stories about her father, has kept his picture and for years identified herself as his daughter, may need to remain faithful to the biological tie even while looking to her stepfather for everything that a father could provide. It requires sensitivity and the willingness to put the child's needs and desires ahead of your own.

> EXAMPLE: Suzanne tried for twelve years to have children with her first husband. For medical reasons, it was difficult, and the only two times they conceived, she suffered miscarriages.
>
> The marriage did not survive, and Suzanne found herself divorced at age forty, having to adjust to the disappointment of knowing she would never be a mother.
>
> Two years later, Suzanne married a widower with three children. She hoped that the children would call her "Mom." The children frankly said that they still thought about their mother often and talked about her. "We don't want to hurt Suzanne's feelings," the fourteen-year-old confided to her father, "but she's not our mother."
>
> After five years of marriage, when the children were nineteen, sixteen, and fifteen, Suzanne at times resented all that she had done for them. She had, in effect, been their

mother without the formal acknowledgment of the fact. In their kisses on the cheek at bedtime, she had always felt a reserve. Five years later, however, when the children were adults, they found the words to express their love and gratitude. It had taken ten years of patience, devotion, and frequent reminders to herself that she was an adult and the children were only children. But she had a parent's pride in the three young adults' accomplishments, a happy marriage, and a good enough relationship with her pregnant stepdaughter to be able to say, "Don't you dare tell that baby to call me Stepgrandma!"

EXAMPLE: Mark and Chris have been married for two years. He is thirty, and she is twenty-five. Chris has a six-year-old son who never knew his biological father and a three-year-old daughter by her first husband, whom she divorced after a violent, on-again-off-again marriage lasting about a year. The ex-husband refuses to have anything more to do with either child and has expressed willingness to have Mark adopt them. Chris is eager for this to happen, and the children also seem to want it. They both call Mark "Daddy" and have a good relationship with him.

Mark has reservations about going ahead with the adoption. He feels it is probably best for the kids, and the best way to show his love and commitment to Chris. Yet he doesn't feel they are really his children. Although he is fond of them, he knows he will probably feel different about the children he and Chris plan to have together. "Maybe adopting them would change that," he admits. "But what if it didn't?"

I encourage Mark to share these feelings with Chris. The two of them can work toward an agreement, based on mutual understanding, through which Mark can express his commitment to Chris and her children without having to conceal any feelings that may be stirred up later, feelings of less attachment than to his biological children. This kind of understanding will be important whether Mark adopts the children or not.

≡Summary

The two adults in the child's home—parent and stepparent —are both parents in that home, so far as rules are concerned. You need neither biological nor legal status as a parent to use the system described in Part I. All that matters is that you are helping to meet the child's needs on a daily basis. If you sense that you are being tested because the child is ambivalent about whether you are a "real" parent or not, do not let that be the issue. The important issue is whether you and your partner can give the children an explicit list of what actions are expected of them and what consequences will follow if those expectations are not met.

For some stepparents, the role involves all the thankless tasks of a parent, the same conflicts with the children that their natural parent suffers, the same worries and frustrations, without the fullness of joy and satisfaction that comes to the parent. But you can have it exactly the other way around: sharing in all the joys, priding yourself on your accomplishment as a partner in raising the children, relating to them in a very special way, yet remaining freer than their biological parent can be from those inevitable fights and worries and frustrations. Many stepparents have a better and more satisfying relationship to the children than their natural parents have. The goal of this book is to make *both* kinds of relationship better.

SUGGESTED BOOKS: Stepfamilies

Berman, Claire. *Making It as a Stepparent: New Roles, New Rules.* New York: Harper & Row, 1986.

Gardner, Richard. *The Boys' and Girls' Book About Stepfamilies.* New York: Bantam, 1982.

Lewis-Steere, Cynthia. *Stepping Lightly: An A to Z Guide for Stepparents.* Minneapolis: CompCare Publications, 1981.

Visher, Emily, and Visher, John. *How to Win as a Stepfamily.* New York: Dembner Books, 1982.

CHAPTER NINETEEN

Parents Without Custody

When I was divorced, my ex-wife was "awarded" custody of our five-year-old son. It seemed like the appropriate word, because we both felt that he was a prize. The court's assumption that he needed her day-to-day care more than mine made it natural for the "award" to go to her and the aching void to me. The parent without custody—most often, but not always, the father—suffers a painful loss in addition to the pain of the divorce itself. He is not going to be there when the children cut themselves or scrape their knees, not going to tuck them into bed at night or be bounced out of bed by them in the morning. No matter how well the weekend visits go, they always end with the wrenching bitterness of taking the children "home" to alien territory. In a way, one recapitulates the divorce every weekend, with its mixture of sadness, guilt, anxiety for the children's welfare, and helpless rage over the injustice of it all.

One does recover. For me, those feelings lasted about five years, but they did wear off. One thing that helps is that both parents begin to realize that except for the sadness, the one without custody actually has the easier role of the two. The one with custody is more frequently the one whom the children engage in power struggles, the one nagging them, rushing home to drive them to soccer practice or the orthodontist, waiting up for them after curfew.

If you are a noncustodial parent, you can cherish the joys of being with your children and watching them grow, while taking advantage of the fact that you don't have day-to-day responsibility for their comings and goings. Once you get over the idea that a weekend father (or mother) is supposed to provide constant upbeat entertainment, you can settle into a more normal relationship. There are certain advantages to being with your children for a day or two at a time, then having a week or two to yourself.

It is all a matter of your attitude. I found that it helped, whenever I felt myself resenting the arrangement, to tell myself that it was as if I were paying for a first-rate boarding school. "My son is away at school," I would say to myself. "He comes home every other weekend."

Let me share what I have learned from my relationship with my son and his mother. I certainly have not managed to follow this list of principles perfectly, but I have done well enough to be what the great British pediatrician D. W. Winnicott would have called a "good enough father." I have a "good enough son" to show for it.

- Use the system described in Part I to make at-home rules, which take precedence over the custodial parents' rules whenever the children are with you. You can be as consistent with the other parent's rules as you think advisable, but the children will not be disturbed by any differences that are made clear. If you have a new partner, then the two of you can collaborate as in any stepfamily, when the children are with you.

You may not need many rules. I know a father who has only one rule, because he has only found a need for one: If the children cannot agree about what radio station to listen to in the car, he turns off the radio.

Noncustodial parents generally will not need any elsewhere rules, because that is the other parent's job. If you make a rule that conflicts with hers, your rule will have to be disobeyed. This may sound obvious, but the divorced fathers I know, including myself, sometimes find it hard to give up all that control to the mother. We have to struggle to accept the fact that we simply do not have the power to shape our children's experiences as we would like to do. That is where the boarding-school fantasy helps. Someone else is in charge.

• Have as little to do with the other parent as possible. I cannot make this an absolute principle, not knowing your situation and feelings. However, in the first years of my own divorce, almost any innocent conversation could lead to a fight, which only produced distress for all of us. The best period was during the second year, when for four months we exchanged not a word; I simply picked up and delivered the child on schedule, and neither of us found it necessary to call the other to request any revisions. (In recent years, I should add, we have amicable, constructive conversations about our son, every few months.)

• On the other hand, when you do have to negotiate something, be businesslike. Be as courteous and cooperative as you would be with a coworker whose help you might need in the future. No matter how you feel about the people with custody, anything that makes life easier for them will work to the benefit of your children. Anything that makes it more difficult for your ex-spouse and his or her current spouse to be effective parents will in the long run harm the children. I can't think of any exceptions to that principle. Be as uninvolved with those other parents, as independent in your relationship with the children, as you can be. But in certain areas, such as pick-up and drop-off times, health care, coordinating birthday presents, and, most of all, in avoiding backbiting remarks, you and your children have everything to gain when you manage to cooperate.

• Keep money issues entirely separate from visitation. Pay your assigned child support with unerring regularity. Refuse to discuss other questions, such as extra money for camp tuition or music lessons, when the child is present. If the child wants to ask about money—for example, why you declined a request to pay for half his music lessons—treat it as a sincere and legitimate question on his part. Don't let yourself get defensive, assuming that his mother put him up to it. It doesn't matter if she did. Explain your reasons just as you would have done if there had been no divorce.

• Be absolutely reliable on pick-up and delivery. It is important to let the child know he can count on you. The fact that you are not a constant presence in his life is far less important than your consistency and reliability. If you have to change a date with your child, suggest an alternate date; don't just cancel it. Keep other promises, too—for example, don't promise a ski trip unless it is definite.

• Don't be hurt if the child, at times, seems to forget about you. There are reasons, having nothing to do with you. As children grow older, they have more interests outside the family. Inducing guilt is counterproductive. Just be patient. My son has often forgotten to call me back—if I call at dinnertime, for example. This leaves me feeling pretty unimportant. Then a few days later, he may call to tell me there is something on television I would be interested in. He cares! He thinks about me!

When the child calls, express your joy at hearing from him, not your hurt about his not calling more frequently. You could have called him. You are the adult; he is the child. The separation from you is not his fault. The fact that he was born into an unstable marriage is not his fault. Your sadness is a consequence of your own mistakes—not of the child's neglect.

• Don't be jealous of the stepparent or of other significant people in the child's life. He would have had a number of other attachments even if there had been no divorce. If you continue to do your job, whether it is every weekend or only a few weeks a year, *no one* will replace you. I guarantee that.

• Many divorced parents, with custody as well as without, make the mistake of assuming that any problem the child has must be due to the divorce. Don't forget that children in intact families have problems in the course of their development, too. Basically, you are a normal parent, and your relationships with your children are normal. The divorce should gradually become a relatively minor consideration. So should the fact that you don't have custody of the child.

• Ultimately, your principal effects on your children's development will not come from what you do to them or for them. It will come from the kind of respect they have for you, as a person. And it will come from the respect they see that you have for them.

SUGGESTED BOOKS: Parents Without Custody

Rowlands, Peter. *Saturday Parent: A Book for Separated Families*. New York: Continuum, 1982.

Ware, Ciji. *Sharing Parenthood After Divorce: An Enlightened Custody Guide*. New York: Viking, 1982.

(Also see books suggested in chapters 17 and 18.)

CHAPTER TWENTY

Crisis

Beyond Liberty and Probation is a third mode of life, which I call Crisis mode. It is a temporary measure for parents whose teenage children are so far out of control that they cannot be made to respect the ordinary rules of Liberty without first undergoing a Crisis. It requires a powerful confrontation with reality in which the consequence of continued defiance will be expulsion from the home or withdrawal of financial support. Crisis mode requires professional help.

The Crisis comes when you announce an ultimatum, such as "The next time you are arrested, I will not post bail" or "If you do not stay in this drug rehabilitation center for three months, you will not be allowed to come home." It may or may not culminate in actually kicking the kid out of your house, but as with any ultimatum, you must be prepared to carry it out if necessary.

In this chapter, I shall explain how parents can decide whether they have to impose Crisis mode. I shall discuss how to do so, and connect the principles of this book with the ToughLove movement, of which you may already have heard. However, the main purpose of this book has been to *prevent* your children from ever abusing their freedom to the extent that Crisis mode would be needed.

═Crisis mode: When?

There is an easy test you can use to decide if it is time to go beyond Liberty and Probation. If you find your family in either of two situations, it is time for Crisis mode.

Crisis situation one: Child in grave trouble. When certain kinds of events happen *more than once*, nothing short of a parent-induced Crisis is likely to produce a change. These events include being arrested for any reason, being suspended from school, staying out overnight without permission, physically assaulting anyone (not counting fair fights with a male of his own age group), carrying a switch-blade or a pistol, or using any drug to the point of losing consciousness or memory. *One* incident of this kind is sufficient cause to seek family counseling. But if you have a second incident, either before or after starting counseling, then you should enter Crisis mode.

> EXAMPLE: Teddy is a fourteen-year-old who repeatedly fails to do homework, lies to his parents, and is in danger of failing eighth grade. After trying to implement a system of rules and consequences, with no positive results, Teddy's parents ask the school counselor for the names of some child psychologists in their community who specialize in family therapy (see chapter 21). *They do not need to use Crisis mode;* Teddy's behavior problems are not comparable to those listed in the preceding paragraph.

> EXAMPLE: Bud is a fourteen-year-old who has been suspended from school for selling marijuana. His parents try to deal with this problem by making a set of clear rules and consequences. Unfortunately, soon after returning to school, Bud is again caught selling marijuana. This time he is arrested. It is time for Crisis mode. The juvenile officer recommends family counseling, and the judge appoints a social worker. However, professional counseling is not enough. Bud's parents ask the social worker for referral to a local chapter of ToughLove, the parents' support network. They work with both sources of support. Their fellow ToughLove members help them set a "bottom line" for Bud and follow through with it. The therapist helps them understand why

this is particularly difficult for them, helps Bud deal with the impact of his parents' stand, and helps all members of the family begin to communicate effectively with each other.

Crisis situation two: All reasonable consequences exhausted. If you have a child who ignores your rules, you don't need to go into Crisis mode; you simply need to enforce the consequences. If your child is taking the consequences for ignoring rules but his behavior is not improving, that is usually not sufficient cause to switch to Crisis mode. You can escalate the consequences or use Probation. But if your child defies your consequences to the point where you cannot escalate them any further without physical violence, it is time to precipitate a Crisis.

EXAMPLE: Tom has defied his curfew so many times that he is now supposedly on Probation until he serves a thirty-day grounding. But Tom shows no remorse, denies that his parents' concern is valid, and cannot be trusted to come home after school to be grounded. Short of locking Tom in his room for a month, there is no way his parents can enforce the restriction on his freedom. Hence they have to switch to the mode in which his right to continue living with the family, not merely his freedom, is at issue.

This example assumes that Tom's parents have already withheld all such unnecessary luxuries as allowance, transportation, the right to have friends over. If you simply feel helpless but have not sat down and made a list of all the things you provide in addition to food, shelter, and nurturance (see chapter 10), then that is the thing to do first. Most parents who cry, "Nothing works," have not been imaginative enough about what they have tried. In Crisis mode, your ultimatum or "bottom line" is absolutely your last resort. The last freedom you can withhold is the child's freedom to continue living in your home.

EXAMPLE: The Davises had drawn up a list of all the things they were doing for their daughter Marsha. Except for providing food, clothing, a bedroom, medical care, praise (on the rare occasions when they could find something to praise her for), and affection (on the rare occasions when she let them close enough to give it to her), the Davises had systematically withdrawn everything else on the list as conse-

quences for ignoring their rules about curfew, school attendance, cleanliness, and courtesy. Eventually, praise and
affection were withdrawn, too, simply because the Davises
could no longer sincerely give it. Marsha continued to ignore
their rules, coming and going as though the house were a
hotel. She showed contempt toward her parents and brother.
Finally, with the help of a family therapist, her parents in-
stituted Crisis mode. They established a bottom line—the
maximum misbehavior they would put up with from Marsha
—beyond which she would be sent to live in a group home in
another town.

≡Crisis mode: How?

The foregoing examples of when to institute Crisis mode also
illustrate what I consider its two distinctive features. First is the
"bottom line." In Crisis mode, as in Liberty, you will use written
rules and consequences. The difference is that you will have to go
beyond the freedom-versus-restriction type of consequence, upon
which Part I of this book is based, to the more radical question of
whether to continue providing a home for your child. I shall not
put it more delicately. You may feel that you could never deny
your child shelter. But the truth is that it is only a question of *how
much you are willing to put up with* before you would do so. That
is what we mean by a bottom line.

The bottom line raises powerful legal, moral, and emotional
issues. (Many of the issues are discussed in the excellent book
ToughLove, by Phyllis and David York, whose argument I shall
summarize below.) "Kicking the child out of the house," to put it
bluntly, is a very big part of what you may have to do in Crisis
mode. You will want to find somewhere for the child to stay,
which you can do with the help of a social worker and with the
help of your support group. Once you have found a place, you
present "structured choice." If the child chooses to reject the
place you have found, there is nothing more you can do. You have
fulfilled your moral as well as legal responsibility, and now you
can only hope that the child learns to survive in the world.

A structured choice that is often effective in changing teenagers' attitudes is to threaten to send them to a foster home in a

distant part of your state, away from all their friends and drug sources. (The choice is "If you defy this bottom line, you will be sent to a foster home at the other end of the state.") Obviously, it becomes all the more important to know the law, to know what your options are—and this is one of the benefits of a support group like ToughLove.

In Crisis mode, when a teenager gets himself in trouble with the court, one of the difficult decisions parents may have to make is whether to let the teenager take the consequences, and refuse to keep bailing him out. Fortunately, ToughLove groups are skilled in the use of informal hearings in judges' chambers, judges' signatures on unofficial documents, and other procedures to impress the gravity of the situation upon teenagers without tying matters up in the formal paperwork, trials, and bureaucracy of the court system.

The second distinctive feature of Crisis mode is the need for mutual support among parents. You can withhold allowance from a child who leaves the kitchen messy, all by yourself. But you will need a friend by your side if you plan to refuse to post bail for one of your children.

I am impressed by the ToughLove movement, especially by the materials prepared by the Yorks to help nine hundred local support groups get started around the United States. On only one point do I disagree with some of the ToughLove literature: I do not see such groups as a substitute for professional counseling.

Crisis mode = getting tough + support groups + counseling. The right way to join ToughLove or one of the other self-help support groups for families—Parents Anonymous (mainly for parents who have abused or neglected their children, or are afraid they might), Families Anonymous (mainly for parents of teenagers with drug problems), Al-Anon (for family members of alcoholics), or similar groups within your church, synagogue, or community—is by first contacting an experienced professional, then getting some advice from that person about the type of self-help support that will benefit your family the most.

I certainly would not want family therapy or any other type of counseling to be an obstacle to self-help. No responsible professional would discourage you from making use of all the re-

sources in your community. What I do want to discourage you
from doing is assuming that a self-help group can do the whole
job.

You can count on your fellow group members for solid,
heartfelt support when you do what is hardest for you: drawing
the bottom line for your teenager. You can count on them to help
you find a place for your kid to stay when he is no longer able to
stay with you. You can count on them to come with you to the
police station or to court. And you can count on them not to
blame you for what your child has been doing.

What you cannot rely on fellow members of a support group
for is understanding the special patterns of interaction in your
particular family, as compared to others. There is a danger that
you will get "prescriptions without diagnosis." The group members may have strong ideas about how you should tackle the problem, but their prescription will be based on their own experience,
not on a discerning analysis of the dynamics of your particular
family. It is as though you were to tell a friend that you had an
itchy rash on your arm and the friend gave you some medicine
that had helped her when she had a similar-looking rash. But her
rash was due to an allergy, while yours is a reaction to skin para-
sites. What helps in one case could be disastrous in another.

Although I feel confident in advising parents in Crisis mode
to make use of *both* professional counseling and a parents' support group, I am aware that this can be difficult. Despite the fact
that ToughLove's founders themselves were family counselors,
there are apparently some ToughLove parents who have had
negative experiences in therapy and who regard their group as an
antidote to professional advice. They may have been blamed by
counselors for what their children had been doing, or they may
have been told to be more patient and nurturant while their children were running rampant. Having swallowed this bad advice for
years, they are fed up with it. They have become antiprofessional,
though they lack the training and experience to do the professional therapist's job.

My advice is to shop around among ToughLove groups in
your area, as well as any other groups that look appropriate.
Look for people with whom you feel comfortable, from whom
you feel support, but who do not pretend to be able to do the
whole job of counseling you. At the same time, you should shop

around among professional counselors to find someone whom you trust, like, and can afford. One question to ask in the initial interview is whether that person can recommend additional resources in the community. He or she may strongly recommend ToughLove. On the other hand, he or she may have serious reservations based upon your description of the situation, or upon his or her own knowledge of the particular group in your community.

In the next chapter, I discuss at length how to find an appropriate family therapist. As for ToughLove, you can telephone (215) 348-7090 for the current locations and meeting times of the chapters nearest you. For Al-Anon, look in your local telephone directory under Alcoholics Anonymous. Check with school and hospital social workers for information about other appropriate groups.

≡The "Ten Beliefs"

Phyllis and David York, counselors whose own lives were torn apart by their teenagers' wild, irresponsible behavior, built the ToughLove movement upon what they called their "Ten Beliefs." Listing these ten important principles will be a good way to summarize their approach and at the same time point out how well it relates to the ideas in this book.

Although the Yorks created this list to help abused parents become ToughLove parents, most of the principles apply long before your children become teenagers. And the principles also apply if your children and teenagers never act in the extreme ways ToughLove is designed to combat.

1. *Family problems have roots and supports in the culture.* This is not a "cop-out" for parents; the Yorks do not fall for the "peer pressure" myth. They emphasize that children must be held accountable for their own decisions about whether to yield to peer pressure, and that parents are not powerless against peers. However, the Yorks refuse to tell parents, "These problems are your fault." We counselors have to acknowledge that this generation of American parents faces problems in the society with which our own parents did not have to cope in the fifties and sixties: easily available and socially glamorous drugs, widespread crime

both organized and unorganized, unemployment, a majority of all marriages ending in divorce, the necessity for both parents to work, a foreboding sense of nuclear apocalypse, worldwide terrorism and chaos. Against all those odds, we parents try to sound a hopeful message: "Work hard, adhere to decent human values, obey the law, and you will have a wonderful life ahead of you." The peer culture says, "Get high while you can."

Parents must be realistic about the forces opposing them in the teenage subculture and in the culture at large yet not be passive and helpless about them.

2. *Parents are people, too.* This means, "Stop letting your children walk all over you." It also represents a rebellion by thousands of parents nationwide, against psychiatrists, psychologists, social workers, and other counselors who told them to be more patient, more understanding, more lenient, more loving. The Yorks argue, and I agree, that children do not want parents who are pushovers. If you stand up for yourself as a person, asserting your own rights, you will not only get your own needs met, you will also be helping your kids. Kids need parents who are people.

3. *Parents' material and emotional resources are limited.* "Parents have both the right and the need to say, 'This is my limit. I've had enough. I need something from you now.'" (*ToughLove*, p. 45).

4. *Parents and kids are not equal.* As I have said several times in earlier chapters, a family is not a democracy.

5. *Blaming keeps people helpless.* Amateur counselors make parents helpless by implying that they were responsible for everything that happened in the past, instead of offering specific suggestions to give them back the control they have lost. The same mistake is made by family members themselves. As long as everybody in the family dances around pointing at each other and dwelling on past wrongs, nothing is going to change. The first step in solving problems is to stop blaming ourselves and others, and start planning differently for the future.

6. *Kids' behavior affects parents. Parents' behavior affects kids.* That much seems obvious, and it is the reason for working with a family therapist instead of shipping the

"problem child" out for individual psychotherapy. However, even in family therapy some parents are tempted to say, "We're not going to change unless he/she does." The kid says the same thing, and we have a standoff. Nobody changes. Instead, ToughLove support groups and professional family therapists tell parents, "You change first. Give your kids something different to react to, and their behavior will have to change, too."

One thing that can make a supportive friend or counselor effective is recognizing that the behavior they see in distressed parents is more likely to be a *result* of what those parents have been going through than a reliable picture of the way they were years ago when the problem started.

The Yorks claim that many counselors, when they are meeting parents for the first time when those parents have been driven to the depths of ineffectiveness, hostility, and despair, assume that this is the kind of parents they have always been. None of the psychologists and social workers whom I know are guilty of such simplistic thinking, but I think this is a good reminder anyway. When a family is in crisis, everyone's behavior is a result of everyone else's, and the useful question is not "Who brought us to this point?" but "Who will take the lead in changing the way we interact?"

7. *Taking a stand precipitates a crisis.* In Crisis mode, the parents recognize that their family's situation has reached intolerable proportions. They draw a bottom line, which may cause a crisis for the child, who has to change his behavior or move out.

I don't think it is quite true that taking a stand *always* precipitates a crisis. In fact, Crisis mode will sometimes lead to a peaceful solution of the crisis the family has been in for a long time. I think the Yorks' point is that it is *all right* if the parents' stand does precipitate a crisis. A long stay in a rehabilitation hospital or a year in a foster home may be the best thing that could happen to a particular teenager. As one father put it, "We should have precipitated the crisis right then and there when he was still in school. We didn't do that. I guess that everyone thinks the same thing: No, we can't do it now, he's in school. The really most important thing is to get the head straight and if that means missing school for a whole year, it's worth it" (*ToughLove*, p. 190).

8. *From controlled crisis comes positive change.* This belief is based on a fairly recent discovery by social scientists that social systems, including families, adapt in very much the same way individual organisms do. A plant grows toward the light, a baby learns to communicate in the language of its parents, and, similarly, a family makes positive changes whenever it has to change in order to survive.

At the same time, families, like organisms, resist changes as long as they can do so while continuing to function. So the authors of *ToughLove* realize that parents often resist taking a stand because the distress they have grown used to is less frightening than the unknown results of a crisis. The kind of controlled crisis the Yorks recommend—the same as what I call Crisis mode—often leads to a gratifying resolution. It almost never leads to a worse situation than what preceded it, whereas fear of precipitating a crisis usually results in prolonging or intensifying the problem.

9. *Families need to give and get support in their own community in order to change.* This is what ToughLove, Families Anonymous, Al-Anon, and Parents Anonymous have to offer. I agree that when family problems reach Crisis proportions—not only in the case of an abusive adolescent but also in the case of an abusive parent, an emotionally disturbed child, or an alcoholic or drug-dependent family member of any age—relationships with mental-health professionals are never enough. The member whom the rest of the family labels as the source of their headaches needs to be brought together with peers who acknowledge having similar problems; and the rest of the family also need the support of people like themselves who have been through similar crises. Even if you had your own private family therapist available full-time, there would be many times when you could get more from talking with another troubled parent. The other parent is enough of an outsider to be more objective than you can be, yet has "been there" in a way the professional has not.

Furthermore, you yourself will benefit as much from the support you give to other parents as from what they give you. The greater objectivity and firmness you are able to muster in talking about the other parents' teenagers is sure to echo back in your own response to your own teenager. Urging the other mother to lock her daughter out of the house may help you find the courage to do the same with your own kid.

10. *The essence of family life is cooperation, not togetherness.* This last belief is a restatement of my own central theme—that the direction of family development is toward autonomy. The child's agenda is to acquire more freedom, along with the skills and self-confidence he or she will need in order to enjoy that freedom. The parents' agenda is to relinquish control over the child's actions, one step at a time. That indeed requires cooperation—between the parents, among the children, and between parent and child. Togetherness is fine at certain times and places, but as a way of life it runs counter to what growing up is all about.

≡Summary

This book is designed to help parents prevent a nightmare that occurs in millions of American families. But if you have already lost your adolescent's respect, trust, and caring, and he or she has lost your trust and respect and *almost* lost your caring, Crisis mode is a way of extending the principles of this book to an extreme "bottom line": the point where you acknowledge the possibility that the only way you may be able to save your child and the rest of your family is by expelling the child from your home.

If you have found that it is too late to apply clear and consistent written rules and consequences, if you are victimized by an abusive child who gives no sign of caring about your feelings or about your rights, then:

- *Don't* dissipate your energy in guilt.
- *Don't* cripple yourselves in blaming one another or in blaming the child,
- *Do* recognize your mistakes.
- *Do* recognize that your child is in pain, too. Those intolerable actions are not evil but symptoms of unhappiness; unfortunately, they are the kind of symptoms that only make everyone's unhappiness worse.

• *Do* seek out a competent, professional family therapist.

• *Do* explore ToughLove or similar parent-support groups in your community.

SUGGESTED BOOKS: Crisis

Bayard, Robert, and Bayard, Jean. *How to Deal with Your Acting-Up Teen: Practical Self-Help for Desperate Parents.* New York: M. Evans, 1988.

York, Phyllis, and York, David. *ToughLove.* New York: Doubleday, 1982.

CHAPTER TWENTY-ONE

Family Therapy

This book by a child psychologist and family therapist has been designed to give most parents all the professional child-rearing advice they need. However, the system (written rules, consequences instead of nagging, more praise than criticism, active listening) will not work in every case. This chapter is about the exceptions.

Four different circumstances might lead you to seek professional advice.

1. You waited too long before deciding to make and enforce rules. The kind of problem behavior you are concerned about is already so dangerous or upsetting that you have to go into Crisis mode to produce change. As explained in the previous chapter, the Crisis mode requires professional help.

2. You try to make rules, but you and your spouse cannot agree about them or cannot manage to follow through with them. The communication problem is mainly between the two of you. (How to raise the children may turn out to be only one of several issues that need to be resolved in your marriage.)

3. You follow through consistently with your rules, escalate the consequences by small degrees, yet the problem behavior gets worse. The child continues to ignore the rules and to take the consequences, thereby bringing punishment

upon himself. (This indicates deeper psychological problems than merely a lack of parental structure.)

4. Finally, there are certain kinds of behavior you may be concerned about, for which stricter rules should not even be a first attempt at solution. First on the list is chronic depression, which often manifests itself in irritability and a lack of concern about parents' goals. Depression may grow out of grief, loneliness, anger, unrealized expectations, confused messages from the significant adults in the child's life, low self-esteem, or the chronic unhappiness of others in the family. Children cannot be expected to sort out and deal with those feelings without help. Then there are other emotional disorders, such as phobias and generalized anxiety, which are more likely to be exacerbated if parents take a tough line. The same is true of such compulsive habits as nail-biting. Severe eating disorders (self-starving or vomiting) also need professional diagnosis and therapy. And so does any disorder with a possible neurophysiological basis, such as hyperactivity.

In any of those four situations, parents should consult a child psychologist, psychiatrist, or social worker who specializes in working with families. Therefore, this chapter begins with an explanation of what "family therapy" means and how you can find an appropriate professional to help you help your child. Then we shall discuss in more detail the circumstances that might send you to this kind of counselor.

═What is family therapy?

When children are in trouble behaviorally and emotionally, the clinical professions have two fundamentally different approaches to get them back on the developmental track. In one approach, a therapist establishes a relationship with the individual child, becomes a kind of auxiliary parent, and tries to compensate for whatever emotional injuries occurred earlier in the child's life. In the other approach, the therapist establishes a relationship with the whole family, but primarily as a consultant to the parents.

Individual child therapy is the old way, trying to help the

child directly. Family therapy is the new way, helping parents to help their children.

Family therapy makes more sense for several reasons. One is that children live with their parents seven days a week, and the parents have far more influence on them than any outsider —certainly more than one who sees them only an hour or two per week. Another reason is that a child's troublesome behavior affects everyone in the family, and everyone's reactions then reverberate back upon the child. The whole family is one organic system, with all the parts interconnected. It is like a baseball team: You cannot train one member of the team to use a different set of plays without every other player being in on the changes.

A strong argument against individual child therapy is that it often makes parents look and feel inadequate. The implicit assumption is that the therapist is a better parent. Family therapy, in contrast, respects parents. It conveys a message to children that their parents are competent and in charge, that they care, that they can change the patterns of family interaction.

Dr. Charles Kramer, a child psychiatrist who is my colleague at Northwestern University Medical School and founder of the Center for Family Studies there, has said that prescribing individual therapy for a child who lives at home ought to be grounds for a medical malpractice suit. Those are strong words for a physician to use against his own colleagues, but a growing number of other psychiatrists—as well as psychologists, social workers, pediatricians, teachers, school counselors, and juvenile officers— agree. We should never treat a child as an independent person, as though we could change him without working with the most important people he lives with. (Freud himself wrote that it was impossible, but his closest followers, the psychoanalysts, continue to work with individual children and adolescents. Family therapists, to varying degrees, make use of Freud's insights about the mind and about human development, but we incorporate those insights into the family-centered approach.)

Therapy is counseling. There is no difference between family therapy and family counseling. In this book, I use the two terms synonymously. Perhaps the term *counseling* more accurately conveys the idea that the professional's role is to advise parents, not to "fix" children. Family therapy is counseling. Conversely, family counseling is psychotherapy, as powerful an agent for change as psychoanalysis, behavior modification, or any other form of therapy.

An assortment of disciplines. The distinction between individual and family therapists has little to do with the field in which they received their primary training. There are child psychiatrists, psychologists, and social workers who work only with individual children; and there are those who work primarily with families. In some cases, the family-therapy training came as part of their training in their particular profession. But because family therapy is relatively new, many of us acquired our special training later, after we already had our academic degrees.

Psychiatrists are medical doctors; they may prescribe drugs, and they have more knowledge about any drugs you are already using and about physical ailments that complicate your family's problems. Psychologists are a more varied lot. A clinical psychologist with a Ph.D. who has passed the state licensing examination is a broadly trained expert in testing, diagnosis, and several types of therapy. But there are also more narrowly trained psychologists who specialize in only one type of treatment—for example, stress reduction. In that case, more of the responsibility falls upon you to be sure that the type of therapy this person offers is really what you need. Social workers (M.S.W.'s), too, have a variety of specializations. Because the field of social work has always been family-oriented, it was quicker than psychology or psychiatry to assimilate family therapy, beginning with one of the pioneers of the new approach, Virginia Satir.

There are also increasing numbers of other kinds of professionals who have been trained in family therapy. Some pediatricians, nurses, and family-practice physicians do counseling as one aspect of their work. Many ministers are also trained in family therapy.

A family therapist's type of academic degree is of virtually no importance in determining whether he or she can help you. A responsible member of any profession will not offer you therapy that is inappropriate. A psychologist or social worker will refer you to a psychiatrist if there is a possibility that someone in your family may need medication or hospitalization. A psychiatrist or social worker will refer you to a psychologist if certain kinds of testing are needed. A minister or pediatrician will refer you to a mental-health professional if the problems seem to go deeper than communication among family members.

More significant than the letters after the therapist's name are the following considerations:

- Is the therapist a respected professional? (I shall discuss how to get the names of respected family therapists, below.)
- Is he or she mature and experienced? If not, will your therapy be discussed with his or her supervisor regularly (weekly)?
- Do you feel comfortable with his or her personal style?
- Does the therapist seem to understand what you say in the first interview, answer your questions clearly, and offer a suggested plan for therapy that makes sense to you?
- Are the fees reasonable, and can you take advantage of your health insurance or employee-assistance plan?

Shopping around for a therapist is fine. It is normal to begin by calling two or three people, perhaps even to have appointments with each of them. Remember, you are not "putting yourself in the hands" of a professional; you are hiring a consultant.

Family therapy includes individual therapy. Almost all family therapists also work with individuals when it is appropriate. (Unfortunately, most therapists who see individuals do not work with families.) A family with whom I recently worked consisted of mother, father, fourteen-year-old son, and eight-year-old daughter. I met with the whole family only three times. I had fifteen sessions with the son alone; sixteen with the mother and father; four with the mother, father, and son; one with the mother alone; and two with the father alone. This was not planned in advance; the decisions were made each week as we worked on different aspects of the problem. There are other families whom I always see as a full group, some in which I have not seen the children since the first session, and others in which I work mainly with the adolescent, only occasionally inviting the parents to join us. Sometimes, grandparents and other relatives are invited for special sessions.

Such flexibility is fairly typical of family therapists. The choice of who should come will not be left up to you, however; as the focus of the work changes, the therapist may suggest restricting or expanding the number of participants.

Another possible change in midstream is that one or more family members may be referred to a different therapist with special skills: a behavior therapist (one who uses behavioral conditioning), a play therapist (one who communicates with children through play with symbolic objects), a hypnotist, a group therapist (for example, with a group of adolescents who have similar problems), or a psychiatrist who is qualified to prescribe medication.

A clinic or a private practitioner? Family therapy is available in many agencies that are subsidized by community or private funds, enabling them to charge less than many therapists in private practice. You may wonder, therefore, what a private therapist offers to make his or her higher fee worthwhile.*

What you *don't necessarily* get is better therapy. There are a few benefits of seeing a therapist in private practice, but there are also some advantages to a community mental-health clinic or agency. Although the following points are generalizations, they are worth thinking about when you are looking for a therapist:

> • With a private practitioner, you may be able to count on a longer continuing relationship with your therapist. This does not necessarily mean longer therapy; it might mean stopping when the current problems are resolved but being able to return to the same person several years later. When he or she established the practice, it was with the intention of remaining in that community for many years. At a clinic or agency, where the therapists are salaried employees, they are more likely to leave: to move away, or pursue an advanced degree, or start their own practice. In general, large institutions and those that are known as training centers have the highest turnover in their clinic staffs. However, you can check this out at the first interview. Ask how long you can count on the therapist to remain there. Of course, no one

---

* Many private practitioners have sliding scales, so you should not *assume* their fees are higher than a clinic until you inquire.

can predict very well how long your counseling will need to continue. Despite the best-laid plans, you may have to transfer to someone else at the clinic. That is not the worst thing in the world, just something to try to avoid.

• You may have a wider choice of therapists in private practice than of clinics in your community. It is difficult or impossible to shop around for a therapist you like within any one clinic.

• The private practitioner might have a fancier office, with a quieter waiting room.

• On the other hand, you may get better-supervised therapy in a clinic. Private practitioners consult their colleagues about cases, too, but they are not forced to do so as systematically as the staff of a well-run clinic. The training clinics connected with universities often have the best-supervised therapists.

• A clinic may provide better access to a variety of approaches, unless the whole clinic is too specialized.

• Many of the best-trained, most sensitive and skilled therapists are social workers who remain in salaried positions with agencies rather than moving off into private practice. Discrimination against social workers in private practice is one reason for this. In most states, M.S.W. psychotherapists are ineligible for payment by health-insurance plans. In an agency, a staff physician or psychologist can sign the insurance forms. Psychologists and psychiatrists have an easier time building up their own practices, but that does not mean they are better therapists.

In summary, even if you can afford a therapist in private practice, don't turn up your nose at clinics or family-therapy agencies with subsidized fees. Explore both alternatives, if possible, and make your decision on the basis of how you feel about the therapist.

Finding a family therapist. The ideal source of a referral is someone who knows your family, understands what family therapy is all about and why you need it, and has firsthand knowledge about the work of several therapists in your community. Call the child's pediatrician, the school social worker, or your minister. Or call all three, and ask each of them for a couple of suggestions. (You might also ask each what he or she has heard about the therapists suggested by the others.) If the same clinic or therapist is suggested by more than one person, that is surely the one to try first.

Almost as good a source of information about therapists are your friends and relatives who have been in family therapy. Your sister-in-law probably cannot analyze your situation as objectively as your pediatrician can, but on the other hand, she knows you better. And you can evaluate her recommendation based on how well you trust her opinion.

If those two kinds of sources do not give you enough promising leads, call your local hospital and ask for the social-work department. Tell them about your problem, find out if they offer family therapy (they may work only with patients in the hospital), and ask for some names of private practitioners whom they recommend.

If there is a Family Institute or a university-affiliated family-therapy training program within a few hours of you (again, something a school or hospital social worker would know), they undoubtedly keep a directory of their alumni and can give you several names of qualified family therapists near you.

Finally, the *worst* method of finding a therapist is by calling your state psychiatric, psychological, or social workers' association, or by using the yellow pages or responding to a newspaper advertisement. Reputable people are listed in all of these places, but the listing is no guarantee. Being on the professional association's referral roster means nothing except that they have paid their membership dues.

Now that you know what family therapy is and where to find it, we can deal with the more difficult question: When do you decide that a system of rules and consequences is not going to work?

≡Waited too long?

I don't think it is ever too late to begin setting down rules, warning children about the consequences of their actions, and following through. Crisis mode is based on rules and consequences just as much as Liberty is. So are prisons and mental hospitals. The difference is only in the degree of restriction.

What you may have waited too long for, though, is to be able to put this system into effect without help. In the previous chapter, I mentioned several crisis situations that indicate a professional should be consulted:

- Being arrested.
- Suspension from school.
- Staying out overnight without permission.
- Physical assault.
- Carrying a knife or pistol.
- Abuse of any drug to the point of losing consciousness or memory.

This list is certainly not exhaustive; anything that you consider to be as self-destructive or as dangerous to others as the actions named above should be added to the list. Any such incident is a sufficient indication that you have waited too long before setting clear limits. I would not think a rule such as "If you are suspended from school again, you will be sent to military school" could possibly be sufficient in itself to resolve the internal problems that have led to the child's suspension.

All the actions listed are within the realm in which a child can, with help, turn completely around and get on a positive track. But they are so close to the outer edges of this realm that you have little room for trial and error. Therefore, consult a psychologist, social worker, or other family therapist before cracking down on such actions.

In all likelihood, the family counselor with whom you talk will recommend a system of clearly defined rules similar to what I have described. But you will know that this advice is given to you personally after the experienced counselor has explored your family's particular situation. And you will have the counselor's continuing support through the crisis.

Parents' despair. An even greater danger than trying to crack down on children too late, without professional advice, is that parents will give up trying at all. They will feel so powerless against "peer pressure," so convinced that "nothing works" that their only recourse is prayer, or kicking the child out of the house without therapy, or waiting for natural consequences to catch up with the child.

MISTAKE: Andy's parents are fed up with his school failures, shoplifting, and hostility toward them. "I give up," his father says. "I'm just waiting for him to hang himself." He means this as a figure of speech. But every year, three hundred to four hundred children in the United States do hang themselves, and another fifteen hundred or so commit suicide in other ways. And these statistics represent only those who "succeed."

No parents should ever accept serious problems in their children as something about which nothing can be done. You might choose to accept a messy room or fighting among siblings without making rules about such problems—if you think enforcing these rules would be more bother than looking the other way. But don't accept a school suspension, a deadly weapon, or drug abuse with the same resignation. Such problems don't go away when they are ignored by parents.

Therefore, no matter how much despair you may feel, if your reaction to that despair is to give up, you will probably soon have reason for worse despair. It is part of the therapist's job to change that despair into the energy needed for a systematic assault on the problem.

≡Can't agree on rules?

Some parents put off making rules because they have found from experience, or unconsciously expect, that they cannot agree on what the rules should be, what the consequences should be, or who should enforce them. In other families, the mother and father think they are in agreement, but their child knows how to break their consistency by approaching them separately.

EXAMPLE: *Seventeen-year-old daughter:* Mom, can I borrow your Sears credit card? I need a new pair of running shoes.

Mother: What happened to your clothing allowance?

Daughter: I spent it on clothing. These I need for track; they don't count as clothing.

Mother: I'll give you an advance on next month's clothes-purchasing budget, if you want. I'll discuss it with Dad, but it seems to me shoes of any kind are clothing.

Daughter (later): Dad, my clothing allowance isn't supposed to cover equipment for track and stuff, is it?

Father: What do you need?

Daughter: Running shoes. Look at this pair.

Father: Oh yeah, you can't run in those. But I'll bet you've already asked your mother for the money.

Daughter: She was willing to give it to me if you said okay. She wasn't sure if track shoes would count as school expenses or clothing. But obviously I wouldn't be running five miles a day if I wasn't out for track. Besides, my clothing allowance is a pittance. I'm already going to need an advance for a decent top and some jeans.

Father: All right. Is twenty enough for the shoes?

Daughter: No way. They'll be at least thirty. Give me forty, and I'll bring you the change.

If this sort of thing happens once in a while, you can deal with it. You and your spouse can promise each other not to go along with any requests for "extras" without discussing it with one another. But if you are unable to carry out that policy, it probably means that there are hidden conflicts in your marriage. One of you may be harboring resentment about the other parent's relationship with your children, or about something that has nothing to do with the children. Try to sit down and explore such feelings openly. What is getting in the way of communication? What does your spouse think might have happened if he or she had discussed the issue with you before giving the child a unilateral yes or no? It will soon be clear whether you need some help from a family counselor.

The best way to proceed is to try to enforce a set of rules for your children after reading this book. Then try to resolve any disagreements that you discover between yourself and your spouse. If that doesn't work, then you need to talk with a family counselor. Obviously, both partners will have to see the counselor together; it is not a matter of one of you taking the children to be "reformed." Think of the counselor's role as shown in the diagram: consultant to the parents, as needed.

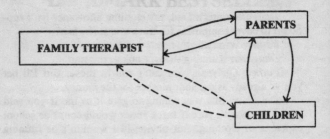

≡Rules don't work?

Another situation in which professional consultation is needed happens when parents have enforced their rules consistently but their child continues to bring the consequences down upon himself. Here, the main problem is not lack of parental agreement, consistency, or structure.

Inappropriate expectations. You may be expecting behavior that is beyond your child's capabilities at this age. Inappropriate expectations can result either from a parent's lack of experience with children, or from a particular child's disability.

If you wonder whether your expectations are appropriate, the best person to ask is probably your pediatrician (except for questions having to do with school achievement, which, of course, you would address to the child's teacher).

Covert depression. The child may be seriously depressed without appearing depressed. Children and adolescents don't always show depression in the way adults do, by looking and feeling sad. A clinically depressed child may be active, rebellious, even violent, much like a child who merely suffers from a lack of limits. When you set limits, the latter child's behavior improves markedly; that of the seriously depressed child does not. The depression may come from loneliness, rejection by peers, grief over the loss of a loved one, anger or confusion about a divorce, remarriage, or adoption. Low in self-esteem, high in guilt (warranted or unwarranted), he may be punishing himself by getting himself grounded or by losing privileges again and again. Whatever the source of emotional pain, once it is expressed in self-defeating actions, a tough parental response might perpetuate the negative feelings, contributing to a vicious circle.

EXAMPLE: Michael's father and stepmother brought him to a child psychologist after a series of lying and filching incidents. Michael was an immature eleven-year-old with a three-year-old half sister. He was a below-average student, repeating fifth grade. He had no friends. The psychologist learned that Michael's parents had responded to the lying and stealing in a variety of ways: lecturing Michael, spanking him, threatening him. What they had not done was to set forth clear consequences, so this was the first step in family therapy.

After two weeks, it was apparent that Michael's father and stepmother could follow through consistently with their consequences. However, this was no deterrent to Michael's misbehavior, even when the consequences were made more severe. He continued to take money and other items from his parents, and for the first time he stole something at school: a small radio.

The therapist insisted that the parents continue enforcing consequences for all such actions, but he also initiated individual play therapy with Michael. Some of those sessions included the father, some both parents, and some were private sessions between Michael and the therapist. It became clearer that the core of Michael's unhappiness had to do with feelings about his natural mother, a drug addict who had not been able to care for him. Michael was angry at having been abandoned, blamed his father, stepmother, and, most of all, himself. He continued to see the psychologist weekly for more than a year, then at irregular intervals over the next several years. The lying and stealing stopped soon after play therapy began, but Michael's school problems and social relations were slower to improve.

Other disorders. Depression is certainly not the only disorder that can be hidden. In the following section, I discuss many problems for which, if you *know* your child has them, rules and discipline are not the answer. However, you may not realize that this is true of your child until after you put into practice a system of written, consistently enforced rules.

In general, the way to know whether a system will work for your children is to put it into effect and follow through with consequences. The results will tell you whether you need to go to the next step, family therapy. And your rules will not have done any harm.

Rules not appropriate?

With certain kinds of child-behavior problems, you can be pretty sure in advance that rules are not the solution. (You may need clearer rules anyway, but not as a substitute for therapy.) One group of problems I have in mind are self-directed: depression, specific fears, generalized anxiety, hyperactivity and attention deficits, compulsive habits such as nail-biting, and eating disorders. Another group are social problems, such as stealing, chronic lying, bullying other children or animals, painful shyness, and promiscuity.

Overt depression. I mentioned above that seriously depressed children and adolescents do not always act depressed. Sometimes, though, they do—behaving socially withdrawn, tired, apathetic, self-deprecating, tearful, melancholy; sleeping too much or too little, eating too much or too little, perhaps being preoccupied with death. A depressed person rarely shows all these symptoms; any three are sufficient for a clinical diagnosis. However, before we apply the official label ("depressive neurosis"), the child must have had either a major episode of acute depression (inability to function in normal daily activities) or a full year of manifesting three or more depressive symptoms.

You may have your own home cure for depression, something you do for yourself when you are feeling blue: a car trip, an extra few miles on your morning run, a new dress. Don't try to treat your child's depression the same way, or any other way except by consulting a professional therapist. I am not saying children never get through depression without help; some do, especially if their life situation improves. But in too many cases, childhood depression leads to chronic adolescent and adult problems, or to suicide. And the longer you wait for the depressive cloud to lift itself, the more the child misses socially, academically, and in terms of self-esteem.

Specific fears. When a child has an intense, irrational fear—of the dark, of being alone, of animals, of water—and does not get over that fear by a certain age, parents sometimes become impatient. If they are sensitive as well as sensible, they gently but persistently coax the child through a series of nontraumatic experiences—allowing them to put only their toes in the water, then on a later occasion going in up to the ankles, and so on. Pressuring the child too much may make him even more afraid; on the other hand, indulging the fear and keeping the child away from the feared situation prevents him from learning not to be afraid. If parents avoid both extremes, children usually gain confidence and master their fears. At the same time, they learn other important things, such as trust in their parents.

If the child refuses to give up the fear despite your best efforts, then this is something to talk with a therapist about, rather than putting more pressure on your child. The therapist may help you carry out a carefully designed series of "desensitization trials," not very different from what you already tried. First, however, he or she will be assessing whether the fear is a *phobia*, which means that the child is unconsciously more deeply afraid of something else. The deeper fears are displaced onto the object of the phobia.

> EXAMPLE: Polly, age six, is knocked down by a large dog. From then on, she is intensely afraid of all dogs, large and small. Her parents indulge her in this for about a year, but then they insist that she must get over her excessive fear. They sensitively control her encounters with dogs, beginning with small dogs and quiet dogs, held on leashes or in their owners' laps. This is not the sort of problem for which a psychologist's help is needed. Polly's parents know what she is afraid of, they know why, and they know what to do about it. Only if their own desensitization cure did not work would they need to seek professional help.
>
> Mary, also six years old, develops an intense fear of dogs without having had any bad experiences with dogs. Correctly defined, the term *phobia* applies to Mary's fear

—displaced onto dogs from more complex, unconscious origins—but not to Polly's, which was in fact caused by a frightening encounter with a dog. Although Mary's parents are just as gentle and thoughtful as Polly's, Mary's phobia only gets worse. At the age of eight, she is taken to a child psychologist, who uses play therapy to discover and help Mary work through her deeper fears. It turns out that her grandmother's death two years ago left Mary with intense fears about dying, mixed with guilt about an incident in which her grandmother had severely reprimanded her for teasing a dog. There is no way Mary's parents could have known what caused her phobia. Their good sense in taking her to a psychologist not only saves her years of unhappiness and embarrassment but also frees her from her confused feeling of having played a part in her grandmother's death.

In both Polly's case and Mary's, the parents begin by putting pressure on their daughters to behave maturely. In one case, the pressure is effective. In the other case, it is not effective, but no harm is done and the child's need for therapy becomes clear.

Generalized anxiety. An anxious child may not have specific fears, but he may be generally fearful, overly dependent, and easily upset in many situations. Since it is normal for all children to be fearful, dependent, or upset at times, you can only judge your child's level of anxiety in comparison with other children of the same age. Again, pediatricians and teachers are the best people to consult about how concerned you ought to be.

If the pediatrician, teacher, or your own experience tells you that your child is excessively anxious, and if you don't see significant improvement over a period of months, don't keep waiting for the child to outgrow this problem. And don't pressure the child for more independence—that may backfire. Consult a child psychologist or other professional therapist who specializes in children and families.

Hyperactivity and attention deficits. Many of us consider our children "hyper" at times. All parents, I suspect, have noticed deficits in our children's attention to such things as table edges, flowerbeds—and rules! The diagnosis of hyperactivity, however, applies to a child who literally can hardly sit still. Such children often show specific deficits in auditory or visual attention, which slow down their learning in normal classes.

In recent years, we have learned more about the neurophysiological aspects of hyperactivity in children and are gaining more control over the disorder through a combination of drugs, behavior modification (administered by the parents), and family therapy. If you think you may have a hyperactive child, ask your pediatrician to refer you to a child psychiatrist, preferably one who is affiliated with a hospital outpatient program for hyperactive children and their parents.

Compulsive habits. Thumb-sucking, nail-biting, blinking, and stuttering should be ignored at first, but if they persist for many months, discuss the problem with professionals. Start with your pediatrician, but if you are convinced it is a bigger problem than the pediatrician thinks, call a child psychologist. *Don't* try to talk (nag) the child out of doing it, but don't try to extinguish it by consequences, either—at least, not until you have consulted someone who can evaluate what the habit is a symptom of. Such habits have a way of becoming entrenched just because the parents are lobbying so hard against them.

The same can be said of bed-wetting, up until age eight or so. After that age, I don't think it does any harm to try the consequences I suggested in chapter 5, but if you don't succeed, talk it over with your pediatrician.

Eating disorders. Refusal to eat certain foods is not an eating disorder. Refusal to eat with the rest of the family is not an eating disorder. These problems are simply challenges to parental authority, and you have the choice of giving the child that amount of freedom or making a rule about it.

Eating disorders are serious mental illnesses: anorexia nervosa (self-starvation) and bulimia (gorging followed by self-induced vomiting, or binge eating alternating with drastic dieting). Simple obesity is not considered a mental illness, though it is often both a symptom and a cause of serious emotional problems. If you have the slightest concern that your child may be anorexic, bulimic, or obese, consult your pediatrician.

I don't need to discuss the symptoms of these disorders in detail, because the diagnosis has to be made by a doctor, not by you. For example, you might think your daughter has anorexia nervosa, but she might actually be suffering severe appetite loss and malnutrition as a result of a neurophysiological disease. That has to be ruled out before psychotherapy for anorexia nervosa can be initiated.

However, there are a few facts that may help to put these eating disorders in perspective and underline the importance of early detection and treatment. First, they are not diseases exclusive to adolescent girls. The most typical age of onset is in the early teens, and there are many more anorexic and bulimic girls than boys, but these illnesses may begin at any time from age three to adulthood, and they do afflict boys as well as girls.

Second, anorexia nervosa is not just dieting carried to an extreme. It is dieting gone out of control, to the point where the young person becomes addicted to hunger. Anorectics will fight almost as hard to be allowed to starve themselves as drug addicts will fight for their fix. Like an addiction, the starvation begins gradually and is much easier to stop if you catch it early. A girl with a normal figure who says she is fat, starts to count calories obsessively, and goes on a diet may be on her way to anorexia. But a few family-therapy sessions can educate her about the dangers of the illness, help the parents make rules about dieting, and help her talk about her deeper worries. Without that prompt help, once she has lost a significant amount of weight, is measuring every bite she eats, and has a distorted perception of her own body, treatment will be a long and harrowing process.

True anorectics (those who are dangerously skinny and have such distorted body image that they deny their skinniness) rarely recover spontaneously. Without treatment, or even with treatment if it begins too late, many of them die. Some, however, consciously decide to become bulimic instead of anorectic. As one of my patients said, "I realized, 'Hey, I could die from this!' Then I read an article about bulimia—how you could eat all you want and vomit and you wouldn't gain weight and you wouldn't starve —and at first I thought, 'That's disgusting.' But then I tried it, and pretty soon I didn't mind it." This is common; it is estimated that as many as 20 percent of all girls and young women try, at some point, binge eating and vomiting. Therefore, when I hear of someone who had anorexia and made a spontaneous "recovery," I try to find an opportunity for a confidential talk about bulimia.

It is difficult, though, because many bulimics burden themselves with shame about their secret "disgusting" vice so that the shame becomes as great a burden as the compulsion itself.

As for obesity, it is not quite as urgent to crack down immediately, but I would not ignore the problem either. Much depends upon the child's own feelings about it. A body may be perfectly healthy even while weighing 20 to 30 percent more than what is considered fashionable. On the other hand, children who are very sensitive to how others see them might consider themselves terribly fat if their weight is merely above average for their height. Rather than impose your own standard, I suggest having frank talks with your child about his or her own concerns about weight. Don't hesitate to get professional help if needed.

Cruelty. Bullying other children—physically or verbally—tormenting animals, and sexually molesting younger children are *never* merely a result of unclear rules or inadequate limits. Such behavior does not come naturally to children. It comes from pain and confusion deep within the child. Not to give it immediate professional attention is a tragic disservice to the child, as well as to his or her victims.

Shyness. The point where shyness ceases to be merely a personality trait and becomes a cause for therapy is fairly easy to diagnose. So long as children go ahead with activities, even if they are the quietest members of the group, their shyness is probably not causing them anguish. But if they avoid things they really want to do, they need help. For instance, a girl wishes she could be a Brownie but won't join unless her mother agrees to come to every meeting. When the mother refuses, if the child goes ahead and joins the troop, no therapy is needed. If she does not, she needs to be seen professionally to prevent the problem from mushrooming. The older the child, the more strongly I would recommend therapy.

Other problems. Elsewhere in this book, I have discussed chronic (prolonged) lying, stealing, drug abuse, promiscuity. You can make a first attempt at dealing with these problems in Probation mode, but if they persist, your chances are poor for solving the problem without help.

I have surely omitted some problems for which neither parental firmness nor parental love and support will be sufficient. The problems discussed above can only convey some general ideas about when to seek help. Whenever you are in doubt—my standard line—call your pediatrician.

≡Summary

In this book, I have presented a system for managing children's behavior and development through clear rules, consequences, no nagging, and an emphasis upon self-esteem and responsibility. The system of rules and consequences outlined in Part I was designed in such a way that parents can use it with no fear of doing harm. It will solve most behavior problems, in most families, without professional help.

There are, however, many situations that parental discipline cannot resolve, without the help of someone who can diagnose the particular problems of the particular family. In general, what a family therapist has to do is figure out what *function* the problem behavior is serving for a certain child in a certain family, what benefit comes to the child or to others in the family when the child persists with the behavior. Then the therapist (who may be a psychiatrist, psychologist, social worker or other professional) can offer more adaptive ways for everyone in the family to act.

Therefore, parents should be prepared to seek help if a clear, consistent system of rules does not work. In the following cases, we can even say in advance that it will not work. Find a qualified family therapist:

• If the child's actions have been allowed to go so far out of control that you are already in a crisis (no room for trial and error).

• If you and your spouse cannot agree upon rules or consequences, or cannot enforce them consistently.

• If you enforce your rules, but the child persists in bringing consequences down upon himself—even as you gradually escalate the consequences.

• If the child appears to be suffering from depression, specific irrational fears, general anxiety, painful shyness, hyperactivity, compulsive habits, or an eating disorder.

• If the child attacks other children or animals, molests

them sexually, lies or steals on a grand scale, or is sexually promiscuous.

If you are in doubt, don't hesitate to consult your pediatrician and/or the child's teacher, counselor, or school social worker.

SUGGESTED BOOKS: Family Therapy

Ackerman, Paul, and Kappelman, Murray. *Signals: What Your Child Is Really Telling You.* New York: Signet, 1978.

Kramer, Charles. *Becoming a Family Therapist: Developing an Integrated Approach to Working with Families.* New York: Human Sciences Press, 1980.

Napier, Augustus, and Whitaker, Carl. *The Family Crucible: The Intense Experience of Family Therapy.* New York: Harper & Row, 1988.

Ramos, Suzanne. *Teaching Your Child to Cope With Crisis: How to Help Your Child Deal With Death, Divorce, Surgery, Being Adopted, Moving, Alcoholic Parents, Sick Parents, Leaving Home, and Other Major Worries.* New York: McKay, 1975.

Sorosky, Arthur, and Baran, Annette. *The Adoption Triangle.* New York: Doubleday, 1979.

Zimbardo, Philip, and Radl, Shirley. *The Shy Child: A Parent's Guide to Preventing and Overcoming Shyness From Infancy to Adulthood.* New York: McGraw-Hill, 1981.

APPENDIX

For Professionals

This appendix is for psychotherapists, counselors, physicians, nurses, teachers, school administrators, clergy, community social workers—any professional who works with parents of troubled children. Its purpose is to explain the rationale of this book in terms of the current state of our knowledge in developmental psychology and in family-systems therapy, and to describe how I use the system in my own practice.

The majority of readers of this book will be parents whose problems with their children are less severe than the average case we see in our offices. They attend PTA programs and church workshops on child-rearing; they talk about these issues extensively with friends and relatives; they read books and magazine articles—and they do a good job of preventive care. They avert crises with their children, or they respond adaptively to a crisis so that the experience strengthens the whole family. Although there were many books already on the market for such parents, there were none, I felt, that delivered the appropriate combination of these three principles:

1. Emphasizing the need for a balance between, on the one hand, attention, active listening, praise, emphasis on responsibility, and other constructive, competence-building, confidence-building techniques—and, on the other hand, a

firm set of rules based on parental authority and consistent consequences.

2. Offering a system or set of procedures for parents to use in designing their own rules, rather than the "expert's" suggestions as to what those rules should be.

3. Acknowledging the role of punishment in child-rearing but showing how all punishments can be designed to restrict children without causing feelings of rejection, humiliation, pain, or deprivation.

These straightforward principles can be understood and applied creatively by most parents without professional consultation. There are others, however, about whom you and I are more concerned. In my experience, the parents who seek counseling for problems with their children are *not* merely people who could have solved their own problems with the right self-help book. Their crisis has come about because they *can't* simply agree on rules, stop undermining each other, and stop hassling their children. Or it has come about because the children *can't* conform to a rational set of rules with appropriate positive and negative consequences. The emotional cost of doing so is too great. A family therapist, in order to be helpful in a lasting way, must identify the recurring dynamics of the family—the patterns of interaction that maintain their problem—and then must intervene to disrupt those patterns and force the system to develop new, more productive adaptations. It would be naive to hand such a family this book and expect them to change.

In writing this book, I was aware that those parents who most need it would probably not read it. I originally began the project because it was a tool that I needed in my work with dysfunctional families. Perhaps it will prove useful to other troubled parents who, for whatever reason, have more faith in the impersonal printed word than in personal counselors. But it is primarily designed to be given to parents by family counselors as a principal intervention in the first or second session of work. I shall outline how I use this tool with families. In the course of that discussion, its theoretical rationale will become clear.

The rules task. Whenever children's behavior is the family's main identified problem, I assign parents a homework task between our first and second interviews. Their task is to sit down together and draw up a list of rules. It is as much a diagnostic task as it is an intervention (Haley, 1976; Pinsof, 1983). This book began as a handbook for that task. Corresponding roughly to chapter 4, it explained the differences between rules and preferences, the "if . . . then" criterion for rules, the idea of starting with small consequences that can be increased, and the guidelines for natural and logical consequences (Dreikurs and Grey, 1968). I sound the parents out on all these points in the initial interview, show them a sample list of rules, and ask them to come back the following week with their own list. (Parents who have previously heard me speak at their school or church may arrive for the first session with a list they have already tried and failed to enforce.)

One function of starting in this way is to establish a clear alliance with the parents. "What have you tried in the past? What worked? What didn't work? What are the things you want to insist upon now? What sort of consequences would work for your child?" It puts the therapist in the role of consultant to the parents, neither a substitute parent who is hired to cure the child nor a critic of the parents whose role is to show them all their failings. If the parents have never tried a set of written rules, I can explain the system in five minutes, and by the next session we can diagnose, together, where they had difficulty implementing it. If they have already tried this sort of thing, we quickly get to whatever obstacles they encountered (or created).

At the same time, I engage the children by frankly asking for their assessment of the problem, their ideas about how the family could change. I empathize with them especially with regard to how confusing life must have been "not knowing exactly what the rules were, hearing one thing one time and something else the next time." I win a little trust from the children by advising the parents to try smaller consequences than they had in mind—setting back the curfew time, for example, instead of grounding the child; or increasing the grounding in units of one day instead of doubling it each time. (This comes as a relief to the parents, too.) Then I ask for help. The parents having come up with a rule (either in the first session or after conferring during the week before the second session), I turn to the child or children and say:

"Your parents are trying to draw up a set of rules with definite consequences. What's in it for you is that you won't be hassled anymore about anything that isn't clearly written in the rules. This will only work if they follow through as they say they're going to do, with the consequences. The only way we'll know if they can do that is if you test the rules. So I need you to do that once or twice, after you post the list.

"On this first rule, I'm worried that you might start getting everything done in time for the bus each morning, before we find out whether Mom and Dad can follow through with consequences. So, without telling them when you're going to do this, and without reminding them about the rule, at least once this week I'd like you to leave without making your bed or washing the breakfast dishes. Then come back and tell me whether Mom and Dad remembered to enforce the rule or whether all they did was the same old nagging and complaining. Will you do that?"

This is not a paradoxical intervention (Watzlawick, Weakland, and Fisch,1974), because it is entirely sincere. I am prescribing the symptom, but the parents have already planned an adaptive solution, which they cannot practice unless the child tests the rule. Many children understand and welcome the chance to cooperate with me. They are dying for some structure, consistency, and security; that is why they pushed their parents to the point of seeking help. Others, however, claim to be unwilling to bring the consequences upon themselves. ("I want to go to bed later, not earlier!") I make a strong pitch:

"I understand how you feel. It would seem crazy to disobey the rules when all that gets you is punishment. But that's what I'm asking you to do. Just once or twice. It's a small sacrifice to make, for the sake of changing the way your parents deal with things. Would you be willing to try it?"

This almost always wins the children's cooperation, whether they are five or fifteen (or twenty-five, in some cases). If not, there is no need to push further. (*Not* to test the parents means obeying their rules.)

I try to reframe the children's misbehavior as well intentioned; thus the label "behavior problem" is lifted off them, freeing them from having to act out that role. At the same time, I add that their misbehavior is doing the family no good and can no longer be tolerated by the parents. The responsibility for solving the problem is shifted back onto the parents.

With most families, I spend the first four or five sessions, or more, talking about the rules, the testing, the consequences, and all the transactions that occur in relation to this new experience. Often there is significant improvement in the "problem" children in those few sessions. They may show one or more positive signs:

- Engaging with me in a friendly, trusting way while still maintaining that "the list" is a terrible idea, not working.
- Helping me by criticizing the parents' failures to enforce the rules.
- Discovering and acknowledging the advantages of the list.

This way of beginning always leads to two results. I help the parents work out the details of a set of enforceable rules as described in Part I. At the same time, the exercise of trying to collaborate on their rules brings out the underlying dysfunctions that need treatment. Thus I have usually accomplished all seven of my goals for the initial phase of counseling:

1. Engaging with all family members—with the parents, empathic alliance; with the children, empathic understanding and mutual willingness to listen.

2. Establishing the assumptions of our work together—that I am in charge of the sessions but that the solution depends upon parental agreement with one another and on their own priorities; that I will not tell them what their rules should be.

3. Destabilizing the system. If the children have been caught between the two parents, I break up the triangle. Parents are treated as one unit, children as another. If there has been no clear boundary between the generations, I force a hierarchy by insisting that the parents are in charge and by refusing to accept their helplessness. If the children have been split into "good" child and "bad" child, I point out that the "good" child's behavior has not been helpful to the family as a whole, and I insist that rules be drawn up for every child. Sometimes I predict misbehavior by a different child if the "problem" child improves.

4. Observing what happens when the parents try, or resist trying, to collaborate on rules and consequences.

5. Taking the focus off the child as "identified patient"; explaining that we cannot deal with the child's behavior until the parents can communicate better and work together.

6. Introducing "active listening" techniques (asking questions, clarifying what one has heard, requesting permission to respond—see chapter 11) and practicing them in the session, between the two parents and between each parent and child. Often I challenge the children to demonstrate these techniques to the parents; children seem to be able to learn this (as most other things) faster than adults.

7. Educating the parents about some basic principles of child-rearing (I see the role of therapist as essentially that of a teacher):

    —The importance of consistency in parental policy-making and follow-through.

    —The value of enabling children to know what is expected of them and what they can expect from their parents.

    —The fact that criticizing, yelling, and nagging are as destructive as the failure to set limits, and that all of those alternatives provide poor role models for children.

    —The idea of priorities: distinguishing between the things the parents really want to insist upon and lesser issues that they might be tempted to nag and complain about but do not take seriously enough to translate into rules.

    —The merits of the freedom-versus-restriction continuum, and the conception of child development as moving in the direction of freedom, with periodic steps backward to safer, more restrictive conditions until the child is responsible enough to handle more freedom.

    —The destructive, ineffective character of three other types of punishment used by parents instead of simple restrictions: physical punishment, food deprivation, and humiliation.

    —The importance of *self-esteem*, including actual

competence and the child's *belief* in his competence and worth. I emphasize that this is more important than any system of rewards and punishments we can devise.

In short, working with parents on their rules is a point of entry for the therapist, entirely different from working on the assumption that something is wrong with the child. Although the rules approach is quite consistent with the structural and strategic schools of family therapy (Haley, 1976; Minuchin and Fishman, 1981), I regard it as far from the whole treatment. It is merely one technique in the family therapist's kit. In the following rationale, I shall indicate how the family therapy proceeds beyond this initial work with rules.

Rationale. This is not the place for a theoretical discourse, nor do I want to publicize the paltry secrets of our art. I do, however, want to discuss my approach to parent/child problems in the context of a particular system of therapy. Integrative Problem-Centered Therapy (IPCT; Pinsof, 1983) is integrative in two ways. First, it integrates the family-system treatment with the individual treatment of each member within the family. Second, it integrates the psychodynamic use of emotion and, to varying extents, personal histories, with the problem orientation of the so-called strategic, structural, rational, and behavioral therapies.

A summary of Pinsof's article will help to clarify my approach to parents' and children's complaints about each other. IPCT has the following essential features:

1. Problem-centered. Therapy begins with the problem as identified by the patient system and clarified by the therapist. He or she does not put new goals on the agenda without a mandate from the patient system (in the present application, the parents). The therapist obtains that mandate by linking his or her suggested goal (e.g., better communication between the parents; more intimacy; or more autonomy) to the family's original identified goal.

2. Problem maintenance. IPCT involves an analysis of how the system has worked to maintain the problem until the present (Feldman and Pinsof, 1983). Rather than seeing the problem as an anomaly that the whole family wants to dispose of, we have to understand it as something that has been serving a function and that the family cannot easily be

rid of. They must either find a more adaptive way to serve the same function or give up their beliefs about the need for that function to be served.

3. Health assumption. Like Haley (1980), Pinsof strongly repudiates the attitude that patients are sick and helpless, that the curative factors come from the therapist. IPCT acknowledges that systems—individuals or families—solve their problems because all living systems have the capacity to adapt. The therapist is like a gardener: watering, weeding, moving a plant into better light, but relying always upon the inherent growing and healing capacities of the organisms themselves. (Note the similarity to Haim Ginott's [1965] approach to children in therapy, and to parents in his books.)

4. Interdisciplinary orientation. Whenever the patient system is unable to adapt, one explores other hypotheses and consults with other professionals. For example, a child who soils his pants needs a pediatric examination; a school phobic may need projective testing or play therapy; an underachiever may need tests for specific learning disabilities, or tutoring. One should *not* view every behavior problem as an occasion for clearer parental rules.

5. Adaptive solutions. The health assumption enables therapists to conceive of our role as helping the family find adaptive solutions to their problems, helping them discover where they are blocked from such solutions, suggesting other possible solutions and exploring the obstacles to implementing those. With this attitude, we invariably find families creating better solutions than any we could impose upon them. An example was the mother I mentioned in chapter 11 whose discomfort with the negative aspect of consequences for misbehavior led her to post, alongside the rules on the refrigerator door, a "Family Newsletter" reporting the parents' appreciation for positive changes they could see in their sons. Her adaptation of my approach was more compatible with her own and her husband's style than anything I could have instructed them to do.

6. "Block" (i.e., obstacle) identification. Several times in any session, Pinsof asks a question like "What do you think would have happened if . . . (you had supported your

husband?/you had followed through with the consequence you promised?/you had told your new wife how you were feeling?/etc.)." When he gets the answer, based either on the person's past experience or on a "catastrophic expectation" (Perls, 1971)—"He would expect to get his way with everything"/"Our son would quit school"/"She would leave me"—Pinsof usually asks the respondent to check this expectation with the other person involved (the husband/the son/the wife). The search for an adaptive solution then proceeds by means of the elicited dialogue and the exploration of each family member's needs, fears, and motives, until they can see possibilities for new patterns of interaction that they are willing to try.

7. Determinant continuum. When change is blocked, the determinants of the block are conceptualized along a continuum from "immediate" to "remote" (Kaplan, 1974). Immediate determinants are recent, actually exist in the current situation, and are interpersonal (what person X is doing to person Y right now). Less immediate determinants would include organic causes—for example, hyperactivity that might respond to medication. The most remote determinants are in the past, involve transference reactions from significant others who are not actually involved in the current situation, and/or are more intrapsychic (what Y projects onto the situation with X because of things that may have happened to Y in early childhood). The philosophy of IPCT is to work with the immediate determinants and attempt to solve each problem at that level if possible. The therapy moves back along the determinant continuum to historical, transferential, and/or intrapsychic determinants *as necessary*, always linking each insight back to the current situation and goals.

8. Emotion. Finally, IPCT differs from other cognitive and behavior-oriented therapies in its strong affective emphasis. The rationale for pushing clients to verbalize the feelings behind their behavior is the assumption that human emotions energize, motivate, and facilitate active problem-solving (Ackerman, 1958; Tompkins, 1962). Often people are in touch with one emotion and attribute their behavior to that emotion (e.g., anger) but repress or deny another emo-

tion that lies beneath it (e.g., the fear of abandonment). Therefore, IPCT is at odds with Rational-Emotive Therapy (Ellis, 1963). As Pinsof (1983) explains:

> Sadness and grief facilitate psychologically reparative solutions to problems of loss. The greater a system's ability to appropriately access the various human emotions, the greater their capacity to adaptively resolve life problems. The therapist's affective task is to teach the patient system to identify and use emotions that will facilitate resolution of their presenting and other related problems.

This brief overview of IPCT indicates, I hope, why the system presented in Part I of this book has been an effective starting point for family therapy whenever a child's disobedience is presented by his parents as a problem. I never see disobedience as a symptom of child pathology, but rather as interaction patterns maintained by the family for a reason. Although maladaptive in some respects—the family is in pain—the intergenerational conflict is an adaptation to some other aspects of the family's dynamics or to its situation with respect to a still larger system. The presenting pain, in effect, relieves or protects the family from a worse pain, real or imagined; and they will not part with it until they have reason to believe the worse pain will not replace it.*

The system of rules deals with the immediate end of the determinant continuum. If it is effective in meeting the parents' goals —producing respect for certain basic rules and eliminating the intergenerational warfare—then we have no need to deal with remote determinants. If, on the other hand, the parents are unable to do this task, then I have my mandate for exploring more painful issues. If they resist that, they can try again to get together on their rules. Each time they acquire as much insight as they can tolerate about how they are maintaining their problem, we return to the immediate end of the determinant continuum and the here-and-now task. I keep them engaged, praise them for their successes, and empathize with their failures. They feel that I am *with* them—which I am. But at the same time, they are caught in a

---

* Freud himself (1920) had that insight about the families of his patients, which convinces me that if he had lived another decade or two he would have changed his couch for a set of conference chairs and insisted upon working with the whole family.

squeeze: Either they must change their parental behavior or they must undertake more difficult work further back on the determinant continuum. In that sense, the position I put the parents in with respect to the structure of therapy is a model for the position they need to put their children in with respect to rules, choices, and consequences. They cannot honorably escape until they are functioning demonstrably better, as a family, than when they came.

Different kinds of families. The system described in this book forces parents to be firm about a small set of rules, continually reassessed as their children grow and demonstrate responsibility. It forces consistency in following through with consequences but keeps the consequences small and nonabusive. It facilitates open, supportive communication without any need for nagging, complaining, or character assassination. For these reasons, parents who have leaned toward too much control, too many rules, and too severe consequences will be pushed away from those extremes. Parents who have not had enough control, not enough rules, no consequences, will be pushed in the opposite direction. The system is just as useful in *blocking* parents from being authoritarian, arbitrary, and abusive as it is in *promoting* discipline in parents who feel impotent and distraught.

In other words, the same basic approach can have opposite effects on different types of families. Obviously, the metaphors one uses and the reasons given for rules, consequences, praise, and active listening must be suited to the individuals. One codes the same message in entirely different language for different clients, as a pharmacist might put the same medicine in tablets, capsules, or liquid for different patients.

At the same time, I believe these different parents share a great deal of similarity. When I work with extremely punitive parents, it is probably not their punitive side that hears me but the part of them that would give anything *not* to be punitive if they can be reassured about certain fears. When I work with parents who are putting up with chaos, manipulation, and abuse by their children, it is not their helplessness and despair that I speak to but the part of them that believes in their rights and responsibilities as adults. If those conflicting opinions were not already being voiced within either type of parent, my therapy would not change them.

The push toward a moderate amount of structure and discipline, from either too much or too little, is the *direct* benefit of this approach. I have already said, however, that there is an even greater benefit in the way the task serves as a diagnostic tool. Two families might look similar in terms of their presenting problems and their apparent structure, but what happens when each set of parents is told to confer about rules and consequences?

In one family, the mother is unable to get her husband to set aside time for the discussion. He is never home, or, when home, is uninterested in helping her. The problem, as he sees it, is that his wife is an inept mother. He works hard at his job and expects her to discipline the children. He undermines her in my office by disparaging her, just as he undermines her at home by ignoring the children's misbehavior and failing to back her up whenever she does try to deal with a problem herself.

In the next family, the parents have a serious, intense discussion in response to the task I have given them. They hear and understand each other, but they fundamentally disagree. The mother is fed up with her daughter's behavior and wants to set strict limits and consequences. The father says that he knows he would never follow through with those consequences. Standing up to his daughter chokes him up, and he prefers to back off and let her have her way. Our work leads into the father's depression, his inability to stand up to people at work, and his bitter memories of confrontation with his parents.

A third set of parents has no difficulty with the task at all. The mother and stepfather are in perfect agreement. But the rules they come up with seem developmentally inappropriate. For example, the fifteen-year-old is not allowed to touch her stepfather's stereo or take any food out of the refrigerator without permission. Her rebellion seems to me to have been provoked. This mother is being made to choose between her child and her new husband. The problem is too many rules for the child, too little understanding between the spouses about what their marriage entails.

After the initial work with rules, the course of therapy is different for every family. In some families, after the first session I ask the parents to come alone and I do not see the children again for months. Despite a commitment to *conceptualizing* the whole family as a system, I have most often found that the core issues in the parent system have little to do with the children and either are not appropriate to discuss with the children or are more directly addressed without them.

With other families, I may see the adolescent alone for a while, we may alternate individual adolescent sessions with family sessions, or the adolescent may be referred to a group. How we proceed depends partly upon the family structure and dynamics, but even more upon the quality of rapport I am able to establish with the adolescent.

Research on the efficacy of psychotherapy has time and again shown that the therapist's training (social worker, psychologist, psychiatrist) and ideology (psychodynamic, structural, behavioral) are far less important factors than the patients' feeling that this therapist is someone with whom they can relate comfortably, who cares about them, and who understands them. Accordingly, it is not my intention to urge any particular school of family therapy upon the professional reader. What I would like to urge is that you try to incorporate the kinds of parent education outlined above (which I have attempted in the book itself) within your own therapeutic approach. Reports of your experience in doing so, and critical comments on this book, will be most gratefully received. Please write to Kenneth Kaye, Ph.D., 4747 West Peterson Avenue, Chicago, IL 60646.

≡Summary

Although the author hopes this book will be a valuable self-help tool for the average family, he also hopes that it may help dysfunctional families in two ways:

Some parents may read the book, attempt to apply it, encounter difficulties, and follow the author's suggestion to seek professional counseling.

For parents who have not read this book but who seek counseling either for themselves as parents or for one of their children as a "behavior problem," this book or the system explained in it can be used as a preliminary, diagnostic intervention. As such, working on a system of rules and consequences may or may not be sufficient family therapy, but it is an excellent starting point. From that point, the therapist can move back to more remote determinants of parental helplessness, of child misbehavior, of hostility, rage, miscommunication, or despair. On the other hand, if a solution can be achieved or if adaptive developmental processes can be set into motion by working directly on the immediate prob-lem—the lack of clear, consistent, enforced rules that both parents agree upon—then psychotherapy at the level of remote determinants is, at best, a needless luxury.

References

Ackerman, Nathan. *The Psychodynamics of Family Life.* New York: Basic Books, 1958.

Ellis, Albert. *Reason and Emotions in Psychotherapy.* Secaucus, NJ: Lyle Stuart, 1963.

Feldman, Larry, and Pinsof, William. "Problem Mainten-ance in Family Systems: An Integrative Model." *Journal of Marital and Family Therapy,* 1982, *8,* 295–308.

Freud, Sigmund. "The Psychogenesis of a Case of Homosex-uality in a Woman." In *Sexuality and the Psychology of Love.* New York: Collier, 1963, pp. 133–159 (First pub-lished in German, 1920.)

Ginott, Haim. *Between Parent and Child.* New York: Mac-millan, 1965.

Haley, Jay. *Problem-Solving Therapy.* San Francisco: Jossey-Bass, 1976.

Haley, Jay. *Leaving Home.* New York: McGraw-Hill, 1980.

Kaplan, Helen. *The New Sex Therapy.* New York: Brunner/ Mazel, 1974.

Minuchin, Salvador, and Fishman, Charles. *Family Therapy Techniques.* Cambridge, Mass.: Harvard University Press, 1981.

Perls, Fritz. *Gestalt Therapy Verbatim.* New York: Bantam, 1971.

Pinsof, William. "Integrative Problem-Centered Therapy: Toward the Synthesis of Family and Individual Psychotherapies." *Journal of Marital and Family Therapy*, 1983, *9*, 19–35.

Tompkins, Silvan. *Affect, Imagery, Consciousness.* New York: Springer, 1962.

Watzlawick, Paul, Weakland, John, and Fisch, Richard. *Change: Principles of Problem Formation and Problem Resolution.* New York: Norton, 1974.

INDEX

TACKLE LIFE'S PROBLEMS

With Help From St. Martin's Paperbacks!

HOW TO LOVE A DIFFICULT MAN
Nancy Good
_____ 90963-2 $3.95 U.S.   _____ 90964-0 $4.95 Can.

BEYOND CINDERELLA
Nita Tucker with Debra Feinstein
_____ 91161-0 $3.95 U.S.   _____ 91162-9 $4.95 Can.

WHEN YOUR CHILD DRIVES YOU CRAZY
Eda Le Shan
_____ 90387-1 $4.95 U.S.   _____ 90392-8 $5.95 Can.

HOW TO GET A MAN TO MAKE A COMMITMENT
Bonnie Barnes & Tisha Clark
_____ 90189-5 $3.95 U.S.   _____ 90190-9 $4.95 Can.

HAVE A LOVE AFFAIR WITH YOUR HUSBAND
Susan Kohl & Alice Bregman
_____ 91037-1 $3.50 U.S.   _____ 91039-8 $4.50 Can.

LANDMARK BESTSELLERS
FROM ST. MARTIN'S PAPERBACKS

HOT FLASHES
Barbara Raskin
_____ 91051-7 $4.95 U.S.   _____ 91052-5 $5.95 Can.

MAN OF THE HOUSE
"Tip" O'Neill with William Novak
_____ 91191-2 $4.95 U.S.   _____ 91192-0 $5.95 Can.

FOR THE RECORD
Donald T. Regan
_____ 91518-7 $4.95 U.S.   _____ 91519-5 $5.95 Can.

THE RED WHITE AND BLUE
John Gregory Dunne
_____ 90965-9 $4.95 U.S.   _____ 90966-7 $5.95 Can.

LINDA GOODMAN'S STAR SIGNS
Linda Goodman
_____ 91263-3 $4.95 U.S.   _____ 91264-1 $5.95 Can.

ROCKETS' RED GLARE
Greg Dinallo
_____ 91288-9 $4.50 U.S.   _____ 91289-7 $5.50 Can.

THE FITZGERALDS AND THE KENNEDYS
Doris Kearns Goodwin
_____ 90933-0 $5.95 U.S.   _____ 90934-9 $6.95 Can.

Publishers Book and Audio Mailing Service
P.O. Box 120159, Staten Island, NY 10312-0004

Please send me the book(s) I have checked above. I am enclosing $_____
(please add $1.25 for the first book, and $.25 for each additional book to
cover postage and handling. Send check or money order only—no CODs.)

Name _____

Address _____

City _____ State/Zip _____

Please allow six weeks for delivery. Prices subject to change without notice.
Payment in U.S. funds only. New York residents add applicable sales tax.